D0370131

MetaPhysical Fitness!
The Complete 30 Day Plan For Your
Mental, Emotional, and
Spiritual Health

By David Harp
and
Dr. Nina S. Feldman

Important

We believe that meditation is one of the healthiest habits that you can cultivate. But if you are currently under the care of a physician or undergoing psychotherapy, please discuss this program with your doctor or therapist before you begin.

We would also like to stress (if you'll pardon the use of that word) that this program is not meant to be used in lieu of either medical or psychological help. Should meditation raise your awareness of physical or emotional issues that need to be dealt with, please seek the help of a competent professional.

Other Books By David Harp

Instant Blues Harmonica, or Zen and the Art of Blues Harp Blowing
Instant Flute
Make Me Musical: Instant Harmonica Kit for Kids
Instant Blues and Jazz Improvisation for the Chromatic Harmonica
Instant Guitar
Me and My Harmonica
Instant Blues and Rock Harmonica (video)
Bending The Blues
Harmonica Positions
How To Whistle Like A Pro

and with Dr. Nina Feldman:
The Three Minute Meditator
The Three Minute Meditator Audio Cassette

Copyright © 1989 by David Harp
All Rights Reserved
Printed in the United States of America
First Edition: September 1989

mind's i press
P. O. Box 460908
San Francisco, California 94146 - 0908

Contents

Contents

Contents

Contents

Dedication

We'd like to dedicate this book to all of the many people who are working to save the planet through mindfulness and compassion rather than violence and confrontation:

People who recognize that the world can be changed only by acknowledging and altering in themselves that which would be all too easy to simply condemn and deplore in "the other".

People who recognize that we can work with enormous zest and energy without becoming so enwrapped in a desire for results that we place ends above means and put those who seem to stymie our efforts out of our hearts.

People who recognize that, in a very real sense, we are all one — one planet, one race, one consciousness. From our hearts to yours, we thank you.

Acknowlegements

We'd like to thank all of those who have touched our minds and hearts in ways so numerous that to mention them would require a book longer than this one: our friends and family, our clients and therapists, our teachers and students.

Special thanks are due to many, but we'll name just a few:

Our mentors, without whose encouragement we would have hesitated to either begin or complete this project: Ram Dass, Stephen Levine, Jack Kornfield, and Charles Garfield.

Rita Ricketson: David's partner, in every sense of the word, whose editing, computer expertise, and moral support are mainstays of our collaboration.

Katherine Grace Ricketson Feldman: Age five months, opener of David's heart and generous provider of many anecdotes.

Fred and Frieda Feldman: Without whom David and Nina would have had to locate another opportunity to extrude their twinship into physical reality.

Bert Smiley: For his loving acceptance of Nina and all that she is (including her time consuming and sometimes obtrusive relationship to her twin and co-author).

Margie, Ana, Stephanie, Anita and the others: For walking Nina through so many "don't knows"...

The Women's Vipassana Group of Washington D.C.: For providing Nina with a traditional environment in which to "practice what she would preach".

David and Nina in 1956, age 5

And to our readers, whose appreciation and feedback brought this book to fruition. Thank you all....

David and Nina today, age 37

Read This First

A Very Brief Overview

We'd like to begin by briefly describing the rest of the book, so that you know exactly what you're in for. As you perhaps already know from a glance at the rear cover, our 30 day plan is not "just " a how-to instructional on meditation. Instead, it's a complete program for integrating the many-levelled benefits of meditation into your daily life.

Learning to do this will improve your *mental* health, by changing the way you relate to your thoughts. It will improve your *emotional* health, by helping you to understand and work with your feelings, your relationships to other people, and your relationship with yourself. And it will improve your *spiritual* health, by helping you to develop and maintain a connection with the Universal Consciousness (or God, or the Higher Power, or whatever term you prefer to use).

A tall order? Perhaps — especially in only ten minutes a day of formal practice, plus as much "real life" use as you choose to do *while* you go about your everyday routine. But tall order or not, this is how we plan to help you do it:

We'll spend a few pages presenting our concept of MetaPhysical Fitness, and then tell you just who we are, and why we need to meditate. We'll talk about why you probably need to meditate, too, and give you some historical and physiological background on meditation. We'll present an overview of the means and ends of our method (on p. 30, if you can't wait), and finish up with a few general instructions before starting you out on Day 1 of our 30 day program.

A Shortcut: The Box System

We understand that some of you may be in a rush to jump right into the actual practice plan. So, since the introductory information discussed above is not *absolutely* essential to the plan, we've boxed the most important paragraphs of these earlier chapters, like the one below. Thus, people who want to go right to the 30 day plan can still get the gist of the opening sections by reading just the boxed chunks.

> If you're really itching to begin the 30 day plan, you can read only the boxed sections between here and page 47. As you skim through the pages, going from one box to the next, look at each **boldface** section title as well, and read any section that particularly appeals to you. This shortcut scan will get you to the exercises in no time at all! Then, after you have a few minutes, days, weeks, or years of meditation under your mental belt, you can come back and read the entire beginning of the book, word for word, at your leisure. So if you're "boxing" it, skim your way on to the next one, on page 11.

For Readers Of *The Three Minute Meditator*

For those of you who have read our earlier book, *The Three Minute Meditator*, welcome! (If you haven't, please go on to page 11, "What Is Meditation?") You're coming to *MetaPhysical Fitness: The 30 Day Plan* as old friends! And like communication between old friends, much of what we say here will be familiar, although some of it will be new, and the way in which it is presented will be quite different (and, we hope, more accessible).

In fact, we're writing this book largely in response to your urgings. Many Three Minute Meditators (3MMers) have written to let us know how much they liked our earlier book. Most told us that meditation was changing their lives in a more relaxed and compassionate direction and had become a valuable tool for stress reduction. But some readers said that it was "hard to know how to begin." That their well-paged 3MM sat in an easy-to-reach spot on the bedside table, but was not used often enough throughout the day. That, even with the best of intentions, fitting meditation into a busy lifestyle did not always happen spontaneously — and that some systematic suggestions would be very welcome.

Several readers described the array of meditations in 3MM as a sumptuous buffet brunch — such a large array of choices it was hard to know where to begin. They found themselves relying on one or two meditations and thinking that "someday" it would be nice to explore a few more. But again, the question of "Where to begin" seemed to be a stumbling block.

We were, of course, delighted to hear from you and interested to learn that more structure would help some get started. And so, *MetaPhysical Fitness: The 30 Day Plan*.

3MMer's: Use This Book To Meet *Your* Needs

You old friends may want to follow the Program a bit differently from new readers, perhaps picking and choosing your own eclectic patterns throughout the 30 days. And that's okay, since there's no right or wrong way to proceed. But, we do urge you to at least skim through the entire book. Although many of the exercises will be familiar, we have arranged them in a progression so that later experiences build on earlier ones. And: A Word To The Wise — during the writing of this book, both of us worked the 30 day plan, and found it to be very satisfying and helpful.

Speaking of "us", you'll notice that we have changed most of the "I"s in *The Three Minute Meditator* to "we"s in this book. We did this in the interests of readability, and didn't mean to imply that our experiences are the same. More the opposite, in that we hope that the upgrading of Nina to a full co-author will add another dimension to the book, since her life, personality, and meditational needs are not at all the same as David's.

We'd love to hear your thoughts about this book, and we thank you wholeheartedly (double-heartedly?) for your feedback and support. Keep in touch, and keep on meditating!

What Is Meditation?

We'd probably better define meditation before talking about it too much more. The following is our basic definition.

Meditation is the art of mental self-control. Each of the Three Minute Meditations in this book is an *exercise* that will help us to understand and to practice what we call the three levels of meditation. From now on, we'll use the words "exercise" and "meditation" pretty much interchangeably.

The first level of meditation involves relaxing the mind, and learning to focus mental attention. Many meditation methods never get beyond this step, so this is often what people think of when they think of meditation.

The second level of meditation involves understanding and learning to work with the way thoughts arise and depart in the mind.

> The third level of meditation helps us focus our mental awareness on an alternative way of being in the world. Ultimately, meditation can enable us to participate in this very different way of living, which can be called by a tremendous variety of names such as "Living In The Now", "Enlightenment", "Living A Spiritual Lifestyle", "Realization", "Christ Consciousness", "Acknowledging a Higher Power" or simply "Investing In The Meditator's Worldview".

The Benefits Of Meditation

> If you know enough about meditation to even pick up a book with a title like this one, chances are that you already know that meditation is just full of benefits. It will calm you down, and help you to deal with the stresses of daily life. It will probably allow you to sleep less, while increasing your available energy. It can be used to lower the blood pressure and heart rate.
>
> Meditation is also a wonderful tool to help deal with thoughts and emotions. Your fears and desires can actually become your teachers, rather than the tormentors that they may now be. But there's an even more important reason to meditate. No one can control the events that befall them to more than the most marginal degree. So learning to control your attitude and your thoughts about those events will help you to appreciate life more, and to face change or loss with greater acceptance and compassion.
>
> Finally, there is another whole level of benefits that await the diligent practitioner, because meditation can help you relate to yourself and the world in a radically different, and more spiritual, way. But we'll talk more about these matters metaphysical after you've had a taste of the meat-and-potatoes of a daily meditation practice!

MetaPhysical Fitness: A New Concept In Meditation

As we've worked to develop a way to best present the art of meditation to our readers, we experimented with a number of different analogies. We wanted to choose an analogy that would be familiar to everybody, and one which would stress the day-to-day usability , the immediate and practical rewards, of meditation. We came up with the idea of comparing meditation to physical fitness.

It's often tempting to think in terms of specific, concrete "things" rather than in terms of ongoing "processes." And it would be so convenient if "the meditative lifestyle" or even "Enlightenment" were things, that we could obtain or achieve once and keep forever, like rowing machines or law degrees. But they're not. They're ongoing processes, and they require ongoing practice, rather like getting (and staying) in shape...

The benefits of physical fitness are obvious. We look good, and we feel good. Everything that we do, whether work or play, we do with increased vigor and enthusiasm. If we should find ourselves in an emergency situation that requires physical action, our bodies are well prepared to do whatever is demanded of them.

Getting in shape isn't too hard. A few weeks or months of weight lifting combined with the Scarsdale Diet and we look and feel great! Jogging and the Pritikin Diet will work also, or Aerobic Parachuting and the Rutabaga Diet. But just a few months of indolence and over-indulgence, and we're again ready to enter the Pillsbury Doughboy Look-Alike Contest. Of course, even sporadic and feeble attempts at getting into shape are better than none, although the long-term effects of such lackadaisical efforts may be almost imperceptible.

We really like the comparison of meditating, or even of Enlightenment, with the idea of getting in shape. Like getting in shape, there are a great variety of equally effective ways to go about meditating. Like getting in shape, anyone can meditate, although it sometimes seems easier or more natural for certain people than for others. (Usually someone other than ourselves.)

Once a person has become physically fit, *everything* they do reflects their fitness and helps to increase it. They walk with bounce and balance, and climb stairs instead of taking elevators. Once a person begins to meditate, everything that happens to them presents a great opportunity to both demonstrate and to improve their meditative skills. Fears and desires, annoyances and disappointments, all become grist for the meditative mill. And a person who has developed a meditative mind has a wonderful tool with which to deal with whatever life can throw their way!

Unfortunately, just as with getting in shape, if we stop meditating, we lose most of the benefits, even though we at least now know that a tremendously useful tool awaits us when we choose to return to it. And finally, like getting in shape, we have to begin meditating somewhere. Very old or infirm persons wouldn't start their exercise programs by trying to run the Boston Marathon, but might instead begin with daily walks around the block. A modest beginning, but certainly steps in the right direction!

Someone new to meditation, or someone lacking time and commitment to a meditative practice, surely wouldn't buy a prayer mat and a one way ticket to India. Even 20 minutes twice a day at home might be more than they could do at first. But ten minutes each day of the following MetaPhysical Fitness program might be just what the (meta)physician ordered!

Martial Arts Of The Mind

Each of the Three Minute Meditations is an exercise for the mind. Like exercises for the body, they must be first practiced under controlled conditions in order to later obtain the benefits that they can provide in "real life" situations.

The karate student practices in the "dojo," or karate studio. He (or she) first practices a variety of punches and kicks, doing each one separately, carefully, repeating each movement tens of thousands of times. After mastering each move in isolation, they begin to practice more complicated combinations of blows, performing each sequence hundreds or thousands of times. They then spar with other students or instructors. Finally, if one day they need to use their martial skills on the street, in a real combat situation, their practice has fully prepared them to do so.

Similarly, whitewater kayakers must learn a technique known as the "Eskimo Roll" which enables them to turn their kayak right-side-up after it has turned bottom-up in a river rapid. They first learn this technique in a swimming pool. Once they feel comfortable "rolling" in the pool, they go out and purposely capsize their boat in a very small rapid, and then try to roll. Gradually, they progress on to roll practice in larger and more dangerous rapids, until they can confidently roll *anywhere* on the river.

Dancers begin by practicing certain standard foot and body positions while holding on to a rail in a dance studio. They focus their attention on getting the positions exactly right, before going on to more complex combinations of these positions. Eventually they are able to combine everything they know in a performance before an audience.

You'll begin by practicing a simple type of Three Minute Meditation called the "Clearing The Mind" Exercises. At first, you'll try to do them in calm surroundings, often devoting a full three minutes to each one. Then you'll begin to practice mind clearing meditations in non-stressful real life situations. After you learn to gain a moment or two of mental clarity at a time, you'll add another type of meditation, called the "Watching The Mind" Exercises. Again, you'll initially practice these exercises under conditions of relative comfort, so that later on you'll be able to perform them skillfully under stressful circumstances.

Once you become familiar with the mind clearing and watching exercises, you'll begin to use your new knowledge to increase mind control in "real life" situations, starting with practice during easy, non-threatening events. Instead of getting anxious or angry, you'll just *watch* your thoughts as the omelet arrives slightly overdone, or do a moment of mind clearing as the elevator refuses to stop at your floor. This practice will improve both the quality of your life, and the quality of your meditation. Although you may not ever reach the enlightened point of *welcoming* painful or difficult circumstances in your life, you will become able to see them (as Castenenda's Don Juan said) as challenges rather than obstacles!

As you gain practice and confidence, you'll be able to apply your meditative skills to more serious mental and interpersonal predicaments. Having the ability to calmly and confidently deal with *whatever* comes into our lives is truly the "Master Skill". As dealing with events through meditation becomes a part of our life, we begin to see problems and obstacles as opportunities to use our new meditative tools, just as the kayaker sees rapids not as problems to be avoided, but as exciting challenges to be faced. These challenges then hone and sharpen our skills, rather than frightening or defeating us!

The Scientific Approach

We're not asking you to believe us, or to take our concept of MetaPhysical Fitness or anything else on faith. We're both trained (Nina with her Ph.D. in psychology, and David with his Masters Degree) in the scientific or experimental method. We've both tried meditating, and it's worked for us, as we'll describe below. We've developed a simple method that you can try for yourself.

If you were an experimental scientist, and we told you that we had done an experiment in which guinea pigs fed on a daily diet of tequila and Pepto-Bismol® learned to run a maze 23% faster than guinea pigs fed a normal diet, you might tend to disbelieve us. But, since it would be a simple enough experiment to duplicate, you'd certainly try it yourself before ridiculing us and our results.

In the case of MetaPhysical Fitness, you, dear reader, are the scientist, the laboratory, and the guinea pig rolled into one! With a time investment of only minutes a day for 30 days, how can you lose by experimenting with meditation?

Confidence Comes With Practice

In virtually everything that we learn, whether a new language, a new game, or a new job, confidence comes with practice. As we do more and more of whatever it is that we're trying to learn, we get better and better, and more and more confident, at it. It's the exact same with meditation. When you begin, it may feel strange and awkward. As you give yourself the time to continue, even for a few minutes a day, it will become familiar and comfortable, and eventually an old and trusted friend and helper.

Levels Of Involvement: Swimming And Meditating

When we take up a new hobby or pursuit of any kind, we can get involved with it to a number of different degrees. Let's consider swimming, for example.

We can learn to swim, and then pursue swimming as an occasional pastime, once or twice a week throughout the summer. Or we might decide to learn to swim now as a kind of safety net, because we plan to take up sailing, and want to be able to save ourselves should we fall overboard. We might even choose to make swimming the focus of our life, and become serious competitive swimmers, swimming for hours every day.

We can likewise meditate with similar levels of involvement: as an occasional pastime or relaxer, as a lifesaving tool to be reserved for the emergency of a lifetime, or as a daily companion or even a lifestyle. A desire to use meditation at any level of involvement is a perfectly valid reason to learn to meditate now.

Feeling Resistant To The Idea Of Meditation?

Yes, there are reasons not to meditate. But they are not *good* reasons. So if you feel resistant to the idea of meditating, and especially if you think you have reasons for not meditating, please take the "Why I Don't Meditate" quiz in the appendix. You may also find the section on Commitment (page 35) useful. We believe that these portions of the book will help you to see how erroneous beliefs about meditation and about yourself can prevent you from enjoying one of the world's oldest and most useful forms of self-help!

Who We Are

We, David Harp and Nina Feldman, are twins. Although one of us lives near San Francisco and the other near Washington D.C., we work together by writing on twin Macintosh computers connected by phone modem. The following sections will tell you more about us, and about our relationship and experience with meditation.

First Person Plural

There will be considerable use of the pronoun "we" in much of the book. Not Mark Twain's "editorial we", which he called valid only for kings and people with tapeworms, but the "we" that states that we're all in this together, and that we, Nina and David, are trying to live this program as we write about it. Not issuing Olympian directives from our higher plane, but two ordinary people, like you, who are seeking a deeper and more satisfying way of being in the world.

Occasionally, we'll present ideas, hints or feedback from a few of the many 3MM fans who have called or written. These will be vignettes, with names changed for anonymity. Some are composites.

And in spite of being twins, we're discrete individuals as well, with very different experiences and attitudes on certain subjects, so we'll also want to talk separately. When we do, we'll use "DAVID:" and "NINA:" to indicate our separate voices, as follows.

DAVID: My name is David Harp. Although my training is mostly in psychology, for the past fourteen years I've been primarily a musician, music educator and writer. I've taught over a hundred thousand people to play the blues harmonica, and have written instructional books about a variety of other musical instruments. But that's not what you really need to know about me.

You see, I used to be a pretty unhappy guy. My harmonica classes and concerts were popular, and I may have looked successful and popular to other people, especially those who didn't know me too well. But inside I was vain, insecure, and prone to depression; compulsive about nearly everything, and a hypochondriac to boot. My thoughts and feelings seemed to control me, rather than the other way around...

It's no exaggeration to say that learning to meditate has transformed my life. Although my life is still far from perfect, every time I meditate, my ability to handle old fears, insecurities, and desires grows stronger. Thus my relationships with friends and family have become more loving and less needy or critical. I put less energy into worrying about my business, and more into doing whatever it is that needs to be done. I don't spend days or weeks each year in useless and miserable depression like I used to, so I have time to do volunteer counseling work with terminally ill or grieving people. Since I no longer need an endless series of new infatuations to make me feel loved, I've been able to become a husband, and a father. I truly believe that none of this would have been possible, without meditation.

But what's perhaps most important is that I like myself better. And I'm beginning — for the first time in over 35 years — to feel some minimal control over that mysterious, mutinous creature called the mind.

NINA: My name is Nina Feldman, and I'd like to tell you a little about myself. As far as my career goes, after receiving my Ph.D. in Psychology from Princeton University, I taught at the University of Maryland, then worked as a research psychologist for an international marketing/public relations firm. I'm currently a member of a "think tank" within the American Association of Retired Persons, located in Washington, D.C. But I now think of myself as a "person who meditates" at least as much as I think of myself as a "person who works."

I came to meditation much more recently than David. In fact, David was one of the major reasons I started to meditate. Having known David with greater or lesser intimacy throughout all of our lives, I was very intrigued when I noticed a tangible change in his behavior. The old "Super Dave" who was larger than life — wilder, more colorful, more visible than anyone else I knew — was mellowing. My brilliant "enfant terrible" twin brother was becoming more compassionate, with himself and with others. Intrigued, I started to watch and to listen... and to learn.

When David began to write *The Three Minute Meditator*, he invited me to help him with it. Discipline was not usually his strong suit and he suspected the book would get done months, if not years, earlier if I were involved to brainstorm, edit and provide an on-going impetus for completing the project. Never shy about sharing his enthusiasms, David also told me that if I were going to be involved, I'd darned well better get serious about meditating. Well, that push was all I needed.

I've always been interested in meditation and metaphysics, and have done a lot of reading on my own. But I'd lacked the follow through to make meditation part of my daily life. As a college undergraduate of the early 70's, my stated goal at one time was to "wear flowing white robes and float about two inches off the ground." Of course, that was *before* I went to grad school at Princeton, an eminently sobering experience!

I had several opportunities to begin meditating during my college years. I now regret letting them slip through my fingers, but I simply wasn't ready at that time. For instance, I and hundreds of thousands of other college students were trained in Transcendental Meditation™, only to drop it sometime thereafter. And, when a friend was living in an ashram in Cambridge one summer, I was fortunate enough to obtain an interview with a very well-known guru on his visit to the house. He gave me a mantra, which I regret to say I never used.

But, fifteen years later, meditation is bringing a new serenity and joy into my life. I've been meditating "seriously" for over a year now, although my "seriously" has covered quite a range of behaviors. I've gone from weekend retreats, sitting with a women's vipassana meditation group and integrating meditation throughout my waking/working days — to lapses of days, if not weeks, where I can't quite find the time to meditate. And then, back again to using these mind clearing techniques. My bottom line is, I keep coming back to meditation because it works. Life just plain feels better when I'm meditating. So why argue with success?

Why We Needed To Begin Meditating

DAVID: My own transformation into a Three Minute Meditator illustrates the way in which you can use meditation to shift from an "armed camp" relationship with your own mind to a peaceful and interesting co-existence.

My mind used to be a judgmental, nit-picking boss, and my life generally felt great when absolutely every little thing was going my way, and awful the rest of the time. I spent a lot of time feeling depressed, for no obvious reasons. But that was how it had always been for me, and I had no reason to think that things should, or even could, be different.

In 1984, things changed. I was about to publish the first nationally marketable edition of my "Instant Blues Harmonica for the 'Musical Idiot'!" package, of which I was enormously proud. But while my book was at the printers, a larger publisher (whom I had trusted, and taught to play harmonica) came out with his own version, with a distressingly similar title! My own brainchild, I felt, had been kidnapped, and I was terribly angry, hurt, scared, and depressed.

But, in my acute misery, a single healthy thought kept recurring: The idea that if I could somehow learn the "master skill" of *coping* with a situation like this, that skill would ultimately be worth more to me than a dozen successfully published harmonica books.

That thought persevered. I bought psychology, philosophy, and metaphysical books, and read and re-read them slowly and carefully. Previously, I had read these books for entertainment, or to learn the newest (and hippest) theories. Now, it felt like I was reading for my very life.

Virtually all of my favorite books strongly recommended some sort of daily meditation practice, so I began, after a twelve year hiatus, to experiment again with the Transcendental Meditation- technique that I'd learned but never really practiced in college. I also signed up for a 10 day meditation retreat with psychologist/poet Stephen Levine and Buddhist teacher/psychologist Dr. Jack Kornfield, where I learned that a tremendous diversity of meditation techniques exist.

I began to study meditation, and to make it a part of my daily life. As I learned some "mental self-control," my own thought processes became clearer to me. I found myself slightly less dominated by the usual old feelings of fear and desire. Hypochondria, my favorite bugaboo, would still surface occasionally, but I would generally recognize it quickly and let go of it. My previous day-long or week-long depressions began to disappear in seconds or minutes, hours at most. And even the insecurities that had obsessed me since grammar school started to fade quietly into the background noise of my mind.

I surely don't mean to imply that I'm really together now. I'd better not! Firstly, because it's not true, and secondly, because if I did, and my friends ever read this, I'd face a barrage of well-deserved ridicule, just as I did when "PM Magazine" ran a TV segment on me and called it (their idea, *not* mine) "The Harmonica Guru!"

But I am more together than before I began meditating. Today, outside events affect me less, and I can understand and deal with my thoughts and feelings much more easily. As my boyhood pals Ben & Jerry say, "It's cheaper than therapy, easier than living in a cave in the Himalayas, and if it can work for Harp, it can work for you too!"

NINA: Although David and the Three Minute Meditator project were the immediate causes of my leap into meditation, there were many other factors leading me in that direction. I was working at breakneck speed in a job that never ended. Morning, noon and night, weekends included, I'd find myself facing — and generating — masses of information and having to make sense of it all. Although I loved the work, I could feel my insights getting stretched and my intuition suffering as the impact of "information overload" began to hit me.

Meditation came into my life at a point when I really needed it. As I began to meditate, I could see the ways in which I "set myself up" to get stressed on the job. I began to realize that, yes, deadlines were important, but they often were arbitrary and a day or two more could usually be negotiated. As I began to clear my mind and feel some compassion for myself, I remembered how good it felt not to be stressed all the time. Oddly enough, as I stopped playing "beat the clock", I seemed to have more psychic "space". Things were getting done more easily and even more quickly. The same kind of project that would drive me crazy before, was now "no big deal." The *project* was the same, but *I* was different.

Around that time, I changed jobs to focus on an area that strongly attracted me. The transition was painful, as was giving up a prestigious job in which I'd invested huge amounts of energy and enthusiasm, but meditation helped smooth the way.

Do I believe in meditation? My answer is a resounding "Yes!"
I knew it would be useful, but I never expected to see such subtle — or
dramatic — changes. I've come a long way. But, there's still a long
way to go. What an incredible journey!

We're No Gurus

As you've doubtless already realized, we're not "guru types",
whatever your image of gurudom might be. We love to eat, drink
(moderately), and be merry, whenever possible. We don't levitate,
walk on fire (or water) or claim to be Enlightened Beings (with a capital
B, of course). (Speaking of capital B's, we capitalize all words whose
importance we want to emphasize, like Enlightenment. Hope you don't
mind!)

We are highly experienced teachers. And whenever we learn to
do something, we like to teach it, in the simplest way possible, in order
to offer "immediate gratification" to our students. We've done this, in
a dozen books, for harmonica, flute, guitar, and meditation. And while
developing each edition of each book, we've conducted tests and
experiments with groups of human "guinea pigs", so as to understand
how best to teach.

In the process, we've learned a lot about how people learn.
Perhaps our most important finding is this: keep it simple. Most people
would prefer learning to perform some skill "a little bit" right away,
rather than taking a long time to learn to do it well. And that's what we'd
like to help you do with meditation, today!

In short, we believe in meditation. We believe that it's been
good for us, and we believe that it will help you too. And that's why
we wrote this book.

Why You Probably Need To Meditate

Are you ever bothered by anger or fear? Distracted by desires?
Depressed, bored, or restless? Are you only able to feel happy when
everything is going right? And does life sometimes seem meaningless,
even during those rare periods when everything happens to be going
your way?

If you never have problems with feelings like these, then you
probably don't need this book. You're probably not human, either,
since just about everybody manages to make themselves unhappy at
least once in a while.

"Make themselves unhappy?" What a strange notion! Why would anybody want to *make* themselves unhappy?

Of course, it's much easier to believe that circumstances, or other people, make us unhappy. But that's a load of baloney! Because we've all met, or at least read and heard about, those few rare people who are able to be happy no matter what adversity shows up in their life. And we can all name a dozen rich, famous, healthy people whose lives were made miserable by themselves, from John Belushi to Howard Hughes. Make ourselves unhappy? You bet we do!

It's not really what happens in the outside world that makes a person happy or unhappy, satisfied or unsatisfied. What matters is how you feel inside your own mind. And this is no new idea: over 2,000 years ago, the philosopher Epictetus stated that "Men are not worried by the things that happen, but by their thoughts about those things."

He was clearly correct. For instance, during the 1929 Stock Market Crash, many of the brokers who dove to their deaths from Wall Street windows had more than enough money left to maintain a modest lifestyle. The stock market didn't kill them, and the window didn't kill them. The thoughts and feelings of their own minds did.

You see, for most of us, the mind can often be a cruel and demanding master, constantly criticizing and making judgments. It churns out a storm of contradictory, confusing thoughts. Makes you buy that 1989 GarbonzoMobile on credit, and then worry about the monthly payments. Makes you eat that extra helping, and then obsess about being overweight. Lets you forget about an anniversary date, but reminds you of the time you accidentally wore a pajama top to class in second grade. Makes you feel angry about demands from your child or parent, and then feel guilty for not being the "perfectly giving" father or mother, daughter or son. Jobs, sex, money, health — the list of potentially disturbing thoughts that your mind is just aching to throw at you goes on and on. But it doesn't need to be that way.

Think about having a good-sized dog as a pet, let's say, for example, a Saint Bernard. If it was a spoiled brat of a pup, it could make your life absolutely miserable, chasing the terrified postman down the street, destroying your neighbor's lawn, chewing your shoes into un-identifiable blobs, and even threatening you if you were bold enough to try to curb its depredations. But if it was well-trained by a few months at obedience school, it could be tremendously helpful, acting as a watchdog, fetching your slippers and paper, and generally being "man's best friend".

Likewise, with a bit of training (mind obedience school?), you can make your mind into your own best friend!

> Your mind doesn't have to be a weight around (or, rather, on top of) your neck. Meditation, the art of mental self-control, can quite literally "change your mind"— from a pain-in-the-butt boss to a useful and lively companion! Why let your own mind continue to work *against* you, when you can train it to work *for* you?

Now that we've talked you into starting a daily meditation practice (that is, if you weren't already convinced, which you probably were, since you're taking the time to read this book), we'll give you some historical and physiological background on meditation and the human mind.

Historical And Physiological Background

You don't need the following information in order to meditate. But understanding some of the historical and physiological background may help you to appreciate it more. We are indebted to Willis Harmon and Howard Rheingold's book "Higher Creativity" (see bibliography) for many of the following ideas.

Many millions of years ago, the ancestors of our ancestors were small, land-dwelling mammals, not far removed from those adventurous fish who left the water to crawl finnilly along the beach. Millions of years ago, as our indirect ancestors left the ground to swing amongst the treetops, their little brains began to develop in a way that affects us to this day.

Basically, these tree-swingers needed to be able to make instantaneous decisions about what to grab next. After all, mistaking a tree trunk or a large leaf for the limb of a tree would be a serious or terminal mistake when attempting to travel from branch to branch!

So their brains began to evolve the ability to recognize common objects instantly . Their eyes would scan an object, and if it generally looked like a branch, their brain would give them the go-ahead to grab.

As the brain enlarged and our predecessors evolved towards humanhood the brain maintained and expanded on this habit of generalizing. Primitive people also had to make instantaneous decisions, most importantly, whether to fight or flee when another creature suddenly appeared. Deciding to flee from a flamingo would result in the loss of a meal, while deciding to fight a bear would result in death.

React First, Think Later

So, instead of making an exhaustive analysis in cases like these, the brain learned to leap to conclusions. These conclusions were based on mental images implanted in the brain, which would be triggered by the general size and shape of any visible object. *After* reacting instantly, the object, or approacher, could then be examined in more careful detail, and from a safer distance.

In effect, then, our prehistoric forebears were learning to react to an *image* in their minds. Many a caveman, suddenly perceiving a tree stump at dusk, doubtless jumped for cover as his mind showed him a picture of a stalking tiger. Shortly afterwards, comparing tiger image to stump reality, he perhaps felt embarrassed, but if he hadn't jumped, and it *had* been a tiger...

Fight Or Flight...

Many psychologists and metaphysicians believe that this generalizing function of the brain still causes us to react to a thought, a mental image, as though it were an actual visual image. Thus, as we walk down a dark city street, the *thought* of a mugger in the next doorway causes us to react physiologically in much the same way as the sight of an *actual* mugger. The entire nervous system mobilizes its resources, adrenaline and other hormones rush through our body, blood pressure increases, and we feel anxious, as the "fight or flight" response is triggered.

The thought of a nuclear war, an auto accident, the boss approaching with a pink slip in hand — or any other stressful thought — all can cause our body to react with the fight or flight response. Thus many of us spend a large part of each day in a state of chronic anxiety.

...Versus Meditation

The unhealthy effects of excess anxiety have been chronicled for over fifty years. Fortunately, an equal but opposite reaction also exists, known as the "relaxation response," which balances the anxiety of the fight or flight response by calming and relaxing the nervous system.

It has been scientifically proven that a particular type of meditation, which we call "Clearing The Mind," is the most effective method of producing the relaxation response. For more clinical evidence on this subject, read Dr. Herbert Benson's book, "The Relaxation Response" (see bibliography).

But important though it is, the relaxation response is only the first of the benefits of meditation. If we also learn to observe, understand, and control the thoughts that unceasingly flow through our minds, we can begin to actively use our mind in a positive and tremendously empowering way, rather than allowing our mind to control us. This is the second main benefit of meditation. And we'll introduce, discuss, and help you to practice the third — the Meditator's Worldview — in the latter portions of this method.

And speaking of the method, it's time to discuss the whats, whys, and hows of Three Minute Meditations and the MetaPhysical Fitness Program!

What's So Different About Our Method?

We realize that there are thousands of psychologists, philosophers, and metaphysicians who have already written books on the subject of meditation. But most of these are not for the beginning, would-be meditator, nor for the busy Western meditator who has only limited time and energy with which to practice. Few, if any, provide a concrete daily plan of action, a clear-cut method for exploring the places in which meditation may best fit into your own life.

Our MetaPhysical Fitness program presents a progressive array of mind exercises for you to try while examining the ways in which you can most easily and effectively begin to integrate them into your daily schedule. By the end of the 30 days, you'll actually be creating and implementing the customized meditation plan that best suits you!

Why We Had Problems With Certain Other Methods

Some meditation books and methods are unbelievably complex — full of long words and torturous, tortuous, concepts. When we began to study meditation, even such useful phrases as "manifestation of the unpotentiated noumenon" or "nididhyasana sadhana" were a turn-off.

You don't need to know lots of big words to meditate. That's like asking someone to learn Chinese so they can play Chinese checkers!

Once you understand the basic concepts, meditation is a *simple* thing to do — though not always *easy*. There's no need to complicate a beginner's book with strange and esoteric jargon or terminology.

Another problem that we encountered when starting our study of meditation was that some meditation books are dogmatic. According to them, there is just one "right" way to meditate. Not surprisingly, the "right" way is usually tied in to a particular religious, social, or business organization, with which the writer is often affiliated. Any other method is considered ineffective at best, if not downright sinful. To us, meditation is a tool or method that can be used by anyone, regardless of religion (or lack thereof), creed, culture, or country of national origin.

Between the two of us, we've read hundreds of meditation books, and learned a great deal from them. But we've especially learned that we prefer our meditation straight: no jargon or cults, and hold the dogma, please!

Condensing The Common Characteristics Of Meditation Methods

While studying many of the available "Enlightenment" methods, we found that most share certain underlying characteristics, although the surface details may vary widely. We've analyzed and excerpted these meditational "bottom lines" and we'll try to present our synthesis of MetaPhysical Fitness ideas, exercises, and techniques to you as clearly as possible, drawing the concepts together and elaborating on important themes. This will give you a solid meditational foundation, if somewhat condensed.

We believe (and many others agree, as the quotes in the front of the book indicate), that our program, diligently used, can be the only meditation book that you'll ever need. But we also strongly recommend that *after* you've learned to meditate, you go back to the metaphysical literature, and explore your areas of special interest. We're certain that you'll enjoy and benefit from further study, and have provided a bibliography at the end of this book which will help you to do so.

By the way, contrary to some popular belief, the study of meditation does not have to be all consuming, difficult, painful, or other-worldly. You don't have to "pay your dues" by *struggling* to obtain a meditative consciousness. In fact, struggling is *not* what this book is about. We believe that meditation should be an exciting and pleasurable new skill to learn, a skill that has a natural and satisfying flow of its own. And the 30 days of this program are enough to get you flowing on your way!

More About MetaPhysical Fitness And The 3MM Method

As we said earlier, our MetaPhysical Fitness program is based on the exercises that we call Three Minute Meditations (3MMs). Each 3MM is a specific exercise to help us gain mental self-control. Each one helps us to focus our mental attention, to become more aware, more mindful.

The Three Minute Meditation/MetaPhysical Fitness program is unique, in that it teaches you to meditate *while* going about the affairs of your daily life. Most other meditation methods advise that you set aside a certain time or times each day for meditation. Some demand that a shrine of some sort be built, and that meditation only take place there. The most extreme programs require you to live in a monastery, far from the distractions of the world.

But limiting meditation to specific times or places can have two negative consequences. Firstly, such demands can be hard to adhere to, especially for the beginning meditator who has not yet felt the positive results of a daily meditative practice, and thus is not yet heavily committed to it. Secondly, a time-and-place-specific meditation program somehow sets meditation aside from "normal" existence. Practicing the Three Minute Meditation way avoids both of these problems, although of course once you begin meditating, you can then explore and pursue *any* style of practice that appeals to *you*.

It's obviously easier to find time to do a number of short meditations during a day than to set aside one or two chunks of twenty or thirty minutes every day. Many of the Three Minute Meditations can be done while walking, or eating, or even stopped at a red light. Others can be practiced during a quick visit to the bathroom!

Once you get the hang of Three Minute Meditating, you'll find yourself doing many "mini-meditations" that will be amazingly effective in calming or centering you — even though they only take a few seconds! You'll also probably find yourself wanting to do some longer meditations, of ten or twenty minutes or more, as both of us do.

> We, and many others, find that integrating our meditation practice throughout the day helps us to use meditation skills in daily life. Ideally, meditation becomes a way of life, a way of relating to the world, rather than "something that you do for a little while every day."

DAVID: I recently attended my annual ten day retreat in the Vipassana monastic tradition. No talking, no eye contact, no reading or writing. Approximately sixteen hours a day of alternating walking and breathing meditation, with eating meditations strongly advised during mealtimes. It was great, and I felt very high and clear. But then it was over, and I had to come home!

Long retreats, and esoteric disciplines, can be of great value — monastic traditions exist in nearly every culture. But sooner or later, unless you're a monk, you'll have to come home — that is, you'll have to make your experience apply to daily life. With Three Minute Meditation, you're *already* home. As the old joke goes: "What's the difference between a monk and a Three Minute Meditator? Monks live in order to meditate better, and Three Minute Meditators meditate in order to live better..."

What You're In For: An Overview Of The 30 Day Plan

The next section will provide a general overview of our program. Knowing what to expect may help you to understand and appreciate the rest of this book.

What To Expect Each Day

Each day of the 30 consists of five or six elements, which we'll describe as follows.

The **practice plan,** at the beginning of each day, gives you a general idea of what you'll be doing that day.

Some days will have a **preliminary instruction section,** in which we present information that will be useful to you when you read the actual instructions for the exercises.

Then we'll give you the **specific exercise instruction** or instructions for the day. Reading these sections will probably take between three and ten minutes a day, depending on the day and your reading speed.

Exercises will be used in both **formal practice** and **real life use**. By formal we don't mean wearing tuxedos or evening gowns. Nor do we mean to imply that formal practice is somehow more serious or valuable than real life use — if anything, the opposite is truer. Rather, we're using these terms formal and real life to refer to two different types of training: the swimming pool practice versus the in-the-river use of the kayaker, or the in-the-karate studio practice versus the on-the-street combat use of the martial artist. Scientists make this same distinction between in vitro experiments (in the test tube) and in vivo experiments (in real life situations), actors and actresses differentiate between rehearsal and performance, and football teams between drilling and playing. In all of these cases, what we would call the formal practice (or rehearsal, or drill) is the training that makes the real life use possible.

Formal practice, limited to no more than eight or ten minutes a day, will take place under controlled conditions, in a quiet and comfortable place, where it will be easy to focus on learning and doing the exercise. This will most often involve being seated with eyes closed, except for the walking meditations, of course.

Real life use will take place throughout the day, while going about the course of daily life. You'll begin doing your real life use meditations at times that are non-stressful and convenient. And since helping you to integrate meditation into your everyday routine is an important part of our method, we'll give you exercises that work anywhere, whether jogging or commuting, walking the dog or waiting for the bus, phone calling or computing, cooking, babysitting, or doing the dishes. Gradually you'll start to use your increasing meditative abilities in slightly stressful situations. And eventually you'll find that you can make the techniques work regardless of conditions, during smooth sailing or hurricane weather alike!

At the end of each day, we'll offer some additional inspirational material, or "thoughts for the day". These few pages may present some extra technical hints or tips, or some ideas that will help you to use the day's meditations, or to understand the following day's exercises. Feel free to read these sections before doing the exercises, if you think that doing so will inspire you to work the program. But remember— theory without practice is empty indeed!

Sometimes, especially in some of the later days, all of these above daily components will be blended together, inspiration with instruction, and formal practice with real life use. But by the time you reach this point in the program, you'll have no trouble understanding how to use the material, even if it's not presented in quite as structured a format as the earlier days.

New Exercises And Review Days

We've found that grouping similar types of meditations together is the most manageable way to present information. You'll always have a few days of new exercises, followed by a Review Day in which we'll repeat selected exercises and give you a chance to go over some of the building blocks once more before moving on. It seemed that certain chunks of information "wanted" to stay together, so rather than arbitrarily break up pieces in order to have nice, regularly sized chapters, we've allowed the length of daily chapters to differ widely.

It All Fits Together Just Like Baseball Training

As you work on the simpler exercises, we'll discuss and preview more complicated concepts and meditations, because all will eventually work together to create a whole that is far more effective and satisfying than any sum of its parts. So if some of the early exercises seem hard to do, be assured that the later ones will help you with the earlier ones. Does it seem paradoxical that while the earlier exercises prepare you for the later ones, the later ones will also help you to enjoy and refine your practice of the earlier ones? If so, let's return to our metaphor of physical fitness.

Consider some young would-be baseball players. They might begin with a program of calisthenics to build general strength, while starting to learn the rules of the game. They would soon begin to practice throwing, catching, and batting skills. These specific baseball skills would increase their strength and agility, and probably both help and encourage them to do the calisthenics better. Shortly thereafter, the coach would introduce the principles of strategy and teamwork, and our young ballplayers would be expected to simultaneously study all of the above elements, physical, analytic, and interpersonal.

Days 1 Through 30: What We'll Be Doing

Likewise, we'll proceed on a number of levels at once, because as we said in our definition of meditation, there are three main levels of meditation. These are, once again, first learning to relax the mind, then learning to work with the thoughts and feelings of the mind. And finally, learning to understand, accept and see the world in the excitingly different way which we call the Meditator's Worldview.

We'll begin with the mind clearing meditations, a series of simple exercises designed both to help relax the mind's constant chatter, and to teach the mind to better focus its attention. Within a day or so we'll start (in our inspirational sections) to discuss the Meditator's Worldview.

A quick analogy: learning to focus the mind's attention is rather like learning to control the light beam of a hand held flashlight. Anyone can shine a spotlight on a rock. With just a bit of practice, we can learn to keep our light on a car driving past us. After a great deal of practice, and perhaps some arm exercises, we might be able to keep the spotlight on a slowly moving bird as it flies through the night. And it would take a tremendous amount of hand/eye co-ordination to illuminate the flight of a swooping and darting swallow through the night sky.

When learning to clear and focus the mind, we'll shine our mental attention on physical processes like walking and breathing. We'll begin by counting these processes (counting things is something we all learn very young, so it's easy to do). Then we'll label them. Finally, we'll dispense with numbers and labels and simply experience breathing and walking, looking and listening, in a meditative way.

After a week of mind clearing, we'll be in good shape to go to the second level of meditation, working with the mind. We'll practice the two wonderful mental tools of Relaxation and Visualization. In fact, we'll begin to use them to enhance our meditation practice by visualizing ourselves using the various techniques in real life situations. Then we'll go on to spend a week with the Watching The Mind exercises. We'll learn to understand the process by which our minds work, which will enable us to better control the specific content of our thoughts and emotions.

In this second level of meditation, we'll shine our mental awareness not on physical processes but on mental ones. We'll learn to treat our own thoughts as objects of our attention, once again by counting, labelling, and experiencing them. Treating our thoughts this way will soon give us great awareness, power, and control over our fears and desires, feelings and emotions.

In the third week we'll expand our study of the second level of meditation by learning some new mental tools. Most important will be the fine art of Compassion towards self and others, a tool without which any meditation practice would be dry and dour indeed. We'll continue to work on our Compassion as we study the subjects of Judgement, Don't Know, and Living In The Now, all of which will help us with Softening Around Physical And Mental Pain. On Day 24 we will begin to deal with what for most of us is the greatest pain, that of Imperma-nence. And hard though it may be, we'll find that the grief and loss of Impermanence can be used to sweeten the poignancy and piquancy of a life on Earth.

The metaphysical third level of meditation will be woven into the first weeks of the program in a slightly indirect way. In the last days of the fourth week we'll approach it head on as we focus our attention on the subtle question "Who Am I?", a question that cuts to the very root of existence.

Thus the first twenty-eight days will be spent learning and reviewing a variety of new skills and ideas. The last two days will focus on developing your own meditation maintenance plan and on the ethical questions that face the meditator.

> You don't need to study the above description of the 30 day program in order to do the program. But if you'd like to know what you're in for, you may want to read it in its entirety.

What Can You Accomplish In 30 Days?

Clearly, thirty days is just a drop in the bucket over a meditational lifetime. But, even this mere month can give you a grounding in a variety of exercises and levels of meditations, which will allow you to explore your own meditational preferences and needs. Perhaps you'll decide that you simply want to use meditation as a relaxation tool. Maybe your interest in meditating will extend principally to observing and working with your thoughts and feelings. And should you choose to take what some philosophers call "the high road without guard rails", we believe that the method we present here can, if diligently used, take you as far as a human being can go on the path of (dare we say it?) Enlightenment! And now on to a few general instructions, before be-ginning with Day One!

General Instructions: The "Three C's"

There are really only a few important general instructions for following the MetaPhysical Fitness program. Below, we'll discuss the "Three C's": Commitment, Conscientiousness, and Compassion. We'll also talk specifically about a few of the common difficulties (or, we should say, challenges) that a new meditator may encounter.

On Commitment

By commitment, we mean the degree of desire that you have to work this program. And, even though working the program can be exciting and enjoyable, it does take work. Like anything else, from a sport to the study of any subject, the rewards that you obtain will be in direct relationship to the amount of time that you devote to your MetaPhysical Fitness. The more time and energy you put into it, the faster and greater results you will see in yourself.

One of the most unique aspects of the 30 Day Plan is that although we "require" only a maximum of ten minutes a day of formal practice, you can put as much time into the exercises *while* going about your daily existence as you like. So if you can commit yourself to integrating the exercises into your routine as often as possible, especially during time that is usually "wasted" (waiting for the bus, driving, walking between errands, on telephone hold, etc.), you can actually spend a great deal of each day meditating. If you do this, even for a few days, your rewards will be swift and striking.

One last word, or perhaps a warning, on the subject of commitment. We both know people (in fact, to be honest, we've both done this ourselves) who begin a study or a project and, almost immediately after starting, hit a snag or frustration. They (we?) then throw up their hands and say "I can't do this!" or "I'm just not cut out to do this!". What they really mean is that they are not willing to take the time necessary to overcome their resistance to learning the new skills, or the energy necessary to overcome their old self-image as a person "who just can't meditate (or ice skate, or play harmonica)".

If you find this happening to you, please try to be honest with yourself and recognize what is happening. If you've gotten this far (finding and reading this book up to here), you're already well on the path to a meditative lifestyle, since the realization that such a path exists and the desire to be on it are two of the most important precursors for the person seeking a way of higher consciousness. We sincerely believe that if you take a few hours to read the entire book, *without* doing the exercises at all, and take the "Why I Don't Meditate" test on page 226, you'll overcome any momentary blockage. Please give it a try — it's well worth it!

Conscientiousness: On Buckling Down

Learning to meditate is a bit like training yourself to wear a seat belt. At first, you're likely to forget to buckle up when you get in the car. But if you have decided to be conscientious about using seat belts, as soon as you notice that it isn't buckled, you put it on, every time, no matter what reasons you may have for not doing so. Perhaps you're just going to the grocery store. Perhaps it's a safe, straight road, without traffic. Perhaps you're only three blocks away from your destination. No excuses — you just buckle up. Soon it becomes a habit (and a healthy one, at that).

DAVID: Perhaps an even better analogy would be learning to buckle my beloved new daughter into her car safety seat. She hates it (we call it her "torture seat"), and I'm sometimes tempted to let her ride without being buckled in. But that would be a perfect example of letting *indulgence* take the place of love. Sure, she'd be happier riding in a lap, but because I'm truly concerned with what's best for her, I'd never let her do that, even for a block or two.

Similarly, it's important to be conscientious about your meditation, to keep in mind that while you're meditating, meditating is the most important thing to do. Your intention should be to keep your attention focussed on the chosen object of meditation, be it your breath, your steps, your feet, a sound, a candle, or whatever. That means *as soon as you notice* that your attention has strayed from the meditation, you bring it gently but firmly back. That means not spending even an extra second on the daydream, no matter how exciting it is (so forget the old "but wait — this is a really important thought I'm thinking — I'd better stick with it, and meditate later" trick). Don't waste even a second on self-critical thoughts like, "Darn it! There I go, thinking again. I'll never get this right" Simply *let go* of whatever thought it was that passed through, and come back to the meditation. Just for these three minutes, the meditation is your *preferred* thought — any others can wait. Even though it might seem to be more satisfying to stick with that lovely daydream or that important idea instead of returning to the meditation, in the long run your self-discipline will be far more healthy than your self-indulgence.

On Compassion: Why Self Love Will Help You Meditate

Learning to be compassionate to yourself (and to others) is one of meditation's most important lessons. Many of us have such undeveloped compassion skills that we can make anything, even meditation, just another opportunity for self-criticism. We'll talk lots more about compassion later on, but for now, compassion lesson number one is to treat yourself with loving kindness during meditation practice. Even if you're not yet brimming over with self-love and able to offer yourself full acceptance, there are practical reasons for doing so during meditation.

You see, spending any amount of time berating yourself for not having been properly focussed on the meditation (because you momentarily thought of lunch, or work, or sex) is just more time spent not focussing on the meditation. And spending valuable meditation time not focussed on the meditation is in direct conflict with our guideline above on being conscientious. So even if you tend to be self-critical, take a three minute breather from it. Catch yourself thinking? Don't agonize, just go back to the meditation.

Building Bridges From The Boulders Blocking Your Path

If you're concerned by the number of distracting thoughts that occur when you meditate, it may help to realize that the thoughts which distract you from the meditation are actually *helping* you. They give you the opportunity to notice that you're no longer focussed on the meditation, so that you can return your attention to it. And it's the act of noticing that your mind has wandered off, and returning your attention to the meditation, that actually teaches you to control your mind! Our favorite Indian philosopher/metaphysician, Sri Nisargadatta (see bibliography), calls this "building our bridges from the boulders that block our path."

Paper Training The Puppy

Think about trying to paper train a puppy. You place it on the newspaper. It wanders off. You gently, patiently bring it back. It wanders off again. *It is the act of being returned* to the newspaper that paper trains the pup. You don't kick it when it wanders off, nor give up in disgust. Likewise, it is the act of *noticing* that the mind has wandered, and *returning* the attention to the meditation, which helps us learn to strengthen the mind's ability to focus.

Twin Examples

DAVID: When I began to meditate, I was "plagued" by distracting thoughts. I'd try to focus on my breathing, but a typical meditation session might have gone something like this: "breathe in, breathe out...wow, I'm meditating...uh-oh, I'm not supposed to be thinking about meditating, I'm supposed to be focussing on my breathing...in, out...hungry...uh-oh...drat, I can't do this, I'm no good...in, out, in, out, in, out...hey, I've got it now!...feelings of pride...uh-oh, better go back to breathing...in, out, in out...wonder what's for lunch...darn...in, out, in, out...wonder if it's time to stop yet...etcetera." Sometimes I'd get lost in a daydream of some sort, and my period of distraction would last for minutes at a time, far longer than I was ever able to concentrate on my breath!

Now that I'm more experienced, I still have plenty of sessions like that! But many times, I can just *quickly notice* that a thought has crept in, and *go right back to my preferred business at hand*, which is meditating. So a current session might look more like this: "breathe in, breathe out, in, out, in, out...ahh, a lunch thought...in, out, in, out...Doing Well!...ahh, that's a pride thought...in, out, in, out...." Of course, sometimes I still spend more time being distracted, than being focussed! But I notice the distractions more quickly, and return to the meditation!

NINA: At first, meditation frustrated me because I kept wondering whether or not I was "doing it right." I'd start meditating, and immediately begin evaluating my own performance: "Breathe in, breathe out...is this how it's supposed to feel...in, out...nothing's happening...in, out...I thought this was supposed to *relax* me...but.I'm feeling kind of restless...in, out...in, out...Ahh, now I'm getting into it...in, out... lost it...drat...I wonder if most people have this much trouble getting started?...maybe it won't work for me...in, out...etc."

Once I decided simply to return to the meditation every time I left it (no matter what the intrusive thought was), I was finally able to stop watching and worrying and just meditate. And when I started to apply compassion and even began appreciating interfering thoughts, I stopped being so self-critical and competitive with myself ("It felt better yesterday").

My meditations still get restless and judgmental at times, but now I'm better able to watch my thoughts, and see how my drive to "do it right" gets in the way of meditating. Rather than trying to distance myself by analyzing "the meditation experience," I just *do* it!

On Enlisting Support For Meditation

If you live alone or in a situation where you have plenty of privacy, then doing the meditation practice should be no problem at all. For those who don't, drawing a line between your own needs as a meditator and the requirements of daily living can, at times, require forethought. Spouses, roommates, and significant others will usually understand and honor the request for an uninterrupted few minutes to meditate. And indeed, this is a perfectly *reasonable* request to make — but not always easy to either make or receive.

Lauren, described her difficulties with an unsupportive spouse. "I've been married 35 years and I recently started meditating. I think my husband felt excluded, because he always seemed to need me just when I wanted a few minutes out. He would interrupt my meditation constantly, and I would let him. Then I realized I was sending him the message that this really didn't matter to me. When I started to take my meditating more seriously, I was able to realize that five minutes sooner or later was not a big deal and began to protect my time. It was hard at first because I felt guilty, but now he's getting used to it. And I feel good about making this commitment to myself."

If someone does begin talking to you while you're meditating, simply saying, "I'll be with you in a few minutes, I'm meditating now," affirms your commitment to this activity without overlooking your companion's request. If the talking continues, however, you may want to cut short your meditation and explain your need for a few uninterrupted minutes. Or perhaps you can find a place and time where you won't be interrupted at all (bathrooms are usually good). Ideally and eventually, rather than getting angry at interruptions, you can begin to use them as opportunities to deepen your practice, but that can easily take a few weeks (so hide if you have to).

Interruptions from children can be harder to deal with. A parent who doesn't "look busy" is often fair game and small children's demands can make it difficult even to do mini-meditations.

If a child is old enough to understand "time outs", you can present your need for a few quiet moments as a "stop, go" game. Try drawing a red and green circle on opposite sides of a page. Let your child know that the red circle is a time out for *you* and that you can't play until the green light comes on again. Training children to respect your need for a few minutes of psychic space, even if you don't look busy, is important to your meditational well-being.

With three young children at home, Chris finds it difficult to meditate. "Two are old enough to understand when I need to be left alone, but not the youngest. I'm learning to use her as the focus of my meditations. When I'm breast feeding her, I meditate on those sensations and when I'm walking her to sleep, I do some step counting. I used to get angry when my meditations were interrupted, but now I'm learning to use whatever comes along as the focus of my attention."

DAVID: I like to meditate while babysitting my new daughter. If she begins to fuss or cry, I try to make whatever I need to do to console her the center of my meditation, whether it's diapering or rocking. If I feel really distracted, incompetent, or annoyed, I make those feelings the meditational focus, and work on softening around them.

The techniques that Chris and David described are some of the more advanced techniques of the 30 day program. These exercises, which allow you to use any physical actions (Days 6 and 7), emotions (Day 15), or the act of softening around painful feelings (Day 23) as meditations, will let you make meditation part of your life, rather than something "that you do" separate from it.

How best to deal with possible skepticism from family or friends? We suggest that you mention this book and the idea of Three

Minute Meditations to your significant others as you begin working this program. Make the idea inclusive rather than exclusive, right from the start.

It will also help later on, when loved ones begin to notice your increased relaxation, serenity, and ability to handle stress. You'll then be able to say, "remember the program I told you about..."

NINA: Mini-meditations don't interfere at all with my schedule. In fact, no one even has to know I'm meditating unless I choose to tell them. But, I found I wanted to talk about the ways in which some of my attitudes were changing. And, without prior notice, my husband might have started to wonder what was going on, for example, when the things that used to upset me "suddenly" became no big deal. Little changes, small differences, but noticeable.

On Sleepiness

Some people find that they get sleepy when they begin to meditate. If this is a problem for you, we suggest choosing the time during the day that you're most wide awake for your formal practice sessions, at least at first. If you drink coffee or tea, try a cup just beforehand. If even this doesn't seem to help, and you find yourself drifting off in the middle of a breath, try meditating while standing up — it's a rare person who can fall asleep that way. If sleepiness continues to trouble you, perhaps you will need to use more active forms of meditation, like step counting, rather than more sedentary ones. Finding what works best for you is one of the reasons that we offer such a variety of techniques — please use them!

Some traditionalists use harsher methods to combat sloth. Meditation teacher Jack Kornfield tells of his battle with somnolence in Thailand, where his teacher made him meditate while sitting at the very edge of a deep well. We emphatically do not recommend that one!

On Restlessness

If a meditation makes you feel antsy, try a few different varieties to find one that suits you better. Or, as meditation teacher Joseph Goldstein says. sometimes restlessness can be overcome by just accepting it ("Okay, I'm restless, so what. I'll just be the first human being to die of restlessness...."). You can then use the restlessness itself as the focus of the meditation, and use the Softening around pain techniques of Day 22 to deal with your discomfort. For many people who feel tense or nervous at first, lots of very short (even less than three minutes) meditations each day may be the best way to start, gradually increasing the time as the comfort level increases.

What To Do If It Hurts Sometimes

For some people, as they begin to meditate, certain painful feelings that have been long suppressed begin to come back into conscious awareness. If you find yourself experiencing some pain after the first day or so (most probably won't, but a few may, and it's no reflection on either your desire or ability to meditate), it might be useful for you to take a break from the actual meditation exercises, and read through the entire book before continuing. If you experience any type or degree of painful feeling, please read our section on What To Do When It Hurts (page 124) before doing any more meditation.

On Timing Yourself

It's important to remember that even though we call our method The Three Minute Meditation method, the exercises don't have to be exactly three minutes long. As you'll find in reading on, some of the exercises can be done for 30 seconds, or even three seconds.

In some of the formal practice sessions, you may want to meditate for a particular amount of time, in which case you can use an egg timer, or a watch with a beeper alarm. Or, you can simply meditate while sitting where you can easily see a clock if you open your eyes. As long as you don't end up making clock-watching the de facto focus of your meditation (unless you invent a clock-watching meditation, which is perfectly alright with us), an occasional glance probably won't interfere too much with your practice. And after just a few sessions, you'll begin to get a general idea of how long three minutes (or two, or four, more or less) are. Once again, the times given are guidelines, not absolutes, so don't spend much energy worrying about them.

DAVID: I wear an inexpensive ($20) Casio wristwatch that has what is called a countdown timer. You set the timer to any particular amount of time (three minutes, just for example), and then whenever you press a certain button, the watch will count off three minutes, and then beep you. What I particularly like about this watch is that I can make the 0:03:00 (three minute timer) appear large on the face of the watch, with the actual time in the background. Then every time that I look at my watch, ("What time is it, Kids? It's time to meditate!") I'm reminded of my real priority — being a Three Minute Meditator!

How To Know What To Do During The Day

For those of you who prefer not to carry this book around during the day, you can write down the few words necessary to remind you of the day's "Real Life Use" exercises. Since most days there will only be one or two of these, it won't be hard to do. If you use a daily memo pad, you can note the exercises there — a few people even write them on the back of their hands!

What Is "Successful Completion" Of The Program?

Success in this program is in no way a rigid concept. Success may be different for each person and does not necessarily mean completing all 30 days in order. It simply means getting what *you* need out of this program. Like exercise, even a few days will be of benefit, although of course it's better to develop a meditational habit and then stay in good MetaPhysical shape.

So there's no right or wrong way to approach this program. Some may pick up the book and go straight through, following the action plan on a daily basis. Others may want to try the new exercises each day, but not follow the action plan. Some may read through the book and decide not to start, and that's okay, too! Just the reading of this book, with its technical and inspirational information, will be of value. Perhaps a meditative seed will be planted and ready to sprout someday when the conditions are right for you...

As with any program, people often start and stop — a week or two on, a week or three off. (We both try to watch what we eat and exercise, but it's always an on-and-off program!) And, as with exercise, if you've had a long lapse and feel the need for a slow re-entry, you may want to start over from Day 1. On the other hand, if you've been meditating "on your own" and feel comfortable with these skills, start with the day at which you left off. The key is being honest about your own level. If you come back at too "advanced" a level, you may get frustrated and stop again. If you re-enter at too easy a level, you may get annoyed and quit.

If you're doing the program day by day and finish only half the practice plan for a particular day, you might decide to do the unfinished practice plan again from start to end on the following day. Or, you might decide to do just the unfinished half of the practice plan on the following day. Once again, there's no single right way to do it. The most important point is that you get a sense of what feels best for you. Learning to approach life through the "Braille Method," simply feeling your way along, as our teacher Stephen Levine likes to say, is one of the most basic lessons of meditating.

In fact, it would be perfectly reasonable and valid, and probably tremendously effective, if you have the time, to do each day's practice plan for an entire week, or even each day's practice plan for a *year*. If you get it together in a mere 30 years, you're way ahead of most people!

In fact, The Buddha once said that Enlightenment takes, on the average, 100,000 mahacalpas. And one mahacalpa is approximately the time it would take for a bird, dragging a silk scarf from its beak over the top of Mount Everest once a year, to wear the mountain down to sea level. So don't worry about *finishing* your quick sprint to Enlightenment, but realize instead that you might as well *start* right now!

So Start Whenever You're Ready

There's nothing special you'll need to buy or do, and not much that you need to know before you begin this Program. No special clothing, no equipment, no limbering up for a lotus position. If you've got a few minutes right now, you're ready to start!

On Thoughts And Clearing The Mind

Just as the principle focus of most physical fitness programs is the body, the principle focus of our MetaPhysical Fitness program is the mind. Just as a well-trained body is able to perform admirably in any physical situation, a well-trained mind can effortlessly perform whatever mental tasks are required of it. And just as a fit body does not need to call attention to itself with aches and pains, a fit mind doesn't need to experience the anguish and suffering that so many of us experience on a daily basis.

We'll have lots more to say about the mind as we gradually unveil our "Meditator's View Of the Universe" sections, but for now, rather than worrying about what the mind actually *is*, let's just consider how the mind *works* — and how we can learn to work with it.

Minds are just chock-full of thoughts — that's just the way they are. You may sometimes be able to concentrate so intensely on a specific task that no distracting thoughts interfere. For a while. But soon enough a moment of restlessness, or doubt, or desire, or fear creeps in. And, thoughts being what they are, when your mind *isn't* strongly focussed — when you're driving, or eating, or just relaxing by yourself — your mind may jump from thought to thought like the proverbial "drunken monkey" leaps aimlessly from branch to branch.

Most of the time, our mental attention is directed outwards, to other people, to the outside world. Our mind is full of thoughts that plan for the future, or analyze the past. We constantly make judgments about *everything* that passes into our mental field of view: I like this person, dislike that one, she's beautiful, he's a jerk. Some thoughts are casual, idle, mere mental prattle. And some thoughts may be powerful enough to last a lifetime, as when we spend years being obsessed by the same strong desire, or beating ourselves endlessly with the same seemingly "unmanageable" fears.

When we work with the mind clearing meditations, we simply focus our attention onto just one thing, whether it's our breath, our walking, a candle flame, or whatever. While concentrating our attention onto the chosen object of our meditation, we try not to be distracted by those same thoughts that harass us normally. They will inevitably sneak in, and that's okay. But even a few seconds of mental clarity can really soothe the mind.

Generally, we'll learn the mind clearing exercises in three progressive steps. We'll begin by *counting* our breaths, or our steps, or some other object of our meditation, as counting is a familiar and easy way to focus our attention. Then we'll progress on to *labelling* the breath, or steps, a process slightly less clear cut than counting, but still quite a customary habit of the mind. Lastly, we'll dispense with numbers and labels, and attempt to simply *experience* the object of our meditation, with as little thought or judgment as possible.

This practice of keeping the mind clear by consciously focussing the attention is a wonderful exercise in mental control. And as the mind clears, we can move on to the next step, "Watching The Mind."

Some of the MetaPhysical Fitness (MPF) exercises operate on what we call the "distraction/subtraction" principle. By giving the mind a very simple but consuming set of instructions to follow, the "normal" mental monologue of fears, desires, memories and predictions can be momentarily stilled. The mind becomes too busy to keep up its usual chatter.

After "subtracting" unwanted and unnecessary thoughts from the contents of the mind, you will gradually be able to directly observe the thought processes of the mind, with the mind watching exercises. You'll then practice ways in which to deal with powerful fears or emotions, and with seemingly insatiable desires. But at first, merely removing these "excess" thoughts from the mind for a moment or two will be your goal.

When asked how he could carve an elephant from an immense block of stone, the master sculptor replied: "I simply cut away everything that doesn't look like an elephant..." Carving away the excess thoughts from your mind will leave you with a clear and peaceful feeling, and eventually allow you to understand and control what really goes on in there!

Day 1 Practice Plan

Formal Practice
- Do the breath counting meditation described below at least three times today, for sessions of approximately one minute, two minutes, and three minutes. Remember, the timing does not have to be exact — if you did three sessions of two or three minutes each, you'd be doing just fine! Choose a quiet, comfortable spot for formal practice, as you want your conditions to be as ideal as possible for now.

Identify Opportunities: An important part of today's practice plan is to identify opportunities to use the breath counting meditation during your daily routine. We'll talk more about this, below.

Real Life Use: None, yet.

Thoughts For The Day: On The Breath
This first meditation involves our most basic need. We can live for days without water, weeks without food, and perhaps even years without sex or a job. But one scant minute without breathing is a long time, for most of us. Yet how often do we really focus our attention exclusively on this most crucial of functions? Fortunately, for a person in good health, breathing doesn't take much thought — and we haven't usually given it much — until today.

The Breath Counting Meditation
Begin by practicing this meditation while sitting comfortably in a quiet place. It's probably best to sit up straight, with your feet on the floor, and your eyes closed. Later on you can experiment with other postures, as discussed below, and with keeping your eyes open.

It's unbelievably simple, though not always as easy as it would seem to be. Just *count* the exhale of each breath, mentally:

"Inhale...1, Inhale...2, Inhale...3, Inhale...4" then begin again with "Inhale...1." See if you can avoid losing your count, and also try not to control or regularize your breathing in any way. Let each breath be just as it naturally is, slow or fast. You may want to try to feel the physical sensation of each breath, both inhale and exhale, as it passes through your nose or mouth, but don't do this if it distracts you from the counting.

If you find yourself thinking about anything except the feel of your breath and the number of that breath, return to focus on the sensation of breathing, and on the number of that breath. If you are not absolutely sure what number breath you're on, begin again with "In...1." No judging, no "I blew the count" thoughts, just back to "In...1."

Right now, consider the focus on the breath and the counting to be your "preferred" thoughts. Other thoughts such as memories, worries, desires, plans, self-criticisms or ideas for lunch should just be gently replaced by "In...1, In...2" and so on, *as soon as you notice them* creeping in. And they will! Of course it's difficult to stay focussed! But with practice, it just gets easier and easier.

The beauty of this meditation is that, once learned, you can do it *anywhere!* Try it while waiting on line, or at the laundromat (no one can even tell that you're doing anything unusual)!

Variations On The Breath Count

Experiment, if you like, with extending each count up to eight or ten. Is that easier or harder to do than a count of four? Want to be meditationally macho (or macha)? Every once in a while, see how many consecutive exhales you can count without losing yourself, and your count, in a thought.

DAVID: My personal record to date for consecutive breath counting is 442, reached one competitive afternoon during a ten day retreat. *Pride* was my downfall: "Inhale...439, Inhale...440, Inhale...441, Inhale...442, Wow, I'm really doing great! I bet I've gotten further than anyone else here. Me! David! — Uh oh, what number breath *was* that last one? — did I skip 443? — #%X@!!!......Inhale...1, Inhale...2, Inhale..."

What To Do Today

As stated above in the practice plan, do the breath counting meditation at least three times today, for approximately one minute, two minutes, and three minutes. Remember, the timing does not have to be exact — if you did three sessions of two or three minutes each, you'd be doing just fine!

Thirtysomething

Please, please, please feel free to do Day 1 (or any other day) over again if you like. This program can work perfectly well as a 31 or a 32 or a thirty something day — or week — program!

Identifying Opportunities: Preparation For Tomorrow

You doubtless remember the two ways in which kayakers, martial artists, and ballerinas practice — first by drilling: in the pool, the karate studio, or the dance workshop — and then by *using* what they've learned on the river, in a sparring match, or in an actual dance number. Tomorrow, you'll begin to use the breath counting meditation in "real life" situations, that is, during the course of a normal day.

Please think about some times (at least two) when you'll be able to take from one to three minutes to do the breath counting meditation. You may not choose to try it during stressful situations yet, so feel free to pick *convenient* times for now. Of course, using the exercises to deal with difficult circumstances is one of the reasons that we need to learn them, so we'll give you a few examples of doing so below, and help you practice this on Day 5.

But for tomorrow, it may be easier to count your breaths in the privacy of the rest room, or while taking an extra moment before getting out of the car after arriving at work or at home. Or perhaps while waiting in line for something, or while riding the elevator. There are lots of potential opportunities for a quick meditation, no matter how busy you are, so come up with some times that seem as though they'll work for you.

How Others Use This Exercise

Dan, a telemarketer for a large computer firm, is constantly on the phone tracking down leads, and all too often on hold. He used to feel annoyed or abused about having to wait, and often his annoyance affected his ability to create rapport with his customer. Dan now uses his hold time to do the breath counting meditation. He is then relaxed and ready to put all of his energy and awareness into making the sale when his prospect comes on line.

Gloria, principal of an elementary school, uses breath counting to make the transition between work and home. "With staff meetings, administrative review, and parent conferences, I'm usually right in the

49

middle of gridlock by the time I head home. When traffic comes to a dead stop, I keep my eyes open and count my breaths until it moves. Sometimes I even manage to feel like a human being by the time I walk in the door. I feel as though I'm doing something relaxing and valuable in what would otherwise be time wasted and resented.

Rick, a partner in a corporate design firm, described to us his own breakthrough in using meditation. "My usual pattern is to arrive at work early and keep going all day, blasting my way through stress points and roadblocks by pushing harder and harder. Towards the end of the day, I'm exhausted. My creativity has bottomed out and I'm only good for the "no brainer" tasks. Trying to do anything original after 3 p.m. is just not worth the struggle."

"But today I tried something different and I'm pretty excited about how well it worked. When I hit a snag at 4 p.m., I decided to slow down and meditate for a few minutes. Instead of dropping the project or forcing myself to work harder, I shut my office door and took three minutes to do some breath counting. It felt so good I didn't want to stop. So I did another three minutes and then looked at the design again. I began to see a new way of approaching the problem and I'm going to explore it. I don't know if it will work, but I feel like I'm making progress. And feeling more relaxed, too."

Rick's discovery was based on his willingness to take a risk, to try doing something differently. Especially in a highly charged work environment, people become afraid to let their guard down, or relax, even for a moment.

Sometimes we don't know what our minds and bodies need until we stumble over it. But once we've discovered that there are other ways to cope with stress on the job, it's difficult not to use them.

The paradox for a workaholic is that as you allow yourself a few minutes to meditate, you'll come back to the job at hand refreshed, relaxed and even more productive than before. It's hard to believe at first and it does feel like a risk. But meditation is a "right brain", intuitive approach to intellectual log jams that often works.

Even if you're lucky enough not to be a workaholic, meditation can help in the workplace, Irene, a secretary in a small office, uses breath counting to escape from a claustrophobic work environment.

"I'm working at a job I don't like. And the office manager is always breathing down my neck, talking at me and watching what I do. I'm looking for a new job, but until I find one, I'm stuck. I have to make the best of this, so I meditate. My manager will never know it, but I don't pay attention to much of her chatter. I sit there nodding pleasantly and doing my work, but my mind is focused on "In...One...In...Two..." It makes the job bearable. Thank goodness!"

Thoughts For The Day: On Body Position

Luckily for you, we don't require a full lotus position for meditation (can't do 'em, ourselves, without enriching the chiropractor)! For most of us, it's probably best to meditate (except for the walking-based meditations) while sitting up straight. Not ramrod rigid, but not slouching either, with feet flat on the floor. Then again, you'll sometimes want to meditate while laying down, on the bus, in the bathroom, or standing in line. So don't worry much about body position. Sit up straight when it's convenient, especially at first, and later on experiment with other positions and see if it makes any difference to your concentration.

NINA: I like to meditate for a few minutes first thing in the morning. In fact, I try to catch myself while I'm still barely awake. I simply allow myself to lie quietly for a few minutes and let my mind be still. It's not a standard meditation posture and some purists might scoff. But I like to just hang out with myself for a few minutes in a very relaxed way, creating a pocket of psychic space in an otherwise crowded day. With these mini-meditations, there's no absolute right or wrong way to position your body. It's more important to experiment and see what works for *you*.

On Hand Position

For many people, it is useful to maintain a particular and consistent hand position while meditating. We favor having the thumb tip and forefinger tip of each hand very lightly touching, with the other fingers either curled or extended out.

Learning to maintain a standardized hand position can help to act as a "memory cue" or "trigger" for meditation. Once you get used to meditating, and begin to associate the hand position with meditating, just recreating the hand position will help you enter into a meditative state of mind.

This can be especially useful in stressful situations, like a job interview, where you cannot take "time out" to go and meditate (unless you fake a bathroom break — a useful tactic at times). But simply touching thumb to forefinger while taking a deep and mindful breath can help to remind you of the peaceful place that you find in meditation, and give you energy to continue the interview with confidence.

On Desire: To Crave Is To Slave

Most of us have spent most of our lives so far trying to satisfy our various desires. We sincerely believe that if only we could get enough money, enough delicious food, enough sex, enough congratulations, enough Pleasure, with a capital P— that life would then be just perfect. Interestingly (and ironically) enough, this above strategy, which we erroneously believe will enhance our lives, actually does much to detract from them. Our attempts to satisfy desire usually end up causing us to suffer.

Desire has a compulsive quality, in that we feel obligated to devote large amounts of energy to satisfying our desires. It also has an insatiable quality, in that the more we have, the more we probably want. Whether it's money, or sex, or delicious desserts, too much is usually not enough. Even though we may be satiated for the moment, within a few hours we're back at the refrigerator, within a few weeks we're back at the singles bar, within a few months we're wheeling and dealing to make the next deal of a lifetime. So satisfying desire becomes an endless and futile search, habitual rather than by choice.

The Indian sage Nisargadatta says "To crave is to slave". Our compulsion to satisfy desire makes us slaves of that desire. It is only by loosening the hold of the desire upon us that we become more free.

Meditation can help us to change compulsive desires into pre*ferences*. When we have a preference rather than a compulsive desire, we'd like to fulfill the desire, but we don't *have* to do so. We're not strongly *attached* to the fulfillment of the desire.

Excessive attachment to any thought, whether desire or fear, is likely to produce suffering. We'll discuss attachment more later, in the context of working with thoughts.

The Fool's Search For The Perfect Chicken

It's an old story: the fool's mother sends him to the marketplace with instructions to buy the best chicken that he can find for Sunday dinner. So he goes up to the chicken vendor's booth, and the chicken lady picks out a fine chicken, holds it up, and says, "What a plump and succulent chicken this is! Why, it's solid chicken fat!"

So the fool, trying to be wise (as fools often do), says to himself, "Well, if chicken fat is better than chicken, I'd better get that" and walks over to the chicken fat vendor. The chicken fat vendor holds up a container of his finest chicken fat, saying "Look at this lovely chicken fat. It's as pure as oil!"

So the fool once again decides to be wise, and heads for the oil vendor's booth. Who holds up a jar of his best oil, declaring, "Such oil! It's as clear as water!"

Naturally, the fool comes home with a pitcher of water for Sunday dinner, and is soundly berated by his irate mother.

Now it's easy to laugh at the fool's misadventures, but often our behavior is more like his than we'd prefer to believe. Most of our search for happiness is no better guided than the fool's search for the perfect chicken.

DAVID: When I was younger, I was awfully lonely and unhappy much of the time. I thought that if only girls would like me, then I'd be happy. And I was certain that if I had the right car, girls would like me. So I put a lot of energy into having the coolest car in town. It really didn't help.

Eliminating The Middleman

Most of our search for happiness through satisfaction of desire is actually a much more basic desire to feel okay about ourselves. And that can only come from inside. Learning to control our minds, and then to use that control to connect with a more satisfying and spiritual way of life is the only way to eliminate the costly middleman of desire for status, cars, sex, money, and all the other things that we try to use to feel good.

We've all heard so many commercials, seen so many advertisements, met so many people who believe that things will make them happy. So it may take a while to learn, through experimentation, that these external things won't satisfy us for long. But once we do, we can turn our attention towards the pause that *really* refreshes: meditation — and the higher states of consciousness that it can lead us to!

Day 2 Practice Plan

Formal Practice
- Do the step counting meditation described below at least three times today, for sessions of approximately one minute, two minutes, and three minutes. Remember, as we said yesterday, the timing does not have to be exact — three sessions of two or three minutes each are fine! Choose a convenient location, perhaps a quiet room at home — since this is a formal practice, you want your conditions to be as ideal as possible, for now.

Identify Opportunities: An important part of today's practice plan is to identify opportunities to use the step counting meditation during your daily routine.

Real Life Use: You'll use the opportunities that you identified yesterday to do the breath counting meditation at least twice, for whatever length of time that you choose (even thirty or forty seconds will give you enough time to count two sets of four breaths) during the day. Feel free to do it as many times as you like, because the more you do it, the faster you'll get results.

On Step Counting

This simple but satisfying meditation is one of the easiest to fit into daily life. And, especially for people who tend to be jittery, it may be easier to stay focussed on movement than on breath counting as in yesterday's meditation. Step counting will provide your mind with just enough activity to forestall most other thoughts, since it involves combined awareness of both breath and step.

Note: We know that many people become interested in beginning a meditation practice while ill or incapacitated. If this is your case, or if you are a member of the disabled community, please substitute a breathing meditation every time we suggest one that involves walking.

The Step Counting Meditation

Walk a bit more slowly than usual, while focussing your attention on the ins and outs of your breath. Begin each inhale and each exhale with a mental label of "In" or "Out." Maintain a thumb to forefinger hand position, unless that feels unnatural now.

Without trying to control the breath too much, see if you can begin each in and each out breath exactly as one of your feet hits the ground. Notice how many steps you take during each inhalation, and how many steps you take during each exhalation.

Then count each step as you walk and breathe, so that in your mind you are saying "In 2, 3, 4...Out 2, 3, 4...In 2, 3, 4...Out 2, 3, 4" or perhaps "In 2, 3...Out 2, 3." Continue to substitute "In" or "Out" in place of each count of "one," to help you stay focussed on the breathing as well as the walking.

Your own personal breathing rhythm may be different from the above. Your exhales may take longer than your inhales as in: "In 2, 3...Out 2, 3, 4." Or your inhales may take longer than your exhales as in: "In 2, 3,4 ,5...Out 2, 3." The step count may vary from one breath to the next — just pay close attention, so that you can accurately count your steps during every inhale and every exhale. Just breathe, and walk, and count. As in all meditations, if your mind wanders, gently bring it back as soon as you notice it's gone. Feel free to re-read these instructions now if necessary. If you liked this exercise, you'll enjoy reading "The Guide To Walking Meditation", by Thich Nhat Hanh, a wonderful Vietnamese Zen Buddhist teacher (see bibliography).

Identifying Opportunities: Preparation For Tomorrow

Tomorrow, you'll begin to use the step counting meditation in "real life" situations, so please think about some times (at least two) when you'll be able to take from one to three minutes to do the step counting meditation. Since your normal day probably involves at least some walking, it should be easy to choose a few times to practice this one. Following are some different ways that we and others use step counting. Once again, keep in mind that convenient times are probably preferable to stressful times when you first start to do the meditations.

Using The Step Counting Meditation In Real Life

DAVID: I always use this meditation at the national publishing and music conventions, which tend to be hectic and demanding for me. Instead of scurrying and worrying from one appointment to the next, I walk and breathe, walk and breathe — so that each step soothes and centers my mind. Then, when I arrive at my next meeting, I'm more relaxed, and ready to deal with whatever may arise.

NINA: On almost any job these days, information overload and proliferating decisions can be a real stress. New ideas, new technology, new techniques all add up to one thing: more information! So many options can be overwhelming. And, just when you've gotten your in-box down to a respectable two inch pile, the mail arrives and it's overload time once again! Sometimes just trying to decide on the next thing to do can be a difficult task.

When I feel my concentration ebbing, meditation helps me focus on where to use my energy more effectively. When I first started meditating, I used to take a coffee break with a few deep breaths thrown in on the side. Now, I use a variation on the step counting exercise to take a *meditation* break — while I go to get a cup of coffee.

When I really need to clear my head, I walk up three flights of stairs to the coffee machine, counting the number of steps between each level. I don't try to coordinate my steps with my breathing, I simply count each footfall and start anew at each landing.

This aerobic variation on the step counting meditation is not only a very effective mind clearing technique, it's also a mini-exercise break. And, it's available to anyone who can find a reason to climb a flight of stairs in the course of a day's work.

Ron, a retired engineer, uses step counting while he plays golf, both in between holes and in between strokes. Clearing his mind helps him to relax, and he claims that it increases not only his enjoyment of the game, but his ability to play.

Michael, a custodial engineer in a downtown office building, uses step counting to overcome the Monday morning blues. "I relax all weekend and have a good time with my family. When Monday rolls around, the last thing I want to do is face what's on my desk. I've always hated Mondays, even as a kid. If I was going to get sick, I always hoped it would be on a Monday."

"A few weeks ago I got tired of my own complaining and began trying something different. I've been meditating for a while and I thought I'd see if it could help with Monday mornings. I began counting steps on my way to work. Now, instead of stewing over what I'll find on my desk, I clear my mind. I'm coming into work more relaxed and refreshed. It's kind of like taking a monkey off my shoulder."

Steve, a respiration therapist in a large inner-city hospital, likes to step count while he jogs during his lunch hour. Without taking even a second out of his busy work schedule, he often manages to meditate for twenty or thirty minutes at a time, and returns well refreshed to his challenging job.

Kristen, another jogging meditator and outdoor enthusiast, commented, "I always liked the idea of meditation, but I could never sit still long enough to do it. And I never realized that I could meditate while jogging or hiking. Exploring different types of meditations has let me find my own style. Now I meditate while I'm moving and I do it more than I ever dreamed I would. It feels great because I'm bringing it into my life naturally, not struggling to fit it in!"

Thoughts For The Day: Doing It Your Way

NINA: When I first started meditating, I felt self-conscious about it. I worried about doing the meditations "correctly," and whether I was applying them "appropriately" in my life.

Of course, this limited my ability to use these skills. My breakthrough came when I finally accepted that there is no right or wrong way to meditate or to use these techniques. Once I got out of my own MetaPhysical way I became increasingly creative, even playful, and found, amazingly enough, that *whatever* I did worked!

So if anyone thinks the exercises we're presenting here cover the universe of meditational possibilities, think again. In fact, if you think for a while, you'll probably come up with a few new meditations of your own. And we'd love to hear about them. (More on that later!) And if you are having any other types of doubtful or resistant thoughts about meditation, the next section should be reassuring.

What To Do With Feelings Of Doubt And Resistance

Minds being what they are, at some point yours is going to say to you: "This just won't work" or "Why bother?" But that's nothing to worry about, because just as smelly old manure can be turned into valuable fertilizer, you can use even thoughts of doubt and resistance to hone your meditational skills, merely by watching them. The mind watching exercises, described later, will show you how to use these very thoughts as objects of focus for your attention. They will then become your teachers, instead of your tormentors.

Remember, it's the rapids in the river that improve the kayakers' skill level, not the quiet stretches. If you can just put these negative thoughts on hold for a few days and continue to meditate, you'll learn to use these obstacles to deepen your meditational skill, instead of using them as excuses to quit.

Also: as our dear teacher Stephen Levine likes to say — if you're even interested in meditation and things spiritual, you've come a long way already. Why, according to reincarnation theory, if you're reading this book, you've not only made it up the karmic chain from amoeba and cockroach to homo sapien status, but you are a human being with the interest and the desire for spiritual pursuits! Quite a respectable place to register on the spiritual meter, even if you're still (after a whole two days of meditating) plagued by thoughts of dinner or TV theme songs during your sessions!

Day 3 Practice Plan

Formal Practice
- 3 minutes Breath Counting exercise.
- 3 minutes Breath Labelling exercise.

Identify Opportunities: For breath labelling in real life.

Real Life Use: Step counting at least twice (for any amount of time) in two real life situations as identified in Day 2 (e.g., desk to coke machine, bus stop to car).

On Labelling

Today's new exercise, the Breath Labelling meditation, is not too dissimilar to yesterday's Breath Counting meditation. Like counting, labelling is one of those mental techniques that we learned at a very young age, and thus is easy and familiar to apply. And of course the focus of our mental attention in this exercise remains with the breath. But in spite of these similarities, there are three reasons that we offer you the Breath Labelling meditation today.

Firstly, in the interests of variety. Different people prefer different meditations. Only by trying a number of variations can we find the exercises and combinations of exercises that form our own unique and customized meditation practice. Perhaps on some days you'll prefer to count, and on others to label your breaths. We often like to begin a meditation with one or two minutes of breath counting, then without stopping switch over to finish the last few minutes with breath labelling.

Secondly, the Breath Labelling exercise can be done in an even shorter time than the Breath Counting one. To do one "set" or count of breaths from one to four will take most people at least half a minute, whereas we can relax and clear the mind by labelling a single breath, or even a single inhale or exhale. This allows us to insert a quick Breath Labelling exercise in situations where there just wouldn't be time to do a Breath Counting exercise.

Lastly, the Breath Labelling meditation will help to prepare us for one of the most important exercises in this book. The Compassion Breath (Day 16) is a tool that can literally change our lives, as well as our minds...

The Breath Labelling Meditation

Just as we did with the formal Breath Counting practice, it's best to begin practicing this meditation while sitting comfortably in a quiet place, sitting up straight, with your feet on the floor, and your eyes closed. Later on, in informal usage, you'll experiment with other postures, and with keeping your eyes open, as you do the Breath Labelling meditation during the course of your daily life.

Once again, it's an unbelievably simple exercise, though not always easy. Just *label* each inhale and each exhale of each breath, mentally, as they occur. You can use the words "inhale" and "exhale", or "in" and "out".

"Inhale...Exhale, Inhale...Exhale, Inhale...Exhale", and so on. Try not to control or regularize your breathing in any way. Let each breath be just as it naturally is, a slow one, and then a fast one, and then a medium one — just label the ins and the outs. See if you can begin saying each label term ("inhale" and "exhale", or "in" and "out") exactly when the action that it describes begins, and draw out each mental word so that it lasts exactly as long as the inhalation or exhalation. This may require the use of some long "innnnnnnnnnnnnn" and "oooooooooouuuttt" or "innnnnnnnnnhale" and "exxxxxxxxxxxxhale" words, especially if you tend towards slow breathing. If there is a moment after the end of the exhale but before the next inhale comes, just wait for a moment before labelling the next "in" — don't jump the gun. Let the breath tell you what to say, rather than letting the labels control or regularize the breath.

You may want to try to feel the physical sensation of each breath, both inhale and exhale, as it passes through your nose or mouth, but don't do this if it distracts you from the labelling.

As always, if you find yourself thinking about *anything* except the labelling of your breath and perhaps, if you like, the sensation of that breath, return to focus on just the breath and its label. If you notice that you're no longer labelling, begin again with the very next inhalation or exhalation. No judging, no self-hating or doubtful thoughts, just back to "Innnnnnnnnnnnnnn...oooouuuuuttttttt". Of course it's difficult to stay focussed! But with practice, it just gets easier and easier.

Identifying Opportunities for Real Life Use

Please think about some times (at least two) when you'll be able to take time (even ten seconds will do, although twenty or thirty would be better) to do the breath labelling meditation during the day. You may not choose to try it during stressful situations yet, so feel free to just pick convenient times for now. Of course, using the exercises to deal with difficult circumstances is one of the reasons that we need to learn them, so we'll help you practice this on Day 5.

But for tomorrow, it may be easier to label your breaths in the same types of situations that you identified in Day 1 for the Breath Counting meditation: in the privacy of the rest room, or while taking an extra moment before getting out of the car after arriving at work or at home. But since Breath Labelling can be done in even shorter chunks of time than Breath Counting, it may be easier to integrate into your daily routine. Can you fit a "quickie" into the time between when you dial a call, and they pick it up on the other end? Or (with eyes open) while stopped at a stop light? You really don't need to do this one for long to get benefits, once you've learned to do the exercise in the formal practice situation!

Jason, a door-to-door canvasser for an environmental organization, inserts a few seconds of Breath Labelling after he rings each doorbell.

Eunice, a waitress in a coffee shop, tries to maintain a habit of labelling her breaths as she waits (sometimes only for long enough to label half a breath) to pick up orders from the kitchen.

Joanne, a poet and meditator, also works full-time as a health service administrator. At the end of a working day, she's physically and mentally exhausted, yet often wants to do something to nurture her creative side. As she describes it, "I get very frustrated when I want to work on my poetry, but feel too burned out to begin. It's like having writer's block. I have all this creative energy churning around inside, but I can't tap into it.

Meditation is helping me relax into my creativity, rather than try to force it to appear on command. I start with some breath counting, slide into breath labelling and let my mind open to poetry. It's a new approach to the creative process and I'm enjoying it."

Thoughts For The Day: A Meditator's Guide To The Universe

As we've said, the third and deepest level of meditation is the development of the meditative worldview. Although our program so far has only begun to introduce first level meditations designed to relax and clear the mind, today we'd like to start to explain this very different and uniquely satisfying way of looking at the world around us.

Of course, merely reading about this higher consciousness is not enough. Fortunately, all of the exercises in this book are designed, either directly or indirectly, to help us integrate this new understanding into our lives.

Even if you are already familiar with this "Perennial Philosophy", beloved by spiritual folk since the dawn of history, it may be worth your while to check out our style of explaining it. And if it's new to you, you're in for a metaphysical adventure! We'll begin by describing the "old" way in which we look at the world.

"I Stand Alone": The Western Worldview

Most of us in this workaday Western world tend to hold on to one rather limited but overwhelmingly popular way of relating to ourselves and the world. We'll call this the "Western worldview," and begin by describing the "Western self-image."

When subscribing to the Western worldview, we see ourselves primarily as a body, a few cubic feet of skin-sheathed flesh, with a specialized chunk at the top end called a brain. Complex chemical interactions in this brain chunk "somehow" (totally beyond the ability of science to explain, as of today) give rise to instincts, emotions, thoughts, and self-awareness.

We believe that anything inside the skin is "me," anything outside is "not-me." This not-me part includes everybody else and everything else, from rocks to raccoons to real estate agents.

"We Are All One": The Meditator's Worldview

But there's more than one way to think of ourselves in relationship to the rest of the universe. For thousands of years, mystics and meditators (the two often go together, though they don't have to) of all persuasions have maintained an alternate opinion, which we call the "Meditator's worldview."

In the Meditator's worldview, the universe is, to paraphrase theoretical physicist Sir James Jeans, "more like an enormous mind than an enormous machine." And each one of us is more like an integrated thought in a great big mind than like an isolated little cog functioning almost independently in a great big machine (as in the Western view). Some people like to refer to this "big mind" as the Universal Consciousness. Others prefer to think of it as "God," the "Higher Power," or the "All-That-Is."

> The important element of the Meditator's worldview is that we are each much more than a tiny, isolated mind/body. We are instead a tiny but *important and integral* part of a collective consciousness which includes all that has ever existed. We've just momentarily lost sight of this fact, when we were born into this culture, with its prevailing Western view.

Some analogies may help to clarify this concept. If you'd like to explore these worldviews further, please read the Watts and LeShan books listed in the bibliography. We also offer, on Day 28 (page 197), an absolutely *ironclad* reason to believe in the meditative worldview, which you may want to check out now.

Invisible Connections

A mushroom growing on the ground appears to be an individual plant. Yet the thumb-sized piece we call the mushroom is actually only a tiny, temporary, part of a fungal network (known as a mycelium) that exists underground, year-round, and which may be as large as a football field. Those thousands of mushrooms spread around a meadow, seemingly separate, are all organs or parts of a single organism.

In the Western worldview, a person is like our erroneous concept of the mushroom. Tiny, temporary, and isolated. When we switch to the Meditator's worldview, we see the mushroom as an integral part of a mycelium field, and the individual person as an inseparable part of the universal consciousness.

The Cosmic Ocean

A wave in an ocean seems to have an individual identity of its own. It appears, and exists for a while. You can watch it, and listen to it, and surf on it. Then it disappears back into the ocean, of which it was composed. Try thinking of yourself as a wave in the ocean of consciousness.

Day 4 Practice Plan: REVIEW

Formal Practice
- Breath Counting (page 47): Once for 3 minutes.
- Breath Labelling (page 60): Once for 3 minutes.
- Step Counting (page 54): Once for 3 minutes.

Note: If you feel adventurous, try one six minute meditation in which you begin with a few minutes of breath counting, then go on without stopping to finish with a few minutes of breath labelling.

Real Life Use: Throughout the day use all of the above exercises as many times as you like for as long as you like.

Note: Begin to do at least two walking, and two breathing meditations during your daily activities each and every day, using the opportunities that you've identified. From now on, we will not tell you to do these, except to remind you on review days. It's absolutely crucial for all of us to take responsibility for integrating these exercises into our daily lives, starting *now!*

More Meditator's Worldview: The Dream Analogy
"Row, row, row, your boat gently down the stream.
Merrily, merrily, merrily, merrily, life is but a dream."

We'd sung that song, like everybody else, since childhood, without ever really stopping to look for any particular meaning in it. Yet for thousands of years, philosophers of every culture have compared the unenlightened person to a character in a dream, whose understanding of reality is limited to the "reality" of the dream world that he or she inhabits.

Think about dreaming. In any dream, there are a variety of dream characters. But you'll probably believe yourself to be one particular character — that is, you'll know which character you are in the dream, even though that character might be somewhat different from who you are when awake.

DAVID: I've dreamed of being older, and younger, of being a Russian, and even a Martian. But whoever I am in the dream, I have a clear sense of personal identity. That is, I *know* that it's me, in spite of the fact that who I am in the dream may even change from one part of the dream to another. And I have no trouble telling *my* character in a dream from all of the other characters, be they monsters, friends, Playmates-of-the-Month, relatives, or other actual or mythical beings.

Yet although I almost never realize it *during* the dream, my "waking-life-mind", the one in the "real" Dave snoring in his bed, is mentally creating *both* the "Dave-character-within-the-dream," *and* the rest of the characters in that dream.

Seen from the Meditator's worldview, we could say that each one of us is now like a dream character in a scenario dreamed by the "big mind." The big mind (or God, or the Higher Power, or Universal Consciousness) is dreaming everyone and everything in this real-seeming dream in which we live.

But since we see this universal dream from our own limited point of view (the Western Worldview), the other people and things in it *seem* separate from us, although they're not. We are all characters in the same universal dream, dreamed by the mind of God. And it's "only" a dream, no matter how real it feels.

On Enlightenment

We should probably talk here about what is commonly called the "State of Enlightenment." For some of us (ourselves occasionally included), the idea of attaining Enlightenment may seem a bit much — just another slice of metaphysical pie-in-the-sky. And it's fine to feel that way, because what we consider to be the first two rewards of meditation (relaxation of the mind, and the ability to work with the mind's thoughts and feelings) are in themselves practical daily tools with almost instantaneous beneficial results.

Yet often, people who don't know much about meditation focus exclusively upon this oft elusive state as the sole "goal" of the spiritual seeker. Actually, this exaggerated focus upon Enlightenment may impede or discourage would-be meditators rather than inspire or assist them. Understanding that Enlightenment is more like a journey than a destination is far more useful than grasping greedily at some supposed spiritual goalpost!

But meditation has a third step, ephemeral and evasive though it may seem. So although a daunting task (fortunately for us, fools rush in where angels fear to tread), it behooves us to try to elaborate on the meaning of the E word, for us.

What is Enlightenment?

As we see it, the metaphor of MetaPhysical Fitness applies very well to the idea of Enlightenment. We believe that Enlightenment is a process to be developed and maintained, rather than a state which is somehow permanently achieved. To us, an Enlightened person (sometimes called the "Realized" or "Awakened" person) is one who has invested in all three levels of meditation. It may be possible to reach an Enlightened state without benefit of meditation, but we tend to doubt it.

Such a person (once again, this is from our point of view, not to be confused with ultimate truth, if it exists) might be described as follows, using our three level system. Please keep in mind that certain of the elements listed below will be elaborated on during the rest of the 30 day program, as we present the exercises that can help us to reach this condition of Higher Consciousness.

1) They would have a clear and relaxed mind, generally free of mental chatter.

2) They would be very aware of their thoughts and feelings, and able to work with them so well that they would probably be quite free from fear, anger, and desire. This doesn't mean that fear, anger, and desire thoughts might not arise. But if they did, the Enlightened person would see them simply as thoughts, and treat them with understanding and compassion, with no need to act on them. Rather than seeing people, objects, thoughts, or events in terms of liking or disliking, they would simply observe both the outer "reality" and their own inner response to that reality without judgment or self-hatred. They would undertake action without expectation of result, and with so clear a focus on their own mental process during such action that every "means" would became an "end" in itself.

3) They would see the meditative worldview as being at least as valid as the ordinary "Western Worldview", so that while they could function in the workaday world, they would also understand, on gut, intellectual, and emotional levels, that things were not as they seem. They'd *know* that people were physical expressions of the Higher Power, as well as discrete individuals. That events were interconnected

to a degree unthought of in the ordinary wordview. And that no matter what occured in the day-to-day physical reality, it could be used, with compassion, as meditative grist for their mental mill.

Neither Dry Nor Dour

All of this doesn't mean that our hypothetical Realized person is a dry and dour individual, lost in thoughts of Cosmic Consciousness to the exclusion of human relationships. Enlightenment doesn't even entail the extinction of the Realized one's prior personality — it only means seeing it in meditative perspective. Thus there's no need for us to abandon our current life or personality in the interests of becoming Enlightened. We just have to learn not to be hung up or overly attached to that life or personality. Perhaps it's rather like learning not to be overly attached to *any* of the mind's thoughts, be they fears or desires, angers or self-criticisms.

Nor do we have to worry that those fortunate enough to be maintaining Enlightened status look mockingly down on us from their metaphysical heights. In fact, it may be that the development of compassion, for all of God's creatures, ourselves included, is the key to Enlightenment.

DAVID: The day after my daughter Katie was born, I remember watching her as she lay in her tiny plexiglass crib in the hospital room that she and my wife and I shared. She had managed to get a corner of her blanket into her mouth, and was sucking on it vigorously. Then she moved slightly, and the blanket flopped out of her reach. She cried pathetically.

I suspect that the fully Enlightened among us, those that live always in the Meditator's Worldview, tend to see the rest of us rather as I saw my daughter that day. Our desires and our fears, all that seems important to us, probably appear as insignificant or limited to them as Katie's loss of the blanket seemed to me. From their all-inclusive vantage point, our fears of loss of pride or money, even loss of life, and our desires for material possessions must seem so petty. Yet just as my reaction to Katie was one of compassion and love rather than of mockery or sardonicism (yes, of course I helped her get the blanket back into her little mouth), the more Enlightened ones see the rest of us with compassion and gentle humor, with a wry understanding of what it means to be human, and with a desire to help us to a more mature and broadly encompassing way of being in this beautiful and awful, exciting and awe-full, world that we all share.

The Awakening

A moment ago, we said that when we dream, we always feel identified with the "character" that we play in the dream. Yet when we wake up, we realize that it was "our real waking life self" who was creating both "our" character in the dream, and all of the other dream figures, no matter whether they seemed friend or enemy during the dream.

So let's play out the analogy, and assume that our "real life" body/mind character that seems so real today is actually being "dreamed" or created (along with all the others on this planet, and elsewhere) by the mind of God (or the Cosmic Consciousness, or however you want to refer to the Higher Power). If that is the case, who do you think you're going to be when you wake up?

NINA: After I had awakened from a dream the other night, I could clearly see that the "sixteen year old Nina dream character" (whom I'll long remember and enjoy, for it was a lovely dream) existed only as a tiny and transient part of my own "real" mind, even though for the duration of the dream she felt very real to herself, and seemed to have complete freedom of action and thought.

It seems likely that if a person *fully* awakens (in the sense of this analogy, and probably a rather rare occurrence), he or she will then understand him or herself to be the Cosmic Consciousness or Higher Power or God, which *includes* the body/mind that they had *formerly* thought themselves to be. The Fully Awakened One will probably identify with the old body/mind personality about as much as Nina identified with her dream character after waking up. That is, cherishing and enjoying the old personality, but also knowing it as a very tiny and transient part of the Universal Consciousness, with whom the F.A.O. is now completely identified.

We'll talk more about the idea of identification with the Universal Consciousness in later days. Don't worry about it much now. We don't, and at the rate we're going, we may never have to!

Day 5 Practice Plan

Formal Practice
- Breath counting or breath labelling for two minutes.
- Radio/TV breath count for three minutes.

Identify Opportunities: Think about situations in which you might, in the future, be able to use breath counting in stressful situations.

Real Life Use: Just the minimum twice daily walking and breathing meditations that we asked you to do in the box at the beginning of the Day 4 Practice Plan, unless you really feel ready to try some breath counting in stressful situations.

On Breath Counting And Stressful Situations

We've already practiced the breath counting meditation in several different situations. You've done some breathing meditations sitting quietly by yourself and you've also tried them in real life settings. This exercise will help you refine your skills in bringing meditation into your life, at the times when you really need it.

One of the most stressful things that can happen to us is receiving bad news — our job is in danger, a loved one is ill, our own diagnostic test comes back looking bad. Each of these is enough to send us into a panic of fearful, anxious feelings. Even the "lower levels" of bad news — someone we thought was a friend has let us down, a pay raise or promotion didn't go through — are enough to set our hearts racing and bring on a queasy feeling.

Another major source of stress occurs when we are forced to interact with people that we find difficult or disagreeable. Whether they are family members or co-workers, our stomachs tighten, our teeth clench, and our hearts close as we attempt to deal with them.

Unfortunately, being angry, fearful, or upset won't help. If it did, our first reaction would be a fine way of coping with stress. But, these negative emotions only serve to close our minds and hearts against understanding, to block out compassion and increase judgmental thoughts. These judgmental thoughts may be towards ourselves ("It must be all my fault. I should have done it differently..." and so on) or towards the other person ("It's all his fault!" or "Why does she have to be that way?"). If you ever feel this way when interacting with others, try the next exercise.

The Radio/TV Breath Count

To do this exercise, you'll need a quiet room where you can play a television or radio station.

Begin by turning on your least favorite TV or radio station. Turn to the one that really irritates you, the announcer you're most likely to snap off in mid-sentence, unwilling even to hear the report through. Or try an antagonistic sound — if you're a classical music fan, you might try the local heavy metal station. Or perhaps a talk show will push your negative button. If you're of liberal bent, the Morton Downey Jr. show may be just what you need, in this exercise. For some, Geraldo Rivera will be your ticket to teeth-gritting, Vanna White for others.

Whichever format for annoyance you choose, news show, music, or talk (try them all), you're going to listen, but with an important difference. You're going to meditate your way through a few moments of your least favorite show.

Settle into your chair. Close your eyes. Listen and watch your reactions. Allow yourself to begin to feel upset. Then, slowly, calmly, remove your mental attention from your annoyance and begin counting your breaths. Inhale...1, Inhale...2, "Nine missing and presumed dead as an earthquake hits..." Inhale...3, "Dow Jones average fell 43 points today to its lowest..." Inhale...4, and so on.

Once you've established a rhythm, open your eyes. Continue to concentrate on counting your breaths, but now also watch the TV or hear the radio. Listen with "half a mind" to the announcer. Hear what's being said, but continue to breathe and count, slowly and evenly.

On Meditative Listening

Practicing this reaction to bad news or difficult people on the TV or radio will give you the skills needed to deal with them in your own life, with the same relaxed mind that you are cultivating right now. As we learn new meditations, we'll return to this exercise to practice them.

Surprisingly, meditating while listening to another person can often facilitate understanding. Instead of thinking about what you are going to say next, you can truly hear what the other is saying, with heart as well as mind (or half a mind anyways, since the other half is meditating). And listening with empathetic heart and half a mind may well be more effective than listening with the mind alone...

Nancy, a senior secretary at a Fortune 500 company, has had to put up with an unreasonable boss for several years. "I can always tell when he's under pressure from above because he takes it out on me and the other secretaries. It's as if he's transparent. The stuff from above rips right through him and lands on our heads. If he's having a bad day, we all have a bad day. The worst part is that after he's vented on us, he feels great and we're left feeling all chewed up."

Nancy began to use breath counting meditations whenever she could see her boss getting geared up for a venting session. As she became increasingly able to focus her attention on breathing during negative interactions with him, she was also able to feel some compassion for her overwrought boss. "When he's storming around now, I can sometimes see him as a person who's just plain hurting. I still don't like his behavior, but it helps me let go of my anger. He seems more like a two-year old throwing a tantrum than anything else. And I can comprehend the important parts of what he's saying perfectly well, even while breath counting."

Thoughts For The Day: More Meditator's Worldview

Taking either the Western or the Meditator's approach to life shapes our perceptions of some very basic issues. Attitudes towards birth, death, and everything in-between are affected by our choice of worldview. Here are our thoughts comparing the two outlooks on some of these most important topics.

Birth

In the Western worldview, birth is seen as a rather mechanical event, combining egg and sperm like two chemicals that mix to form a compound substance with its own particular properties. Consciousness then results from a bio-chemical reaction in the newly-formed brain.

In the Meditator's worldview, some impulse or desire in the big consciousness to express itself in physical reality causes the interactions necessary to bring man and woman together, then sperm and egg. Thus each individual is a "recycled piece" of the universal consciousness. We'll talk more about this in Day 28.

Death

From the hard-nosed, logical Western point of view, when the body dies, the human experience comes to an end. Since consciousness is considered to be a by-product of the biochemical processes of the brain, when the brain ceases to function, consciousness must end.

From the Meditator's point of view, the brain and the body can be considered by-products, symptoms, or physical representations of the Higher Power's desire to express itself. The individual personality that was developed during a particular being's earthly sojourn may or may not survive physical death. But when one *identifies* with the Universal Consciousness rather than the individual personality, death can no more eradicate that higher consciousness, than a day of skiing or sex can kill you just because a number of your individual cells were destroyed during the day's activities.

God

In the Western worldview, God tends to be seen as above and separate from the world. God is the creator of the universe, almost as a person might create and then run a business.

In the Meditator's worldview, God isn't separate from the world, but *is* the consciousness out of which *everything* is formed. Continuing the business analogy above, God is not the *boss* of a business that "he" created, but the business itself. God *is* the entire universe, which includes Mother Teresa, us, you, Morton Downey Jr., and Al Capone, as well as any particular and personalized conception of God, whether we call "him" Allah, Jehovah, The Christ, or the Higher Power.

From the Western point of view, when someone says "I am God," it probably means that they are crazy, and that they expect everybody else to bow down to them. From the Meditator's point of view, when someone says "I am God," it may mean that they understand that everybody, and everything, is God also, because God is the "stuff" out of which everything, and everybody, has been created.

DAVID: Modern physics tells us that everything in the universe appears to be created from the same atomic and sub-atomic particles. So my body, and yours, and the table are quite literally made of the same stuff. This seems to me to support the above Meditator's view, on a physical level at least.

72

Meditation and Religion

Prayer and meditation don't have to be mutually exclusive. Putting these processes into separate, neatly labelled mental compartments is both unneccessary and unhelpful. The belief that active adherents to religious beliefs "can't" be meditators without somehow sacrificing their beliefs is quite simply wrong. Christian saints (like St. Teresa of Avila or St. John of the Cross), Jewish mystics (like Martin Buber) and a wide range of Eastern avatars all come from religious *and* meditative traditions.

When Marlene, a devout Catholic, first started meditating, she was afraid that meditation would somehow infringe on her religious beliefs. "I was brought up with the Church as a guiding force in my life. I say my rosary every day, go to Mass at least once a week. When I first started meditating, I was afraid to explore it. I used meditation in a very limited way, just working with stress from a specific situation on my job.

As I continued to meditate and get more benefits from my involvement, I began to feel less threatened. Now I can see that prayer and meditation support each other in my life. In fact, when I'm feeling tense now, I'll meditate before I begin to pray. The meditation mellows me out and helps open my heart to prayer."

Competitive Meditation

It's easy to get competitive, or goal-oriented, with meditation (or with anything else), in this high-pressure culture of ours. The late Tibetan guru Trungpa Rimpoche used to call this "Spiritual Materialism!" (See Bibliography.)

Any expectations about what meditation "should" feel like will eventually lead to painful and self-critical judgments. On the days when it's "working" — going well, feeling fine — you start to think of yourself as a "good meditator", a MetaPhysical "success story." Patting yourself on the back, you feel you've mastered this set of skills. But, as things always go, a week of "good" meditation is followed by a day or two or three where you can't find the time to meditate. Or, if you do, it somehow doesn't feel as good as those memories of days gone by. If those were the "good" days, does that mean these are "bad"?

We'd rather avoid all of the good/bad, success/failure labels. Simply *doing* it is what matters. Each meditation will be different, as you bring a new set of experiences, needs and context to the moment.

73

Try to think of meditation as a dance, rather than a race. In a race, the goal is to reach the end faster than anyone else, or faster than you've ever done it before. In a dance, the goal is to enjoy what you're doing while you're doing it. So try not to worry about whether your meditations are "improving," or about whether you're "doing it right." Just do it! Even in a race situation, excessive concern about how you are doing (looking back over your shoulder too much) will actually *decrease* your performance!

Day 6 Practice Plan

Formal Practice
- Breath Counting exercise (page 47) or Labelling exercise (page 60) for two minutes.
- Experiencing the Breath for three minutes.
- Slow Step Labelling exercise (four labels per step) for three minutes. You may want to begin this one with a moment of Step Counting (page 54).
- Fast Step Labelling (two labels per step) for two minutes.

Real Life Use: Just the usual minimum (see page 64 if you've forgotten).

On Experiencing

So often, as we walk or drive, eat or wash dishes, our minds are aflutter with thoughts, thoughts not at all related to our physical actions. As our minds begin to clear through meditation, we become more able to focus our attention only on what we are experiencing, without adding judgment, or mental comment of any sort. In the Japanese Zen tradition, this is called "just walking", "just driving", or "just washing dishes".

Today we'll practice two such exercises, just breathing, and just walking, and give you some hints for creating similar meditations of your own.

The Breath Experiencing Meditation

In this exercise, we need do nothing more than focus our attention on the physical sensation of the breathing process. What does it feel like to breathe? Where do you notice sensation? In the throat? In the nose? In the belly? Does the air pass through quickly or slowly? Is there an open feeling or a constricted one? Does the breath go instantly from inhale to exhale, or is there a point of equilibrium, a moment of no movement? A hotness or coolness? Any taste or smell? As in the breath counting or breath labelling exercises, be diligent in maintaining the focus of attention on the breath. Whenever you catch yourself thinking, no matter of what, gently but firmly return your attention to the sensations of the breath.

Like the breath labelling exercise, experiencing the breath can be used in very short sessions, once we practice it formally a few times. Even experiencing one, or part of one breath can bring us back to a more grounded place when we are busy and anxious, or unsettled.

However, for many of us, experiencing the breath requires a more subtle focussing of mental attention than counting or labelling the breath, since it somehow seems like there's less to focus on. For this reason, we often like to begin this meditation with a moment of breath counting, then without stopping change to a moment of breath labelling, and finish off the session with a few moments of simply experiencing the breath.

For some meditators, making these transitions in a single session, from counting to labelling to experiencing, can be difficult. For others, it helps to engender a progressively deeper meditation.

If you haven't so far tried flowing from counting to labelling, as discussed in Day Three, try a flow from counting to labelling to experiencing today. What do you think? Does it seem easier or harder than doing the count/label/experience parts of the session separately?

DAVID: My friend Wavy Gravy (Of Woodstock and Merry Prankster fame, now clown to hospitalized children and socially responsible gadfly, see his listing under "Camp Winnarainbow" in the Resources Section) likes to put a tiny dot of Tiger Balm or Vicks Vaporub inside his clown nose, to help him focus on the breath. I do this occasionally, too, to spice up my breathing meditations!

The Slow Walking Meditation

You'll probably want to begin practicing this one in a private place, since it looks a bit funny. Pick a spot where you can walk for at least 8 or 10 feet in a straight line.

Now walk very slowly, so slowly that you have enough time to mentally label every part of every step.

Say "lifting" as you pick your foot up. Say "moving" as your foot travels through the air. Say "placing" as you put that foot down again. Say "shifting" as you shift your weight onto that foot. Say "lifting" as you begin to pick up the other foot. And so on. Lifting, moving, placing, shifting...lifting, moving, placing, shifting...

At first, take a minimum of 8 to 10 seconds to complete each four part (lifting, moving, placing, shifting) step. Whenever your attention wanders, bring it back to your walking process. Try slowing it way down, and take 30 to 40 seconds for every complete step. Vipassana meditation students often call this one the "Zombie Walk" — truly life in the slow lane!

Other thoughts intruding? Get right back to that focus on the active foot. Hint: doing this one barefoot may facilitate focus on the foot!

The Faster Step Labelling Exercise

If you prefer (some people find it easier) you can walk faster, labelling only the lifting and placing portions of each step. Or you can say "up" and "down" instead of "lift" and "place." Obviously, it will be much easier to integrate this one into your daily routine than the Zombie Walk!

Experiencing The Walking Process

Yup, you guessed it. After a few moments of the two above step labelling meditations, dispense with the labels and see if you can bring your attention to your feet. No thoughts, just walking. And don't worry if it seems hard to stay focussed for very long — it is!

When It's Hard To Just Walk, Just Breath

If you have a really hard time focussing during the experiencing of the breath or the walk, you may want to do some breath counting or breath labelling *while* you do the breath or walk experiencing. This dual focus seems to help some folk get the hang of the experiencing meditations. As you gain more control over the focus of your attention, you may feel less need to do this anymore.

But wait, you cry — this dual focus seems inconsistent with the idea of "just breathing, just walking!" Perhaps it is. Yet the mind is a tricky sparring partner, and we are more interested in helping you to discover a set of tools that will work for you than in being perfectly consistent, or in telling you what you "should" be able to do. Our teacher Jack Kornfield tells a great anecdote about just this type of paradoxical situation.

The well-known meditation teacher was sitting in the kitchen of his monastery. A disciple came in and was aghast to notice that the master was eating breakfast and reading the morning newspaper.

"But Master," the student stuttered, " You always teach us to just eat, to just walk, to just breathe."

"My son," replied the teacher, "when I eat and read, I *just* eat and read."

DAVID: At times my mind has been so wild and hard to focus that I'd go to a Hollywood movie, full of every theatrical device ever invented to rivet the attention, from bikinis to bombs to car chases, and still find myself worrying about business or my love life. So being able to focus on something as subtle and undramatic as experiencing the breath while counting it seems like pretty good mind taming to me!

Thoughts For The Day: More About Meditation

As you may be beginning to realize, meditation is not anything occult, or esoteric, or "outside" of normal, daily, life.

In fact, you've probably been doing a certain type of meditation all your life, even if you don't call it that. Because whenever you keep your attention so strongly focussed on something that no other thoughts intrude, that's a form of "Clearing The Mind" meditation. Watching the waves break on the beach, or staring into the flames in the campfire can be meditation. Hang-gliding is a meditation for some, harmonica playing for others. As is anything that forces all of your awareness onto just one thing, so that the usual chatter of the mind is momentarily stilled, with no fear or desire thoughts about the future, or "could've, would've, should've" thoughts about the past.

Making It Happen

For most non-meditators, the above sort of experience just occurs spontaneously, without planning. When it happens, it happens. However, meditators make these meditations happen, because we understand the great value of clearing, focussing, and controlling the mind. Allowing this type of meditation to appear spontaneously without learning to help it along is like occasionally finding a wonderful radio station while spinning the dial, without ever learning the call letters so that you could locate it at will.

Many meditations that you'll be practicing won't involve doing anything that you don't normally do. Only your *attitude* will change, as you consciously try to focus your attention on whatever is happening, whether that's brushing your teeth, or washing dishes. Instead of planning for the day, or wishing that the gravy on the bottom of the pot wasn't burnt on quite so solidly, you will make the brushing, or the washing, into a meditation — just by focussing exclusively on it. No future planning, no past memories: just scrubbing, rinsing. This conscious focussing of attention is sometimes called "mindfulness." It is the most powerful tool that we possess, a mental spotlight that can illuminate any action or thought!

Dishpan Enlightenment

Anything done with focus, awareness, or mindfulness is a meditation, and will eventually take us in the direction of Enlightenment, no matter how mundane (dish-washing Enlightenment? teeth-brushing Enlightenment?) it may seem. Once we've learned to meditate, to be mindful — every action and every thought can become the momentary focus of a meditation.

DAVID: I used to hate washing dishes. It seemed like such a waste of time, and no matter how often you did it, in a week or two the sink was again piled high and smelly.

Now I meditate whenever I have to wash dishes — the smell of detergent and the sound of running water have become cues to remind me to focus my mind. Sometimes (especially when my mind isn't very quiet) I do a breath meditation while washing, other times I focus on labelling or experiencing the washing itself: feel of water, slipperiness, rubbing, clinking, rinsing. If I'm feeling metaphorical (as I often am), I think of the cleansing process as taking place both in the dishes, and in my own body and mind.

Mr. Natural Does The Dishes

During college, one of our favorite cartoon characters was R. Crumb's Mr. Natural, a rascally but largely Enlightened guru. Many years later, we were amused to find that our favorite metaphysician, the amazing Sri Nisargadatta of Bombay, was also nicknamed (in Marathi, his native dialect) Mr. Natural. So, just for fun, we asked artist extraordinaire Robert Crumb if we could enliven our book with a few of his cartoons. We hope that you find them as endearing as we do.

© R. Crumb All Rights Reserved

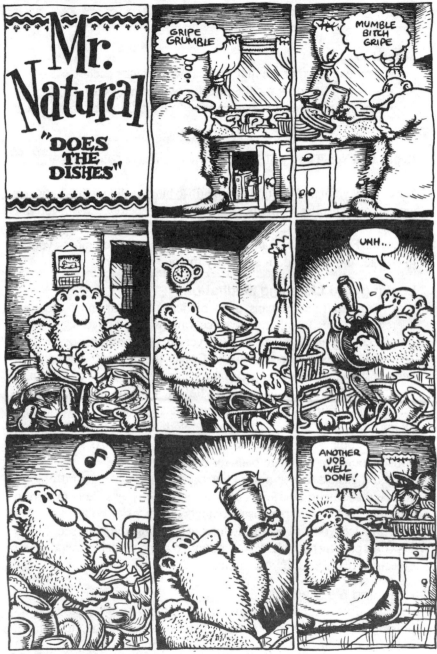

© R. Crumb All Rights Reserved

Day 7 Practice Plan

Formal Practice
- Any two looking meditations for two minutes each.
- Any two listening meditations for two minutes each.
- One two minute "just experiencing" meditation that uses a sense other than seeing or hearing.

Real Life Use: The usual, as per the note on page 64.

Note: Today, for the first time, we begin to blur the distinction between general and specific instructions, as you'll see below. We'll let *you* choose exactly when and how to apply our directions, because (see Thoughts For The Day) learning to meditate is an inside job — you're in charge, and the wisdom is already in you.

Looking And Listening Meditations

Our last (and perhaps most difficult) type of mind clearing exercise involves learning to practice what we may have been doing spontaneously, as we talked about in yesterday's thoughts for the day. To watch clouds, or the flames of a fire, or the foaming waves at the ocean's shore, without trying to make sense of what you see. To watch stars, or fish in an aquarium, or a candle's flame without trying to look for patterns. Without trying to judge or analyze what you're seeing. Doing nothing but seeing. Just seeing. Nothing more than perception, eye meets object, with no mind in the picture at all. As soon as you notice thought or mind, go back to just seeing.

It's easiest to begin Looking Meditations with natural objects such as those mentioned above, as they are slightly less likely to inspire thoughts in the mind than visual objects like faces or bodies are. But with practice, you will be able to look at anything and "just see." Cars or people passing by, a blank wall, or your own hands can provide visual objects for the focus of your attention.

Listening Meditations

You can practice *listening* in the same way. No thought, no judging, no attempts to make sense. Just listening. If thoughts intrude, notice that you're thinking, then focus your attention back on the music.

Instrumental music is usually the easiest type of meditative listening to begin with, as any music that contains words tends to inspire thought when you hear the lyrics.

Other Types Of "Just Experiencing" Meditations

Sometimes touch can become the focal point of this type of meditation—the feel of a piece of material, or the pressure of a wooden seat on the body. Stroking or brushing a cat or dog can become a lovely tactile meditation, as you focus on the sensation of movement of fur against skin. Or, mentally labelling the action, "stroke...stroke...stroke..." you can combine labelling with an experiencing meditation.

Meditate with your nose, by making a smell the focus of a meditation, with attention only on fresh baked bread, or the seaweed at low tide.

Or meditate with your mouth, by making a taste the focus of a meditation.

Try placing the focus of your attention on another person. It may be harder not to think while doing this, since people are so thought-provoking. But the gentle stroking of an infant, child or any loved one's hair or skin can become a rhythmic reminder to attend only to the sensation/experience of the moment.

Want a harder one? Try a just listening exercise with human voices. Begin by overhearing a conversation between people that you don't know. It's tough not to think about the words. If you really want a challenge, do a just seeing or just listening session with the radio or TV, as we did on Day 5. The more emotionally involved we are with Geraldo or Vanna or Morty, the harder it may be — but so important to practice...

The Most Subtle Exercise: Just Sitting, Wide Focus

Perhaps the hardest meditation of this kind is to just sit quietly, and allow *all* of the senses to be perceived without thought. A moment of seeing, as the clouds part and the sun shines into the room. A moment of hearing as a plane goes overhead. A moment of touch, as the knee hurts, a moment of smell, of taste...

All transient, passing through the clear mind without comment or attachment, just sensations.

DAVID: When my mind is fairly clear and I do this one, I experience what I call the "uh huh" phenomenon. On some level I'm aware of the sensations that are being perceived, but I don't need even to attach a verbal thought or label to them. As the breeze hits my skin, it's "uh huh (breeze)". As I smell the potatoes cooking, it's "uh huh (potato smell)". I'm somehow just able to perceive directly, and know that I'm perceiving, without having to take it any further in the mind. Does that make sense? Like the old joke, I guess you really had to be there. But you will be. Especially after you learn to do the mind watching exercises next week...

Living In The Now

When you've *really* gotten the hang of it, *everywhere* that you go and *everything* that you do can become the basis for a mind clearing meditation. We can call this rather advanced state "Living In The Now," and it will be examined in greater detail later on in this book.

If It's Difficult

As we said yesterday, if you find these just experiencing meditations to be difficult at first, combine them with a counting or labelling meditation to quiet your mind. Count your steps as you walk and listen to the birds, or label your breath as you do a looking meditation with the tiny flame of a candle.

And don't worry if during meditation your mind sometimes feels well-focussed and effective, and at other times seems to fly all over the globe. Accept it, because that's the nature of the mind. Try to remember that our goal is progress, not perfection.

It may help to keep in mind our analogy of paper training the puppy (*of course* it runs off the paper, to do its business on the floor — returning it to the paper is what trains it).

Or consider this: one of us has a friend (whose name we'll drop tomorrow, in another context) who worked on the mission to the moon in 1969. Although most of us probably think that the lunar module went straight to the moon, actually it didn't do anything of the sort. Nearly 90% of the time, the module was off course. But it had a self-correcting computer built into it, so it would veer off to the left, then correct itself to the right. Then veer off to the right, and have to correct itself back to the left. So it zigged and zagged its way to the moon. And as long as we keep on meditating — no matter how our mind zigs and zags, clear one day and murky the next — we can stay on the right path, eventually learning to build our bridges from the boulders that only *seem* to block our way.

Thoughts For The Day: Gurus — Not A Prerequisite

What's a guru? A guru is what you might end up with if you crossed a coach or a trainer with a priest or a rabbi — basically, someone who coaches your spiritual development. Of course, the best coach in the world won't help you at all if you don't want to exercise or practice your chosen sport. And the saintliest priest won't help you to be religious, unless you decide to work at it yourself as well.

> Learning to meditate is an "inside job". Although a guru may provide a good role model for the beginning meditator, it is the disciple him or herself who must do the actual hands-on (brains-on?) work of meditation.

Without the desire to work at meditating, having a guru is mostly a spiritual status symbol, a way to appear as though you were following a spiritual path without having to pay the price of hard mental work. If a would-be meditator indeed has the desire to do the work, he or she will be able to proceed along the meditative road quite well, with or without benefit of guru.

In a very real way, once you've chosen to try to walk on the spiritual side of life, you are your own guru. In fact, many metaphysicians believe that, for those on the spiritual path, the appearance of a guru is merely an outward manifestation of their own inner spiritual development.

For these reasons, we believe that it doesn't hurt to begin meditating before you even think about looking for a guru. Once you've gotten some "basic" meditation hours under your headband, you'll be much better prepared to follow any particular meditative discipline (or guru) that appeals to you. And probably, with a well relaxed and somewhat cleared mind, much better prepared to choose a healthy and non-abusive relationship with any spiritual practice and its purveyors.

Perhaps, like us, you'll decide to enjoy and respect the many fine gurus and other teachers whose lectures, writings, and retreats are available, without joining any one group or sect to the exclusion of the rest.

The Wisdom Is In You

It's tremendously important, and empowering, to remember that the wisdom is in you, not something coming from outside. Whenever anything that we say here resonates in your mind, it reflects *your* innate desire to develop a more meditative way of life. That means it's a reflection more on your ability to receive than on our ability to transmit. Learning to trust that *you* know better what's right for you than anyone else will let you create your own path to Enlightenment.

Developing Your Own Meditational Profile

Exploring your own meditational profile is an important step towards developing a set of skills that will stay with you forever. To explore your own reactions to the different meditations, we suggest you occasionally spend a moment at the end of a meditation and reflect on how you felt before, during, and after. These insights can help you to fine tune your meditation practice, as you begin to understand your personal preferences.

Some questions to consider: Did you feel calmer after meditating? Were you comfortable with the exercises? More comfortable with one than another? Which ones? Was there anything that felt uncomfortable? Anything you might change to meet your needs? Did meditation help you deal with an old situation in a new way? Did you have any new insights about yourself or others?

It's also helpful to look at logistics. When did you meditate? Morning? Evening? As needed throughout the day? For how long? Where did you meditate? Were others around? Which meditation did you do? Is there anything you'd do differently next time?

These questions need not be answered "formally." However, on Day 29 when we discuss Your Own MetaPhysical Maintenance Plan, it will be useful to have some idea of your meditational patterns, recognizing that such patterns are likely to change from day to day, if not from moment to moment. But perhaps the most important aspect to keep in mind as you develop an awareness of your own meditational profile is that there's no right or wrong way to meditate. It's simply a matter of finding out what works best for *you*.

DAVID: I probably spend 90% of my meditation time on only a few mind clearing exercises: step counting, breath labelling and just experiencing. I usually do one long meditation of from fifteen to thirty minutes in the morning, and then try to do shorter ones (down to just a few seconds) throughout the day, as I work, play, relax, eat, or do whatever else I find myself doing.

NINA: I tend to do a lot of thought and emotion watching, and less of the mind clearing meditations than Dave. I love to do looking and listening meditations while I jog, and I try to fit in a one and a half hour session each weekend.

Mr. Natural's 719th Meditation

Mr. Natural's 719th Meditation is our favorite Mr. Natural cartoon, although it wasn't quite so meaningful for us back in the old "pre-meditation" days. Now that we're beginning to understand how meditation is a metaphor for the rest of life (as we've talked about, and will continue to explore in the rest of the book), we enjoy the way in which "The Natch" creates an entire world as he meditates, and then allows it to dissolve back into it's original desert as he returns his mind to the meditation. At least that's the way we interpret the cartoon. What do you think? We've arranged the panels so that you can flip through the pages, and see the Old Avatar do his thing!

© R. Crumb All Rights Reserved

85

Day 8 Practice Plan

Formal Practice
- One body relaxation, for as long as it takes.
- One Special Place relaxation/visualization.
- One Meditation Visualization, for at least two minutes.

Real Life Use: One or more Quick Relaxations, as needed during the day.

Note: We've indicated no times for most of these exercises because each person's timing will vary on relaxation and visualization. Try to take the time to do them for as long as it takes you to relax, and visualize. If you're short on free time today, why not take *two days* to complete Day 8?

On Visualization

Simply defined, visualization is the act of consciously choosing thoughts, with the intention of making those thoughts as vivid and realistic in the mind's eye as possible. The fact that our brains and bodies react so strongly to mental pictures (see pages 24 and 25) makes the ability to visualize very important.

A tremendous amount of evidence indicates that after we've spent some time clearly visualizing ourselves performing an activity, it actually becomes easier for us to do. This technique works in almost any sphere, from athletics to music to relaxation, and the key element seems to be the degree of "real-ness" of the visualization. So it clearly pays to spend some time practicing and strengthening this most useful skill.

In a way, the term visualization is a bit of a misnomer, since this technique's effectiveness is increased when senses in addition to the visual can be incorporated into every exercise. In the following visualization, try to recreate, in your mind, a vivid sense of sight, feel, smell and taste. If the idea of learning more about visualization appeals to you, we'd suggest three books to begin with: "Super-Learning," "Psycho-Cybernetics," and "The Silva Mind Control Method" (see bibliography).

DAVID: My mentor Dr. Charlie Garfield, ex-NASA moon shot scientist, world-class athlete, and founder of the Shanti Project (for the terminally ill) now devotes much of his seemingly inexhaustible energy to studying the application of visualization to the "Peak Performance" state, for athletes, business people, those with terminal disease, and the rest of us. Please note his book in the bibliography, as well as those listed above. Charlie taught me not only compassion and technique in the counseling of the dying client, but that I needn't limit myself by self-definition as "a musician" or "a counselor". I'm proud even to flatter myself by considering him a friend to this day.

The Lemon Meditation

Picture a lemon in your mind's eye, as clearly as possible. As yellow as the sun, its thick skin minutely wrinkled, and just a touch oily to the hand. Dig your fingernail into the peel, and see a tiny spray of citric oil arch out into the air. Pull some peel off, to expose the white fibers covering the juicy, wet, pulpy, insides.

You smell the tartness as you bite deep into the lemon, and taste the sourness. The saliva leaps into your mouth.

If you were able to visualize the lemon with any clarity, you probably salivated even before you imagined biting into it. Can you "train" your salivary glands to spring into action at the first thought of lemon? At the word "lemon?"

Most people would consider salivation to be a bodily process rather outside of their conscious control. And yet we salivate when we think of lemons. If the mere thought of the taste of citrus somehow stimulates a salivary gland to produce a secretion, is it hard to believe that other thoughts might affect other glands? Perhaps even glands that control the growth process, the aging process, or the immunological process? The new field of Psycho-Neuro-Immunology is based on just this phenomenon that we've demonstrated to ourselves with a humble lemon. If you'd like to know more about such important matters, please read the books by Joan Borysenko and Bernie

Siegal listed in the bibliography.

We'll continue to use visualization skills in many of the exercises, so practice a few more, like these wild visualizations, just for fun. Can you picture Frankenstein's monster? Now put him into a tuxedo! Change the tux to a yellow tutu! Make him do the Charleston, then replace him with an image of...Robert Redford! When will we ever stop having fun?!!!

The Relaxation Exercise

Being able to relax the muscles of the body at will is a useful ability, and one that visualization skills can help with. You may find it easiest, in the beginning, to practice this exercise while lying in bed, face up and arms at your sides. Take as long as you need, the first few times you do it, even if it takes 10 or 20 minutes.

Make fists with both hands. Really clench your fingers into your palms. Feel the tightness in your wrists, and even up into your forearms. Hold the tension for five or six seconds, then relax it. Tense up again, for a similar amount of time, then relax. This time, as you relax your hands, say "warm and heavy, warm and heavy" to yourself, and visualize your hands feeling warm and heavy, just sinking heavily into the softness of the bed. I like to picture my hands being made of mercury, or molten lead, warm and soft and very heavy.

Perform this same process — tensing and relaxing, then tensing and relaxing, and saying "warm and heavy" (with appropriate warm and heavy visualizations) — for each major muscle group of your body. After doing your hands, do your feet, calves, thighs, buttocks, stomach, chest, arms, shoulders, neck, jaw, and eyes. Tense and relax, tense and relax. Warm and heavy, warm and heavy. Try to cultivate as relaxed a feeling as you can, throughout your entire body, and try to *remember* this feeling once it comes.

The Semi-Quick Face Relaxation

Sometimes we don't have time to go through a full body relaxation, but we do need to de-tensify the physique. At times like these, it's useful to have a shorthand version of relaxation, a way to become aware of accumulated tensions and quickly let them go. Relaxing the face is an instance where the part can represent the whole — as relaxes the face, so goes the body...

Try to identify any feelings of tension in your face. Perhaps you've been concentrating and your forehead is tight with effort. Maybe you've been making polite conversation and wearing a polite little smile for longer than your cheek muscles would like. Perhaps, on a sunny day, or working at the computer, you've been squinting without realizing it.

Take a deep inhalation and scrunch your face up. Like the fist you made before relaxing your hand, hold the tension for a few seconds while you inhale and then, with a sigh on the out-breath, exhale all the tension in your face. Feel those muscles relaxing, warm and heavy, as the tension drains out with the sigh.

The Very Quick Relaxation

Here's an even shorter version. It will work especially well if you've done a few full length relaxations, and been able to memorize that "warm and heavy" body feeling to some extent.

Take a deep breath and quickly scan your body. Consciously relax as many tensed muscles as you can identify, while exhaling with a sigh and mentally saying "warm and heavy". Don't worry about relaxing everything, but focus on either larger muscle groups or those that seem easiest to control. Shoulder and arm muscles are often tight, but often also easy to relax on demand, unlike leg or back muscle groups, which for many people appear to be less amenable to controlled relaxation.

Do this as many times during the day as you can remember to. If you like, choose a muscle or muscle group in which you can easily identify tension, and use it as a tension test, like miners used to use canaries. Canary lying feet up at the bottom of the cage? Air must be getting bad in here. Shoulders rising up to meet neck, pulling arms in and up? Must be getting tense, it's time to do a quick relaxation and meditation.

Some Specific Uses Of Relaxation And Visualization

As you may have already noticed, we love to mix and match our meditations and exercises. So naturally we like to combine relaxation with visualization. If you like, feel free to precede any of today's exercises with a moment of your favorite breathing meditation as well — it may help you to both relax and visualize. And as you continue to follow the program and your mind clears, all of the visualization and relaxation exercises, general and specific, will become easier.

The Special Place Visualization

Spend a moment doing one of the relaxation exercises, or perhaps a combination breath and relaxation meditation. Then imagine yourself in a very peaceful place, a place that you associate with relaxation. Try to develop as clear a mental picture as possible of this place, including the way it feels, sounds, looks, smells, and even tastes. Include as many details as you can, and try to use the mind's eye as a camera to memorize them all.

DAVID: I visualize a lovely tropical beach. I feel the warm sun and the cool breeze, and the sand under me, as I look up at the waving palm fronds. I hear the waves crash, and smell, almost taste, the salt spray in the air.

NINA: My special place is Mohonk Mountain House, a 120-year old resort set in the Shawangunk Mountains, amazingly close to New York City. Mohonk is built like a fantasy castle, with nooks and crannies, towers and turrets. It has a huge porch looking out towards a craggy cliff face that sheers down to a mountain lake.

I imagine myself sitting on the lake-side porch, in a rocking chair. It's early morning and I'm just about to go on a hike. The fresh, cool air is so clean, it smells and tastes sweet. I feel relaxed and renewed — and just slightly awed — by the grandeur of nature around me. Somehow being at Mohonk puts things in perspective. My mental skirmishes become less important in the context of such serenity.

After you've done this exercise a few times, you'll find yourself able to mentally recreate your relaxation place, and feel relaxed, without needing to do the tensing and relaxing, or at least not needing to do it for so long. With practice, you'll be able to return to your relaxing spot just by thinking of it for a second or two. Whenever you're under stress, you'll be able to take a vacation, without even moving!

The Meditation Visualization Exercise

This exercise is a warm-up for the crucial Master Skill exercise at the end of the book. Spend just twenty or thirty seconds (or more) a few times each day, picturing yourself ac*tually* using a Three Minute Meditation technique in a mildly stressful real life situation. For instance, you might picture yourself doing one of the walking meditations as you return to your busy office from lunch. Try to experience the scene that you've mentally created as clearly as possible. Feel your feet as they hit the floor, and feel your thumbs gently touching your forefingers. See the surrounding area, and hear or smell any appropriate sounds or odors. Picture yourself calm, soothed by the meditation.

After you've done this a few times, try to visualize using meditation to deal with a slightly more stressful scenario. Perhaps you can see yourself successfully using a walking meditation on the way to the boss's office for a meeting, or on the way to a blind date!

Thoughts For The Day: Relaxation As A Metaphor For Meditation

In a way, relaxation is a physical metaphor for the mental act of meditation. Just as we learn to identify and then soften or relax tight places in the body, we'll learn to identify and soften or remove painful or otherwise troublesome thoughts and emotions in the mind, as we study the mind watching exercises of the next few days.

On Affirmations

An affirmation is any positive, life-enhancing statement that you affirm, or tell yourself, repeatedly. Affirmations come in all sizes and shapes and can be created at will. Just as relaxation is a physical metaphor for meditation, so affirmation can be thought of as a verbal metaphor for visualization. Instead of picturing yourself doing something, or being or acting in a certain way, you simply say it to yourself. Affirmations may be more effective when preceded by relaxation or meditation exercises, or when coupled with a visualization of the verbal message.

Louise Hay, in her book "You Can Heal Your Life", describes affirmations as a way of "re-shaping" one's mental self-image. And speaking of reshaping Suzy Prudden's new book "Meta Fitness" uses affirmations to reshape the body (see bibliography).

If you like, experiment with a daily affirmation. Try "I am a meditative person", or "I am becoming more serene every day" or any other that feels right to you. Affirmations usually begin with "I am..." and are phrased for the present, not the future ("I will...").

The Master Skill

The Master Skill is the ability to use our meditative techniques in any real life situation. This skill is far more important than the outcome of *any* specific event, no matter how important that particular event may seem. In a very real way, it is better to be able to lose the race, or the job, or the relationship and to *handle* that loss with grace and compassion, and to still feel okay about ourselves, than it would be to win that race, that job, that man or woman.

Our culture tends to stress winning at any cost. Yet sometimes the deepest level of winning is to be a good loser, for not every contest can be won. Inevitably, no matter how smart or rich or powerful or lucky we are, pain, loss and change must enter our lives.

When we begin to see every painful or frightening or disappointing event as a challenge to be dealt with skillfully, instead of as a tragedy or an excuse to be angry, fearful, self-hating, or self-pitying — we are truly the masterful players in the game of life. And the practice of meditation and a progressive investment in the meditator's worldview are the paths that can lead us to this incredibly freeing and satisfying state of being.

Day 9 Practice Plan: REVIEW

Formal Practice
- A full length body relaxation, for as long as needed (page 88).
- A Meditation Visualization (page 91) for three minutes.
- Any of the looking/Listening/Just Experiencing Meditations (page 80) for three minutes.

Real Life Use: Do the *minimum* daily requirement of two meditations *during* your daily activities. By now we hope that you're looking for opportunities to incorporate new exercises, like relaxations and the just experiencing meditations, into your day. It really doesn't matter how *long* you do them for. It's your diligence in returning your mind to a meditative state as *often* as possible during each day that gets results! Do you have any bits of "waste" time in your life, no matter how short, that can be used to good advantage? Make them into "cues" or reminders that it's time to meditate!

DAVID: Whenever I have to use the "save" button on my computer, which I do dozens of times each day, I try to do a quick meditation. Since it usually takes from ten to thirty seconds to save, that's not enough time to do much else. But it's plenty long enough to meditate, to turn my mind towards that which is of real importance, like labelling the breath or focussing on "I Am"!

NINA: Sometimes as I plan to do some short and specific task (like squeezing a glass of fresh orange juice), I decide to do a meditation for as long as the task takes. I usually use breath counting, and sometimes "just experiencing", if I'm feeling particularly meditative.

Our friend Jean is a secretary in a busy office. She tries to remember to meditate every time she walks to the copy machine, a very short but very frequent trip.

> *Robert has a long commute twice a day, right through the heart of the city. He uses every red light as a signal to drop whatever else he's thinking of, and do eyes open breath counting until the light turns green.*

Thoughts For The Day: Thinking About Thinking

Today we'll begin to prepare for the second level of meditation, in which we learn to first observe, and then to work with the thought process itself. Instead of simply thinking, we will start thinking about thinking, for we believe that it is the ability to think about thinking that makes human beings unique. Although animals have awareness (they are aware of food, of physical sensations, of other animals), only humans are aware of the fact that they have awareness. We like to call this awareness of awareness by the name consciousness. We'll discuss more of these metapsychological matters later. For now, let's simply think about thought.

On Watching The Mind

When a thought enters your mind, do you feel obligated to pay attention to it? Perhaps you can simply brush some thoughts aside. Other thoughts, especially fears and desires, seem to expand to fill your entire awareness, although you may consciously want to be rid of them. Often it may seem as though you have little control over your thoughts, especially when a frightening image or unacceptable desire occurs again and again despite your conscious wish to be rid of it. Often it may seem difficult to refrain from acting on such powerful thoughts — the fear seems to literally demand that you take evasive action, and the desire cries out for fulfillment.

After we've practiced our first level of mind clearing and relaxing meditations, we'll start to find it possible to observe our own thoughts, as though they actually were scenes on a movie screen. Our increasing ability to consciously focus our attention becomes a more powerful tool, and the searchlight that we can aim at the dark corners of our own minds. Just as we used walking and breathing as objects of our mental spotlight last week, we will begin to focus on our own thoughts and thought process. This is "Watching The Mind", our second level of meditation.

As with walking and breathing, we'll learn to work with thoughts by noticing them, and counting them, and then labelling them. By doing this we'll soon begin to recognize familiar patterns and sequences of thoughts.

Instead of only paying attention to the specific *content* of each thought (what the thought is about) as we usually do, we'll begin to see the *process* by which thoughts arise and pass away. As we better understand this process through watching the mind, we'll become able to choose how to deal with each thought that arises. We'll see them coming from a long way off, and be ready to pay attention to the ones we want to pay attention to, and gently withdraw attention from those that we don't want to pay attention to. Eventually *we'll* be controlling our thoughts, rather than being controlled by *them*.

On the Fact and Fallacy of Control

No one can control the things that happen in the world. We are all at the mercy of the virus, the accident, the natural disaster, the aging process. Anyone who thinks that he or she is "in control" is a victim of that widespread fallacy, the fallacy of control.

No, we can't always control what happens — in fact we're lucky if we can even influence what happens, some of the time. But we *can* control our *mental* reactions to whatever does happen, if we just learn to understand how our thought process works. And this ability to control our own thoughts — fears, desires and emotions included — is a treasure greater than any amount of money, fame, or power. Find that hard to believe? Just think about billionaire Howard Hughes, rock stars Janis Joplin or Jimi Hendrix, actress Judy Garland or actor John Belushi, or ex-presidential contender Gary Hart.

At The Movies

We'd like to take the analogy of seeing our thoughts as though projected onto a movie screen a bit further now. Please consider these two distinctly different ways of being part of the audience at a film.

If we choose, we can focus our

attention very narrowly on the theater's screen, and watch just the content of the film that is playing. When watching in this way, if sad events occur on the screen, we will feel sad. If happy events occur, we'll feel happy. If the film makers are skillful propagandists, it will be simple for them to manipulate our beliefs and feelings. For instance, the German movie "Das Boot" (The Boat), about a German submarine crew struggling for life, was upsetting to many audiences in this country because it virtually forced them to root for the Nazi submariners.

Alternatively, we can focus our conscious attention more widely, on the entire *process* of "being at the movies." Then we will be aware not only of the action on the screen, but also of the fact that it is "just" a movie. So, as we watch the film, we will also be conscious of many other aspects of the situation. Is the theater crowded or empty? Are the other patrons engrossed, or bored? What special effects or techniques were used to produce the scene that's playing right now? What feelings does each scene or character evoke for us? Do we like or dislike having those feelings? What were the goals of the director and the producer of the movie?

We can relate to our own minds in these same two ways. The type of thinking that most of us do, most of the time, is "content" thinking. We become engrossed in each passing thought. Is that a fearful thought arising? We become anxious. Is that a thought about loneliness? We feel lonely. If two conflicting thoughts happen to arise at the same time, like a dessert-desire thought and a fat-anxiety thought, we feel confused. We are so involved in the content of each thought that comes through our mind that perhaps it seems that we actually are nothing but the sum, the total, of our thoughts.

To repeat (because it's important): In these next exercises, *thoughts in the mind* will provide the focal point for our attention. In other words, we'll be using thoughts as our meditation objects, just as we've already used breathing and walking. As with the breathing and walking exercises, we'll begin by counting, and then by labelling, our thoughts. Finally, we'll be able to focus on the direct experiencing of thought, without counting or labelling.

Day 10 Practice Plan

Formal Practice
- Thought Counting exercise for one minute, two times.
- Thought Labelling exercise twice, for two minutes each.

Real Life Use: Try to label thoughts throughout the day, whenever you can remember to do so.

Note: It may be time for you to start to use the "old dog" method (explained below) of quickly labelling and releasing thoughts that sneak in during your other daily meditations.

The Thought Counting Meditation

This exercise will help you to start withdrawing your attention from the content of your thoughts. Please read this entire section on thought counting before doing the exercise.

Sit comfortably, with some type of timer or alarm clock handy. If none are available, make sure you can see a clock. Set the timer for one minute, or time yourself by the clock. But it doesn't really matter whether you do this exercise for one, or two, or three minutes.

Now close your eyes, and begin to count your thoughts. As soon as a thought appears in your mind, count it, but don't "get into" the content of that thought. If you do, you may only end up with a count of one thought for your entire minute!

Imagine an employee of the Department of Public Works, who has been stationed on a busy road and ordered to count the number of cars that pass by during a day, so that his superiors can decide whether traffic usage justifies upgrading it to a four lane highway. His job is not to think about each vehicle ("Hmm, a Cadillac, must be nice to be wealthy..."), but simply to notice and count. Were his attention to be caught for long by

a particular car ("Oh boy, a red '63 Volkswagen! I used to have one of them. I remember when me and Durstewitz drove all the way to...") the accuracy of his count would be likely to suffer.

You've already gained a modicum of skill at returning the focus of your attention to a meditation (from practicing the mind clearing meditations). So you'll probably be able to let go of each thought after counting it, unless it's one of those particularly stubborn thoughts, which we'll deal with below. And then return the focus of your attention towards looking for another thought to count. If no thoughts seem to come up, either say to yourself "no thoughts" (which is a perfectly valid thought itself, and should be counted), or else just relax and enjoy a moment of spontaneous mind clearing!

So keep a count of your thoughts. This will include thoughts such as "Gee, I haven't had many thoughts yet" or "Uh-oh, was that thought number seven or number eight?" Some thoughts will flash by like speedy and exotic roadsters, perhaps as quick mental pictures or even as single words. Others will lumber like trucks into sight of your mind's eye, and take their time leaving as well.

If a thought arises, and its content is so "grabby" for you that you just "can't" seem to let go of it, try to remember what thought it is. That information will be useful, even though it seems to be preventing you from doing this exercise right now. Write the stubborn thought down, then try the exercise again later on. Fear thoughts and desire thoughts tend to be the hardest to let go of, for most people. But remember — it's not the fear or the desire thought that's the problem — it is the inability to control your reaction to that thought that may create a problem.

This isn't an easy exercise, but there is no way to do it wrong. Its real purpose is not to count thoughts, but to teach us to look, for this moment, at our thoughts as objects, like cars, or rocks, or other people. Nothing to take personally — just thoughts...

On The Thought Labelling Meditation

In the last meditation, we paid no attention to the content of the thoughts that we were counting. Now, we are going to pay just barely enough attention to thought content so that we will be able to label each thought.

Think about a bird watching competition. Competitive bird watchers go out, armed with binoculars, to try to identify as many species of bird as they can in one day. They don't study each bird for hours, or even minutes. As soon as they see one — that's it, a Yellow Bellied Sapsucker — they label it and go on to look for the next. And you're going to be a thought watcher, in this exercise!

Our Favorite Thought

Now make a brief mental or written list of the *types* or categories of thoughts that are commonly featured in the movie of your mind. We each have some perennial favorites, which we'll list below, in general order of popularity. Is your list as high-minded and spiritual as ours? It may be easier to make your list after doing the following exercise once or twice.

DAVID: Planning thoughts are those in which I try to decide exactly what to do, specifically ("I'll write to Doctor John, then have lunch") or generally ("Perhaps I should go to law school"). Desire thoughts include wishes for anything, from sex to world peace. Fear thoughts include any type of worry: hypochondria, money, work, you name it. Happy or appreciative thoughts are often noting pleasurable sensations such as the sun on my face, or the smell of potatoes cooking. Judging thoughts are those in which I approve (or, more likely, criticize) anything or anyone. Righteous thoughts are those in which I am right, and someone else is wrong. Angry thoughts could be those directed at myself, in which case I consider them as falling into the specialized sub-category of self-hating thoughts, or at anybody else.

NINA: My thoughts are somewhat different, but on an equally enlightened plane as David's. They also include planning, but often with a not-so-hidden agenda of wanting to be sure things are under control ("If I wake up at 6:30, exercise, shower and bring breakfast with me, I can get to the office by 8:15 and have time to revise the agenda before my meeting begins"). Fear thoughts are often in the "what if" category with a tendency to "catastrophize" ("What if it snows and I miss my connecting

flight?"). Mind-reading thoughts in which I anticipate others' feelings ("Bert is probably annoyed because I'm not watching the hockey game with him" — when in reality he couldn't care less!) are also frequent visitors. Self evaluative thoughts can be either comparative ("I wonder how often most people come in when they first join the spa?") or competitive ("Am I enough of a success to go to my twentieth high school reunion?"). Wistful, loving thoughts are a mixture of pain and pleasure ("I wish I had more time to spend just hanging out with friends and family"). In all, it's a constant flow of thoughts: feelings, plans, fears, desires and insights, with variations on many themes.

With a bit of practice, you'll be able to detect a thought, label it, and allow it to depart with a bare minimum of thinking. Most of your thoughts will become like the old and well-trained dog approaching the dinner table in futile hope of a handout — a single glance or word, and he'll slink silently away, tail between his legs!

The Thought Labelling Meditation

Sit comfortably, and observe each thought as it swims into awareness. Observe it only long enough to decide which one of your categories it fits into, then go on to look for the next. If absolutely no thoughts seem to be forthcoming right now, simply relax and enjoy a few seconds of effortless mind clearing.

If a thought doesn't seem to fit into any of your categories, quickly make up a more or less appropriate new category ("Ahh, that's one of those 'What-If-I-Had-Been-Born-An-Eskimo' type of thoughts") and go back to looking for the next thought.

As in the last exercise, if a "grabby" thought arises, just notice what thought, and what type of thought, it is.

After the meditation, see if you can tell which thoughts occurred most often. Which thoughts were easy to let go of? Which ones were hard to let go of?

Thought Labelling Throughout The Day

Once we learn to label our thoughts in formal practice, we can begin taking the time to label thoughts whenever they arise during the day. With practice, this can become one of the fastest of the mini-meditations, done as quickly as we notice the thought arising and pin it with a one or two word label. "Ah yes, that's a fear thought." "Hmmm, there's anger."

The key to doing this effectively is threefold. Firstly, it lies in learning to see "our" thoughts as being somehow separate from who we *really* are, which will eventually tie back in to the meditative worldview. The section below will help you to do that. Secondly, it demands that we not get caught up in the specific content of the thought that we are looking at, a wonderful skill to develop. And thirdly, it requires a spirit of adventure rather than judgment.

DAVID: When I began to thought label, I would keep in the back of my mind the image of a very intrepid, stiff-upper-lipped British anthropologist, probably wearing a pith helmet: "Ah yes — cannibals — how utterly fascinating." Somehow this helped me to observe even my less pleasant thoughts with a bit more equanimity.

Relating To Your Mind

When we learn to look at the process of our thinking, to watch our thoughts, we realize that they are not us, any more than that table or this book, or *anything else that we can see* outside of ourselves is us. And we can begin, as Stephen Levine says, to "relate to our mind, instead of *from* it."

> Relating to your mind means mentally "stepping back" to watch exactly what your mind is doing, without getting hung up in the content of any particular thought. It means being able to notice a fearful thought and say "Ahh, there's a fearful thought" without becoming fearful. Being able to notice a lustful thought and say "Uh-huh, there's a lustful thought" without becoming consumed with desire and/or guilt.

As we learn to watch our thoughts, we begin to see habitual thought patterns that are particularly our own. For some of us, tiredness will always cause fearful thoughts to arise. For one person, the sight of an expensive car may result in angry thoughts ("Rich jerk! He doesn't deserve a car like that!"), or for another, result in greedy thoughts ("When I have money, I'll have a car

like that, plus a yacht"). The sight of someone doing better than we are may lead to self-hating thoughts that could express themselves in ways as varied as hypochondria or despair. Or it might produce an envious thought. And that envious thought might then bring up a guilty thought, and so on. We'll learn to work with these chains of thought in Day 11, with the "Rube Goldberg" exercise.

Sneezing Your Way To Enlightenment

An integral part of learning to work with thoughts involves seeing how they arise and how they pass away. Try this unusual analogy on for size — it may help to clarify the process.

DAVID: I used to believe that a sneeze was something that "just happened." Unless I had caught a cold, or gotten pepper or dust up my nose, a sneeze usually seemed to come out of nowhere, and to be nearly unavoidable. Occasionally, of course, I'd notice a "pre-sneeze tickle" in my nose, and then I'd be able to delay or even prevent the actual "ah-choo," if I chose to struggle with it.

After some practice with the various breath meditations described in this book, I often find myself able to observe the entire sneeze process with greater clarity. Instead of noticing the tickle feeling only seconds before it blossoms forth into a full-fledged sneeze, I now begin to note a tiny sensation of pressure or heat at the back of my nose, long before it becomes uncomfortable enough to motivate even a sniff or nose-wrinkle. I then focus my attention on the sensation itself, without labelling it as a nuisance, without wondering whether I'll have to sneeze or not. Just sensation: is it hot or cold, steady or flickering, where exactly is it located, way back towards the sinus or nearer the tip of the nose?

Surprisingly, the urge to sneeze almost always disappears when observed with very focussed awareness, without any need to try to suppress or repress it. The nose tickle dwindles back into nothingness, and I turn the focus of my attention back to my breathing. Most sensations, thoughts, and emotions can be effectively dealt with in exactly the same way. Observing them closely gives us a great deal of power to control them — not by repressing them but by understanding and just observing how and why they arise.

The Chatterbox Mind

Often, we are not even completely aware of all of our thoughts. Many of us suffer from an internal monologue that runs intermittently, a critical, judgmental, internal voice that seems to love to offer gratuitous, and usually negative, comments. These comments slink through our mind half noticed, and, like small leaks in the bottom of a large boat, often have a long term or cumulative effect, which is not a pleasant one. They can be emotional or feeling type thoughts (like the one David describes), or more analytical ones (like Nina's).

DAVID: I used to use the first line or two of the Beatles song "I'm A Loser" to berate myself with. Anytime that I did anything that didn't work out perfectly, I'd subconsciously croon "I'm a looo-oo-ooser..." to myself, thus reinforcing my negative feelings.

Once I began to clear and to watch my mind through meditation, I was able to see what I was doing (at least sometimes), and began to let go of this self-hating habit. Before I started meditating, I couldn't catch myself in the act, so I wasn't able to deal with this behavior.

I feel a lot better now that my mind is no longer singing that darn tune! You'll feel happier and more positive when you begin to quiet the chatter of your mind, too.

NINA: Occasionally, I have to attend business meetings or social events where I don't know anyone. Walking into these situations can be stressful, and certain that all eyes were upon me, I used to tense up.

As I began to watch my thoughts in those situations, I realized that my own internal critic was chattering constantly throughout these events ("I'm being too quiet, should have said something there..." "Did I talk too long? They seemed interested, but maybe they were only being polite..."). Just beneath conscious awareness, I was continually judging, evaluating, and commenting on my own behavior. All these negative thoughts were causing me to feel anxious, without even knowing why.

With increasing awareness, I began to recognize that no one else cared all that much about my behavior. They were all too busy watching their own. And as I learned to be more compassionate with myself, I began to let go of the feeling that I should be performing perfectly in every situation.

Now before I enter a room full of strangers, I take a minute to meditate. Taking a few deep breaths and clearing my mind for just a moment, I can exchange self-centered anxiety for curiosity. All I have to do is show up and be interested. And that's much easier to do with a calm and open mind.

An Interesting Question

As we learn to relate to our thoughts as objects of our attention, an interesting question arises. If we can, for instance, label a fear thought ("Ah yes, there's a fear thought"), the fear thought is being treated as an object by whoever is doing the labelling. And who is that? If a person can label thoughts, it's clear that the thoughts are not the person, but are objects that can be manipulated by the person. So who is the elusive one doing the thought watching? We believe that it may be the sense of "I Am", with which we'll work a lot more later on. What do you think?

Day 11 Practice Plan

Formal Practice
- Thought Labelling meditation twice, for at least two minutes each time.

Real Life Use: The Particular Thought Counting exercise throughout the day, using one thought at a time. Also try to identify thought chains during the day, whenever possible.

On Particular Thought Counting

Yesterday's practice plan encouraged us not only to label our thoughts in formal practice, but also to begin labelling thoughts whenever we remembered to do so during the day. In today's exercise, we'll choose a particular thought and follow it through the day.

The Particular Thought Counting Meditation

You can choose any thought, or category of thought, to notice in this exercise. You would probably get the most benefits by choosing one of those "grabby" thoughts (fears, planning thoughts, or desire thoughts, for most people), as they are the thoughts that you most need practice working with. But if choosing a problematic thought seems scary to you at first, choose one that's not too threatening, the first time you try this exercise. If you like, you can do it for a few hours with a less intimidating thought, and then switch to a tougher one.

Decided on your thought? You are going to try to remember to count the number of times in the course of an hour or a day that you notice your particular thought arising. That's all there is to it. You may want to keep count on a piece of paper, so that you don't forget your score. Try not to get angry with yourself for having these perhaps uncontrollable, or at least repeated, thoughts. The compassion exercises later on will help you to work with your thoughts, and to treat even your own mind with just a touch of mercy.

DAVID: I usually do this exercise with my righteous thoughts, since they are, for me, the grabbiest. I love to be *right*, and it's hard for me to let someone else be wrong without their admitting it, to simply let go of me being right and them being wrong. On a seriously righteous day, I can count dozens of righteous thoughts! Doing so helps me to be aware of the hold that this particular thought has on me, and to diminish it with the use of the judging exercises of Day 19. Sometimes I do the Particular Thought Counting exercise with desire thoughts, and then use the Compassion Breath (Day 16) and the Softening Around Pain exercise (Day 23) to help relax around the desires.

NINA: I usually use control thoughts in this exercise, because I tend to have lots of them. But since my control thoughts are mixed in with what I consider to be valid planning thoughts, it's often hard to know which to count as control thoughts. And of course each control thought does its darndest to convince me that it's actually a perfectly valid and necessary planning thought! So this meditation is hard for me. I usually find it most productive to do in conjunction with the Experiencing Thoughts exercise on Day 12. If particular thought counting seems hard for you right now, don't worry. As you work with the Experiencing Thought meditation, it will become easier.

"Rube Goldberg" Thought Chains Meditation
In a Rube Goldberg cartoon, strange events are chained together to cause a final event. To create a Goldberg alarm clock, for example, the sun comes up, and its rays through a magnifying glass burn the rope that holds up a piece of cheese. Then the cheese falls down so that the mice come out, the cat goes after the mice, the dog goes after the cat from under the bed where he was sleeping, which pulls out a bed slat so that Farmer Ken falls on the floor and is woken up in time for milking!

DAVID: Our minds often work similarly, chaining together thoughts in strange ways. As I began to observe my thoughts more carefully, I found that my frustration or fear thoughts usually bring up angry or "macho" thoughts and images, as I describe below in my "Rambo Thoughts" section.

The Thought Chain Labelling Meditation
After you've tried a few Thought Counting and Thought Labelling meditations, try a Thought Labelling exercise in which you

specifically look for two or more thoughts which often occur together. You may find, for example, that the guilt thoughts that you had perceived as happening spontaneously are actually a result of prior angry thoughts, which themselves are a result of helplessness thoughts. Becoming aware of your thoughts in this manner can really help you to understand why you feel the way you do.

NINA: After I learned to watch my thoughts I was able to see that very few of my thoughts and feelings "came out of nowhere." I discovered that often my thoughts about calling my 92 year old grandfather who lives in a nursing home in Florida were based on a convoluted chain of reactions.

My wistful, loving thoughts ("Haven't talked to Grandpa lately") would bring up guilty thoughts ("I'm a bad granddaughter because I don't write or call more often"). These would be followed by defensive thoughts ("It's very hard to reach him...it's painful when he doesn't even know who I am... I just don't have enough time to do everything...") which would be superceded by even more guilty thoughts ("I really am a bad grandchild to be putting this off"). Occasionally, I'd throw in a few catastrophizing thoughts ("What if something happens to him before I call again?"). By the time I finally called I'd be feeling guilty and angry without understanding why. Uncovering this thought chain helped me face my ambivalence with some compassion and understanding.

DAVID: I used to be troubled by "macho" thoughts. For no apparent reason (but usually while walking the streets of the city at night) I'd find myself having "Rambo" type fantasies of being powerful, tough, even dangerous. I enjoyed these thoughts to some extent, but they also frightened me and seemed inappropriate.

Once I began to observe my own mind with closer attention, I could see that these macho thoughts weren't unavoidable, didn't just "come out of nowhere." Instead, they were always preceded by a fleeting sensation of fear and vulnerability which triggered the Rambo thoughts, just as I found that my sneezes were always preceded by a nose tickle.

I'm now able to recognize these Rambo thoughts as my mind's attempts to avoid frightened feelings of being powerless. With this new awareness, I can acknowledge, accept, and then soothe my fearful thoughts with compassion whenever they arise. I deal directly with them, and no longer have to react by trying to cover them up with macho mind games!

Thoughts For The Day: On Creating Helpful Thought Chains

Most people's unconscious thought chains seem to be negative in nature. But thought chains don't have to be painful or neurotic. Once we learn to recognize thought chains, we can begin to create our own healthy links in the chain, that can help rather than hinder us, as David does (see above) by beginning to chain "macho" thoughts or desire thoughts to compassion and softening around pain thoughts, or as Nina learned to chain her wistful/loving/guilty thoughts to compassion thoughts.

For a physical analogy, instead of following up one caloric and cholesterol filled meal with another (and probably a hefty side dish of self-criticism, as well), you can learn to follow an unhealthy meal with non-judgmental thoughts about what is best for your health, and then some exercise, and a lighter and healthier next meal. As you learn to practice some of the compassion and softening tools in the later days, you'll be able to chain these helpful and self-loving thoughts to your more painful or problematic ones, instead of merely following negative thoughts with more and more of the same.

The Wild And Crazy Mind

After a long, hard, day of observing our thoughts, it's easy to feel dismayed at what we see in there. So it's really important to realize that everybody has a wild and crazy mind, filled with the same type of untamed, tangled thoughts that run through our own minds.

Imagine thinking that you were the only person in the world who needed to urinate every day. You'd be acutely aware that you must continually perform this dirty, "unnatural" act, but you might never see anyone else do it. Einstein pee? Marcus Welby take a leak? Queen Elizabeth give in to such a basic need? Impossible!

It's just as painful, if slightly less ridiculous, not to realize that everybody has the same kind of drunken monkey mind as you do, leaping tipsily from thought branch to thought branch. Few people are open enough to talk to you about the fears, phobias, and fantasies in *their* minds. So your own mind is really the only one whose swirling multitude of strange thoughts you can easily be aware of. But knowing that we're all in roughly the same mental boat can help us to take our own bizarre ruminations just a bit less personally.

Comparing My Insides With Your Outsides

It's also really important to realize that *everyone* experiences pain. Unfortunately, it's all too easy to feel sorry for one's self at times when things are tough, each of us imagining that no one else has ever felt such emotional pain or confronted such overwhelming stress. It's easy to maintain this illusion, because we all try to put on a good front around other people. As we hide our "drunken monkey" minds, we also hide our pain. And, since we don't wear our hearts, or our hurts, on our sleeves, we must always compare our "insides" (our own first hand knowledge of the depth of our pain) to other people's "outsides" (the facade they choose to show to the world). Other people look so together. "How come *they* never seem to falter? Why is it always *me* who's struggling just to stay in place?" is our plaintive cry. But step outside your skin for just a moment. How do you look from the outside? There may be someone looking at *you* and wishing they were as "together" as you seem to be! The "Other's Secret Pain" meditation on page 134 and the "I-Thou" exercise on page 123 will help to deepen this way of perceiving others in a more realistic (and, of course, more compassionate) way.

NINA: I used to be afraid of flying. Not fearful enough to avoid air travel completely, but nervous enough to carry several little talismans and clutch them tightly until safely off the ground. And, if takeoff were ever delayed, I saw it as a clear omen that I should deplane immediately! On the outside, I looked like a seasoned business traveler. On the inside, I was quaking, and also angry at myself, looking with envy and disbelief at fellow passengers who seemed totally at ease.

I began to deal with my fear and anger by watching my thoughts, and found a thought chain. My fear thoughts were engendered by the realization that my safety was out of my control. Flying challenged my illusion of being able to foresee, and forestall, dangers. Once I recognized that my illusion of control was causing me fear, and the fear was causing me to be angry, because I wasn't "as calm as the others", I was able to work on soothing that fear with the compassion exercises, instead of trying to control events with superstitious behavior. And I was able to realize that my anger at myself and envy of other travelers was based on a spurious appraisal of their outside behavior compared to my inside feelings— a classic self-hate/envy trap! Can you find and explore any examples of this in your own mind?

More and more, in the short time since my baby brother got me involved in meditating, I find myself fascinated with the exploration of my own thoughts and mind. I enjoy, as we said, being scientist, laboratory, and experimental subject all in one. And the deeper and more carefully I look, the more I see and understand, in a tremendously satisfying and eminently practical process of growth and change!

Day 12 Practice Plan

Formal Practice
- Two minutes of your favorite breath or walking meditation, just before you do the following Experiencing Thought meditation, and one Relaxation exercise during it.
- One Experiencing Thought meditation, for a minimum of three minutes. If you have time, do a second as well, using the same thought or a different one.
- One Creating A Helpful Thought Chain exercise, for a minimum of two minutes.

Real Life Use: Today is a good day to maintain as meditative a mindset as possible, in order to facilitate the Experiencing Thought meditation. We've purposefully given you a light day of reading and formal practice, so feel free to re-read some of your favorite thought for the day sections, and do a variety of mind clearing and other thought watching exercises as often as you can remember to do so, while going about your daily business.

On The Experiencing Thoughts Meditation

Just as with breathing and walking, we began by counting our thoughts, and then labelling them. Now it's time to just experience the sensation of thoughts, rather as we experienced the physical sensations of walking and breathing in the "just experiencing" walking and breathing exercises.

The Experiencing Thoughts Meditation

Begin with two minutes of your favorite meditation, just to relax and clear your mind a bit. Then call one of your slightly "grabby" thoughts, perhaps a mild desire, or an annoyance, or a not particularly bone chilling fear, into your mind. Or use any repetitive thought — a planning thought, a control thought, what have you. It may be best not to use a *very*

grabby thought yet, until we have presented the Compassion exercises.

Just watch the thought — step back, and turn it around in your mind like an object outside of yourself that you are investigating. Ask yourself: "What does it feel like? Can I feel it as a hot feeling, or a cool feeling? Does my body feel tighter, or looser? Is there an enjoyable element to this feeling, or is it only painful?" It might be useful to re-read the sections "At The Movies" and "Relating To Your Mind". Does looking at the thought in this way change your reaction to the thought? In what way?

Apply your favorite breathing or walking meditation (which you should have just practiced formally) *while* you think your chosen thought. What happens? Do the relaxation exercise, then consider your thought. Does doing these meditations change your experience of the thought? In what way?

If you find yourself getting caught up in the content of the thought ("But I have a *right* to be annoyed, they shouldn't have..."), watch the caught-up-ness. How does it feel to be caught up in a thought like that? And if you cannot back off and relate to this particular thought, try one that's less grabby for now!

DAVID: I began to understand how important it is to take thoughts, especially repetitive and self-hating thoughts, less person-ally, and also how important it is to let go of such negative thoughts as quickly as possible, when I worked at the Haight Ashbury Free Clinic in San Francisco. I sometimes had the job of "talking down" a person brought in on a bad acid trip, and I soon realized that many acid "freakouts" were caused by a person's inability to let go of a disturbing thought.

John was a frequent visitor to the clinic. A somewhat marginal personality, he would come in high on LSD, hallucinating, for instance, that his dead grandmother was crawling up his leg, a knife clenched between her teeth. He'd read of that image in a Hunter S. Thompson essay, and it "just stuck in his mind." So he'd "see" grandma, and then think, "Wow! That's a *crazy* thought." And next, "I must be crazy to even have a thought like that...is she still there?" Half an hour of this, and he'd end up at the Haight Clinic, talking to me!

In contrast, "The Paisley Lady" was a street person who would rarely come to the clinic, except to say hello. She once told me about her method for dealing with potential bad trips — that is, trips in which she would have the same weird thought repeatedly. "Like there's an army of mice, and they're covering the floor. And they're all coming at me wearing little tiny uniforms, with a mouse general in front..." She too would say "Wow, that's a crazy thought." Then she'd laugh, and let her mind go on to the next wild thought, or focus on the patterns made by the hallucinatory mice or the sun on the floor, or her own toes! She'd had plenty of experience with weird thoughts, and was good at letting go of them from one moment to the next!

Creating A Helpful Thought Chain

As we discussed yesterday, many of our thought chains tend to be negative. We go from fear to anger to guilt, rather than from fear to breath counting to meditative awareness. To create a more positive thought chain, choose one of your common but not too upsetting negative thoughts, perhaps a mild fear or a less than obsessional desire that you'd prefer *not* to have to satisfy. Bring the thought into your mind, and then immediately "notice" it (as though it had just spontaneously popped into your head), and label it. Then follow the label with a minute or so of your favorite mind clearing meditation. With practice, you'll form a thought chain that will "kick in" on its own, as soon as the original fear or desire arises. You may find that "experiencing" the thought for a moment after labelling it but before going on to the mind clearing will help strengthen the chain. Eventually, you'll be able to create helpful thought chains around more difficult thoughts, especially once you've begun to use the compassion and softening tools.

Thoughts For The Day: Mind Over Matter

Perhaps the most important point to remember in our exploration of the thought process is that the thoughts themselves are not very important — it's how we *relate* to the thought that counts. As the saying goes, we need to practice mind over matter: if we don't mind, it don't matter!

As we said in our section on desire back in Day 1, when we reduce our attachment to a strong or obsessive desire, one that we simply must

113

fulfill (or nearly die trying), it becomes a *preference*. We'd *like* to satisfy our preferences, but we can continue to feel okay about ourselves and our lives even if we don't.

It has been suggested by psychologist Daniel Goleman that meditation may function as a form of what is called systematic desensitization. Usually this term is applied to a process in which a person is freed of suffering from a phobia or unrealistic fear, such as a fear of snakes. The person is first taught relaxation techniques similar to those of Day 8, and then practices relaxing *while* being progressively exposed to the object of fear (perhaps first to a cartoon of a snake, then to a photograph of a snake, then to a real snake at a distance). Eventually the person can relax knowing that a real snake is in close proximity.

It may be that meditation helps us to desensitize to our thoughts themselves, by learning first to see them as being somewhat outside of ourselves, and then learning to apply tools like the Compassion Breath and the Softening exercises to progressively more painful fears or obsessive desires.

Alchemy And The Midas Touch

For millennia, alchemists have been seeking the touchstone, a magical substance or formula that would turn base metals into gold. Perhaps meditation and the mindfulness that it brings are the mental analog to the Midas Touch, in that whatever thought or situation that we touch with clear mental awareness becomes transformed. Not into gold, but into the material out of which we can continue to enhance our ability to live with skill and compassion. Touch desire with mindfulness, and we begin to learn how to handle desire. Touch fear with mindfulness, and we learn about fear. Our compassion and our ability to soften around physical or emotional pain increases every time we bring mindfulness to any situation.

Midas And Meditation

This mindfulness is a Midas Touch for meditation as well. Every time that thoughts intrude into our meditations, and we respond by remembering the lesson of the paper trained puppy (that *returning* the mind to the meditation, without delay or self-hate, is what matters) — we turn those intrusions into gold. Not the fool's gold of the alchemist, of value only to the greedy, but the true gold of compassionate control over the mind.

Day 13 Practice Plan: REVIEW

Formal Practice
- One Thought Counting exercise (page 97) for two minutes.
- One Thought Labelling exercise (page 100) for two minutes.
- One Experiencing Thought meditation (page 111), for a minimum of three minutes.
- One Creating A Helpful Thought Chain exercise (page 113), for a minimum of two minutes.

Real Life Use: *Lots!* By now, we hope that you are integrating many meditations into your daily routine, choosing the ones that seem most appropriate to you. Continuing to use the mind clearing exercises of the first week will help you to maintain the mental discipline necessary to watch the mind, as you try to label and experience thoughts as they arise. Perhaps you'll find yourself occasionally turning your mind to the consideration of the sense of "I Am". If not, the first of today's Thoughts may encourage you to do so. And if your meditational diligence has generally lagged, perhaps the second of today's thoughts, on Why People Stop Meditating, will give you insight into the ups and downs of your own meditational process.

Thoughts For The Day: Ways To Think About Thought

We'd like to turn our mental attention momentarily to an attempt to oversimplify some rather complex theorizing, which you're quite welcome to skim over if you find it both confusing and unsatisfying. If you find it confusing and satisfying, please mull it over some. And if you find it not confusing (though perhaps still unsatisfying), we'd sure appreciate it if you'd write and make it crystal clear to us!

The Meditator's Worldview And The Mind

Since the meditative and the Western worldview seem so often to disagree on things, it's interesting that in many ways they seem to agree on the nature of the mind, which we'll minimally define as the personality plus consciousness (which we've already defined as awareness of awareness).

Western psychology sees the personality as a construct, created out of an intricate interwoven combination of memories of past experiences, defenses to avoid pain, primitive instincts and drives, analytical abilities, and elements of other people (like our parents) whose memory we have incorporated into our concept of our self. For an explanation of consciousness itself Western psychology has no answer, except to feebly suggest that it may somehow be a biochemical by-product of the brain.

From the meditator's point of view, the personality is also a construct. But there is generally less interest in exploring and delineating the components of the personality, and more interest in investigating the nature of consciousness. The personality is seen as being made up of various thoughts, many based on memory. These would especially include memories of satisfaction (giving rise to desires, and thus habitual behavior), and memories of pain (giving rise to fears). These thoughts are considered to be objects separate from the "real" person—after all, if we can look at our thoughts as objects (as we've been doing this past week), they must be outside of us. The question then arises: Who's looking at the thoughts? The proposed answer: consciousness.

Consciousness is seen as a *reflection* in the individual person of the Universal Consciousness that we variously refer to as God, the Higher Power, the All-That-Is, etc. An analogy: the moon has no light of its own, but reflects the light of the sun. Similarly the individual (who might be referred to as a body/personality unit) has no consciousness of his or her own, but only provides a surface (like the moon does for the light of the sun) from which to reflect the consciousness of God.

In the individual, this consciousness is perceived as the sense of "I Am", which all of us possess. Even an amnesiac, with virtually no memory, or a person suffering from brain lesions, who cannot remember events from one second to the next, has a clear sense of "I Am". It is also the only possession that any of us have that does not change, the only statement that we make in which we mean exactly the same whether we are four years old or our age today. Yes, there's a power and a uniqueness to the sense of "I Am" that makes it well worth exploring.

Why People Stop Meditating

We've probably all had this experience: beginning a program of change with great enthusiasm, committing ourselves to the program wholeheartedly, swearing that *this is it*, this time it (the diet, the exercise routine) will last forever — only to find, by Day 7, that we've had quite enough. Those last five pounds will stay on forever, despite all the on-and-off-and-on-again weight loss programs we attempt.

So it is with meditation. Even three minute meditations take effort. The idea sounds deceptively easy. Of course, we all have a few spare minutes a day — but often the motivation to continue to use them for meditation comes up lacking.

Once having started, why do people stop meditating? Some hit a wall after using meditation as a "crisis intervention". Once their specific problem has cleared up they no longer feel the need to meditate.

Arlene, a beginning meditator described her gratitude at how well meditation helped her through a difficult situation. "My parents were coming to visit and were planning to stay with me for a week. I've only been married for two years and the last time they came it was a disaster. They're lovely people, but after three days, my husband starts to get a little crazy. I felt caught in the middle on their last visit. I was furious with my husband and my parents. It took months to recover.

"This time I started doing mini-meditations about two weeks in advance. I focused on breath counting and feeling compassion — for all of us. Whenever I got upset, I'd try to remember to watch the movie in my mind and not get caught up in my emotions.

It really helped. This visit was much better. But the meditation was like a crisis intervention. Once my parents left, I stopped doing it. I don't know why I stopped, because I could use it to help with a lot of other things in my life. But when things got back into equilibrium again, I just kind of stopped."

Sometimes meditators find the effort of using meditation takes more energy than they want to expend.

John, a student at a top university, described hitting his wall. "Why did I stop? Pure laziness. I got tired of making the effort. Sure it worked. Meditation was great for de-stressing exams. But am I doing it today? Nope.

It wasn't the time it took. But I just got tired of the extra mind-work. On top of all the intellectual stuff I do for school, it was just too much for me. I went back onto automatic pilot. I guess if I start to hurt too much, I'll get back into it."

Many others give up meditation, — for a while — but somehow, it filters back into their lives.

Sarah, a medical technician, recounted her on-and-off again romance with meditation. "I started doing meditation about two months ago and it felt terrific. My mind got calmer and I was able to make some real progress on my temper tantrums, something that's always been a problem for me.

Then my life just got busy and I stopped meditating. But I also found that my temper had returned. I was feeling angry again and taking it out on other people. At first, I ignored it. Then I got down on myself about it. Finally, I went back to meditating because it was the only thing that worked."

On Falling Off The Wagon

Whenever we fall, be it from a diet or an exercise regimen, an alcohol or drug or sex abstinence, or from the good intentions of our MetaPhysical Fitness program, we have two main choices. We can either say, "Well, I really (binged-out) (got lazy) (got bombed) (got loaded) (got wild) (let my thoughts run way out of control) for a few (hours) (days) (weeks) (months). And I feel so lousy and bad about myself, I guess I'll just keep doing it more."

Or we can say, with compassion for ourselves and a wry acceptance of the human condition, "Yup, I sure did blow it yesterday. But I see that I got off track and I'm going to get back on the wagon starting right now."

DAVID: Ironically, at one point while finishing the writing of this book, at a time when I was under a lot of other business and personal pressure, I got so caught up in trying to make the deadline that I stopped

118

taking care of myself. I just worked, didn't eat well or exercise, and was not, shall we say, diligent in my meditation. I began to have lots of negative thoughts, and feel lousy about everything (I call that "putting on my crud colored glasses", which I *used* to wear all the time). After about two days of this (with the help of my wife, who kindly pointed out what a grouch I was being) I made a conscious effort to return to healthy behavior, even though taking the time to do so might mean missing the deadline. After just a few hours which included minimal exercise, healthy food, and as much meditation as I could fit in, I began to feel much better. And, of course, I was able to work better, too.

So if you fall off the meditational bandwagon, there are several ways to respond. You can get right back on, which of course is the choice that we'd prefer to see you make. Or, if you just don't feel much like continuing, perhaps you can keep on meditating for a while and see if the let-down or lack of enthusiasm is a temporary thing, a passing lack of energy. Often a diminution of interest in meditation is just part of the ebb and flow of life — it happens to both of us, from time to time.

If you are really having a problem continuing, you might scale down your expectations about meditation — do some basic breath counting and don't push yourself. Think of this as a plateau phase, and don't feel angry or critical about yourself.

If you find that you're really not willing to do any meditation, simply put it down for right now. But don't feel that you have to reject it. Don't walk away angry, simply walk away. Place your meditation skills on a back mental shelf. They will be there to pick up again as you need them. The very fact that you ever began a meditation program is a tremendously positive step. Remember, David successfully resisted meditating (after paying a good sum of money to learn a method) for over ten years. Nina received a mantra from a top-of-the-line guru in 1971, and hasn't used it to this day!

Day 14 Practice Plan

Formal Practice
- The Compassion meditation, for as long as you need.
- The Compassion Visualization exercise, for at least three minutes.

Real Life Use: The I-Thou exercise, as appropriate.

On Compassion

Probably *the* most important meditation we can do is just to spend time with ourselves in a state of compassion and forgiveness. It sounds easy, it even sounds simplistic, but it *works*. And until we can forgive and feel compassion for ourselves, we can't truly offer it to anyone else.

In this high pressure, performance-oriented society, we often judge ourselves, and find ourselves lacking. We're not as beautiful as the movie stars, as rich as the stock speculators, as wise as the scientists that we constantly see in the news.

We monitor, we judge, we boss ourselves mercilessly — as though our mind were an administrator, seeking to constantly improve some personal bottom line. But when compassion becomes our guideline, even for a moment, we learn instead to *investigate* ourselves as an anthropologist studies a foreign culture. Alert curiosity replaces the usual disdain or denial, the usual attempts to avoid pain by closing off the heart.

Stepping away from a place of critical judgment, we can seek to find out what is true, even if it's not flattering. Then we can bring compassion to these "rough spots." It's easy to love our finer points and nobler qualities, but the unflattering aspects of ourselves — our fears, greeds, stupidities — are exactly the parts that we most need to be compassionate towards!

Thus, the art of compassion will aid us also in those later meditations involving both "Judging" and "Investigation Of The Truth". And, as we've said before, an awareness of compassion will prevent us from letting meditation become just another race to lose, just another way to be hard on ourselves.

The Compassion Exercise

Picture yourself as a small child, at the youngest age that you can remember. Visualize your child-self as clearly as possible, then send feelings of love and compassion to that small child-self. Wrap your arms around yourself, or at least place one hand over the other in a loving, compassionate way. In your mind's eye, see yourself hugging your child-self.

If feelings or thoughts other than love and compassion enter, gently return your mind to thoughts of love and compassion for your child-self.

For many of us, compassionate feelings for ourselves at any age do not come easily. Do this exercise with as much loving kindness as you can muster, and try not to be judgmental if it seems difficult. Can you see the irony of judging yourself harshly for not being able to do a compassion exercise "perfectly enough?" Just do the best that you can, and recognize that it will become easier with time.

Next, picture yourself as an older child, and do the same thing. Don't forget to hug yourself, at least in your mind. Move up to puberty (an age where we all especially need compassion, and hugs) and do it, then in steps of five or ten years until you reach your present age. Now do the same thing you've been doing for younger selves — bathe yourself in love and compassion, while hugging yourself. Only this time, do it right now, with your own arms wrapped lovingly around yourself.

If you feel resistant to doing this exercise, examine your resistance. How does it feel not to want to do it? Perhaps you'll need to first do the Forgiveness meditation (page 132) for yourself, or for a parent who has taught you to be self-critical rather than compassionate.

Rather than using yourself as an object of compassion, you may find it easier to begin developing a sense of what compassion is by visualizing Jesus blessing the children, his wise and compassionate eyes full of love. Or visualizing Mother Teresa tenderly washing the feet of a dying Indian beggar. Possibly thinking of the relationship that you had with a beloved childhood pet will help. Once you start to have an emotional inkling of compassion, you can return to the exercise above. If you can't seem to do any form of the compassion exercise at all, it may help to read Theodore Isaac Rubin's books listed in the bibliography, and Stephen Levine's "Who Dies".

Compassion And Pity

For us, the difference between compassion and pity is that when we pity someone, we usually feel separate from them (feel pity *for* them), and our tenderness is tinged with fear and perhaps a sense of "glad it wasn't me".

With compassion, we feel very connected to the person, and have a clear realization that we are all fragile and vulnerable. And if we do feel fear, the same compassion that we lavish on the other is also turned on ourselves, our own fear and pain, so that we are compassionate *with* them, not *for* them. As John Donne said, "Ask not for whom the bell tolls — it tolls for thee." The same bell of fear and insecurity, of transience in a world over which we can have only a fallacy of control, tolls for us and for those with whom we share compassion. Unlike pity, compassion transcends the split between "us" as subject, "them" as object...

On Subjects and Objects

Think back to eighth grade, for a moment, when you learned (and probably forgot) how to diagram sentences for subjects and objects (and other parts of speech that fall outside of the sphere of this investigation). In the sentence "I saw Robert", "I" is the subject, "Robert" is the object. Or consider "Robert saw Phil", in which "Robert" is the subject, and "Phil" the object. Subjects are actors, and objects the acted upon. Moreover, the action is from the point of view of the subject, hence the terms, "subjective view" (from the writer or speaker's viewpoint) and "objective view" (from an unbiased point, not filtered through human prejudice).

We often act as though we are the only subject, and everyone, and everything else is an object. Kurt Vonnegut, writer, had his fictitious sci-fi writer write a story in which a man discovered that he was the only real person on the planet, and that everyone else was a robot. Many of us live our lives as though that were largely the case, and see all that is from the sole vantage point of our own narcissistic eyes. Even those whom we love are mainly there for the purposes of satisfying our own needs. Sometimes we even relate to our own body as though it were an object, or a possession, owned by us but not of us. It may be that this way of looking at the world is engendered by the Western Worldview discussed on Day 3, in which we are inside our skin, and all else outside is "other". Certain emotions, like compassion described above, transcend this subject/object split. Increasing investment in the meditative worldview overcomes this division between us and the rest of the world, an idea we'll continue to elucidate in later days.

I — Thou and I — It

Jewish theologian Martin Buber coined the term "I — Thou," to indicate a relationship in which you (the "I") relate to another person with the understanding that the other has as many feelings and needs, fears and desires, as you do, and as much right to pursue them. Buber contrasts this with the "I—It" relationship, in which you act as though the other person is mostly an object, whose principle purpose in life is to help you gain satisfaction.

It's easy to be smug, and to say "I don't do that." But how often, especially when you're in a hurry, does a clerk in a store or a gas-station attendant seem to be a real, complete person, with their own history and feelings? When someone cuts ahead of you on line, do you usually perceive them as a person who has problems and fears and needs of their own, just as you do, or are they just some "impolite jerk," getting in between you and the candy counter? Can you see that the beautiful woman, or "hunky" man walking across the street has a full and complete life of their own, and does not just exist as an object for your visual (or perhaps fantasized sexual) gratification?

The I — Thou Meditation

Begin by choosing someone, a bank teller, or telephone sales person, to whom you usually *don't* relate, and try to perceive them as a "thou" instead of an "it", as described above. If you have time, think about how you think *they* feel in the situation that you're sharing? What history, needs, motives led them to be who they are?

What led them to this interaction or place? And what do *they* think about *you?*

With a bit of practice, you'll be able to do this with a surly waiter, an aggressive panhandler, or a politician not from the party of your choice!

Thoughts For The Day: What To Do When It Hurts

Sometimes, as we look deeply into ourselves, old or hidden pain can arise. It may not happen to you, but if it does, please be sure to read this section carefully.

If you are already under a doctor's or psychotherapist's care, you should definitely discuss this book with them before using it. By the way, psychotherapy and meditation make an especially effective combination! As you continue to meditate, previously unconscious material will come clearly into view, where it can be worked with. Please also see our section on therapists and clients, page 219.

If you are in great mental pain now, perhaps you should carefully read the entire book before doing any of the exercises, and then start out with the "Compassion" meditations. They are probably the most effective exercises in the book for dealing with suffering of any kind.

There are two distinct types of mental suffering. There's the suffering that occurs when we are not meditating, or before we've learned to meditate, when our thoughts, our fears and desires, cause us pain. This is the type of suffering that many of us experience on an *ongoing* basis. Since many non-meditators have little control over their thoughts, this kind of suffering is hard to deal with. It may possibly diminish if we can change various circumstances in our lives. But it probably won't. Instead, the pain will merely change to suit the new circumstances!

The type of suffering that may arise during meditation is different, although it can, on the surface, feel the same. But it is suffering whose purpose is to *end* further suffering. So if painful feelings arise while meditating, try to remember that these are the *temporary* pains that will help us to end the *ongoing* pain, just as the pain of the extraction is intended to end the ache of the infected tooth.

As long as we remember to use the mind watching exercises to *observe* our pain, rather than just getting lost in the contents of the painful thoughts, we can *utilize* this temporary pain to reduce ongoing pain. We know, from personal experience, that this is a difficult concept to believe, especially when in a state of suffering. Using the Compassion exercise may be especially helpful, to ease the pain. It's what we try to do, when in pain, if we're "together" enough to remember to do so.

When we learn about ourselves, old pain may be recalled, or we may sometimes see elements of our personalities that we'd prefer to deny. If this happens to you, as it so often has to us, please re-read the preceding section on Compassion, then go directly to the Compassion exercise (page 121). And please consider working with a therapist. Increasing numbers are integrating meditation into their work with clients, a wonderful use of meditation which we strongly recommend!

Day 15 Practice Plan

Formal Practice
- Emotion Visualization meditation for three minutes.

Real Life Use: Counting Emotions for one or two hours during the day. Labelling Emotions for a few hours (or all day) during the day.

On Emotions

To us, emotions are simply a sub-category of thoughts, simply thoughts that have a lot of energy or feeling (the proper psychological word is "cathexis") in them. Often, emotion thoughts are less analytical than other thoughts, and seem to be more connected with physical sensations. Early psychological researchers even thought that physical sensations actually caused emotion thoughts (for example, that we would feel sad because we were crying), although this belief has been discarded, and psychologists now believe that the physical states are largely caused by the thoughts.

Whatever emotions may be, they can act as the focal points for our mental attention. So we will count, label, and experience them just as we did breathing, walking, and other types of thoughts.

The Emotion Counting Exercise

This exercise is extremely similar to the Thought Counting Meditation on page 97. But since, for most of us, emotions do not occur with the regularity of other thoughts (a dozen a minute, or so), it's easier to count emotions over a period of an hour or so, while going about our daily activities. Just try to notice when a thought with a lot of "juice" goes through your mind, and even keep a running tally. If you are not sure whether the thought has enough weight or feeling behind it to be an emotion, it probably isn't. But the point of this exercise isn't to keep score, it's to learn to notice emotions.

The Emotion Labelling Exercise

Once again, it's just like the Thought Labelling Exercise on page 100, except that unless you're a particularly emotional person, you probably won't have many emotions to label in just a minute or two.

Just watch your thoughts for a few hours, and see which emotions show up most often, which are hardest to let go of, which are easiest. By definition, emotions will probably be harder to let go of than most other thoughts.

The Emotion Visualization Meditation

Invent and imagine a situation that is not likely to occur but which would give rise to a thought that would be a powerful one for you. In other words, an emotion. For example, you might visualize the Boss calling you in to yell at you for something that went wrong which wasn't your fault. Visualize yourself (using as many senses as possible) in the situation. Once you've created the visualization, see if you can practice relating to the emotion that arises as nothing but a thought in your mind. Nothing to get excited about, just a thought passing through.

If this seems hard, spend a moment right in the middle of the visualization doing a mind clearing exercise, such as counting the breath. Does that help?

Eventually, working with your thoughts and doing exercises like this one will help you to handle emotions with as much skill as any other thoughts, without pain or fear.

"I have a boss who likes to bark out orders. It's never a request, like 'Would you please rank the results of our last survey and get a summary to me as soon as possible?' It's always 'Where the *&#% are the rankings? We can't move without them!' and then I feel attacked, as if I should have read his mind and finished yesterday."

Denise, a market analyst in a pharmaceutical company, de-  *scribed her reactions to her supervisor's abrupt interpersonal style. "I tried to use compassion, to see him as another human being with pressures of his own, but that didn't work. I just don't like being barked at. I'm not ready to cut him any slack!"*

She continued, "The meditation that seems to be helping me is labelling emotions. Instead of trying to suppress how I feel, I'm watching what goes on inside. It helps me gain

127

perspective when I can say, 'Uh-huh, there's anger. Now I'm feeling self hate because I haven't been perfect. Here comes fear, afraid of getting fired. And, a twinge of jealousy. How come no one else is getting picked on? Anger, again.' And so it goes.

Somehow, when I'm watching my feelings, I feel more whole. Even if these are negative emotions, they're all my own."

NINA: Anger is a very difficult emotion for me. As soon as it arises, it tends to transform itself into fear, sadness, frustration or self hate. Using meditation to label and experience my emotions has helped me understand what I'm really feeling.

Observing the many disguises of anger, I'm better able to face it more directly. I *know* it's going to come out somewhere. At least if it's out in the open, I can feel compassion for all of the fear that goes along with it. I can also use meditation to soften around it, as we describe on Day 23, in Softening Around Emotional Pain.

Thought For The Day: Applying Compassion To Thoughts

DAVID: For me, frustration often leads to anger. When business dealings, relationships, or other events don't go the way I want them to, I first feel frustrated, then threatened by my own lack of control. Almost instantaneously the feelings of frustration and fear turn into anger, as my mind attempts to cover up these insecure and painful feelings with more aggressive ones. Acting upon these aggressive feelings, I may then lash out at myself, or at loved ones, without even knowing why.

But when I can recognize the initial frustration and fearful feelings as they arise, I can meet them with compassion, create a new thought chain that has "a happy ending". A moment of Compassion and Softening will often break that old chain of frustration-to-fear-to-anger, and allow me to face the frustration and fear directly. It's not easy to face up to my own inability to control people, events and things. But I'd rather directly face these feelings and the pain that they bring, than encounter the far greater pain of the mis-directed anger, with its warlike attack on myself or others.

Even if I do get angry, I may be able, after a moment, to remember to be compassionate towards myself, both for my pain, and for having gotten mad. All humans feel anger and must somehow learn to deal with this emotion. Feeling compassion for my anger is far more healing in the long run than feeling guilt for my anger, or feeling angry at myself for my anger. Feeling compassion for myself allows me to "watch the movie" in my mind and step outside my old knee-jerk reaction of pain, anger, and self-hate.

NINA: I recently went to my first American Booksellers Association convention with David. He warned me ahead of time that facing countless rows of exhibitors, all selling books competing with our own, could be an overwhelming experience. It was! And humbling, as well.

David and I looked at each other. "Uh-oh, better meditate." We did some thought watching, and saw fear ("What if our books don't sell?") and a desire to be special ("But *our* book is *really* special!") come into mind. From then on, throughout the day, we used our special Compassion Breath (as described tomorrow on page 131) to deal with those painful feelings so that we could concentrate fully on the challenge and opportunity of being at the convention.

Tomorrow, we will practice the Compassion Breath, an easy-to-use tool that will allow you to inject a dose of compassion directly into your life, wherever and whenever it's needed.

Day 16 Practice Plan

Formal Practice

- The Compassion meditation (page 121), for a *minimum* of three minutes.
- Compassion Breath for three minutes.
- The Forgiveness meditation for at least three minutes.

Real Life Use: Compassion Breath during day, as often as possible.

On Opening The Heart

For so many of us, the fears and pain that we've experienced throughout our lives have caused our hearts to close, to harden. Instead of spending most of our time in a state of loving, compassionate openness to ourselves and others, with a few occasional flashes of hard-heartedness (after all, we are human), we spend most of our time in a somewhat suspicious, judgmental, or at best neutral state, with only occasional episodes of openness towards our closest relatives and friends.

Much of this next week's work will be on learning to open and soften our hearts. The tools of Compassion, Living In The Now, Don't Know, Acceptance, and Softening will allow us to do this, even when our minds are tight and painful. And when we open and soften the heart, the mind will follow.

On The Compassion Breath Meditation

Although the full length Compassion Meditation is important to use for identifying and developing a sense of compassion, it's not always quick or convenient to use. So we've developed a quicker and more easily usable version, the Compassion Breath, an immediately effective tool to use in working with thoughts, emotions, and thought chains.

Perhaps it would be more accurate to say that we've developed the *concept* of the Compassion Breath exercise, which we hope that you will customize into the version that works best for you.

The Compassion Breath Meditation

The idea behind the Compassion Breath is to create a one breath "cue" or "trigger" that prompts you to both remember and to bring a sense of compassion into any situation where it is needed (which is, to us, most situations). If you've done the longer Compassion exercise from Day 14, and have some inkling of what compassion feels like, it will be easier to devise a Compassion Breath of your own. As you'll see from the variations below, the important element of the Compassion Breath is that it can be used to intervene during negative thoughts or thought chains by reminding you to have some compassion and loving kindness for yourself.

Some Variations

DAVID: During my Compassion Breath, I usually visualize myself (as I am now) hugging my young child self. I simply take the very detailed image that I created in the Compassion Exercise, and focus on it as clearly as I can during one inhale and exhale. In some ways, I must admit that I prefer to use the Softening Breath exercise of Day 23 instead of the Compassion Breath, since I often tense and "harden" my heart in situations where I most need compassion.

NINA: I like to use the label "Compassion" during my in breath, and visualize myself filling up not just with air, but with a golden light that symbolizes the sense of compassion that I feel for myself at the end of a good, long, Compassion Exercise. I use the label "pain" during the out breath, and visualize any pain or tension flowing out of me with the exhaled air.

A Compassion Breath: The Heartgill

Some people report good results with this one. All you need to do is visualize yourself breathing through your heart instead of your nose or mouth. Perhaps the air enters via a "gill slit" located in your chest. Or maybe you don't need to focus much on the mechanics at all, but can just feel the flow through your heart instead of your lungs.

131

A Compassion Breath: The "Ahhh, Oooh" Variation

This Compassion Breath variation integrates both awe and pain, by seeing each as necessary to the other. In a world of beauty and splendor, how can there not be awe? But in a world where everyone who is born must die, how can there not be pain? And in a world filled with both pain and awe, how can there not be compassion for those who must live there?

As you breathe in, say a mental "Ahhh," the "Ahhh" of going outside on a beautiful spring morning, the "Ahhh" of watching the sun set over the ocean.

As you breathe out, relax your face (and body, if possible) and mentally groan "Oooh," the "Oooh" of seeing a war on television, the "Oooh" of seeing homeless people rummage for food in garbage dumpsters. "Ahhh, Oooh, Ahhh, Oooh." It's painful, living in this strange, lovely, terrible, unfathomable world. It's awesome, living in this strange, lovely, terrible, unfathomable world. The two just can't be separated. How can you not feel compassion for any creature who must exist here, including yourself?

The Compassion Sigh

We've found that some people prefer to just inhale without a verbal image, and relax and simply sigh on the outbreath. It really doesn't matter whether your variation is simple or ornate, as long as you try to use it whenever possible. And if you have trouble doing this type of exercise, the Softening exercises of Days 22 and 23 may help.

On Forgiveness

We've been practicing being compassionate towards ourselves. We've been practicing treating others as "thou"s. Now it's time to begin cultivating a sense of compassion towards those it's hardest to open up to: people that we are angry at, the ones who have done us wrong. Before we can feel compassion for them, we have to forgive them, hence the following exercise.

The Forgiveness Meditation

This one is very simple, although not always easy. Just picture someone whom you think has hurt or wronged you in some way. It's important, for now, to choose someone at whom you're no longer very angry. Visualize them as clearly as you can. And tell them "I forgive you. I forgive you for hurting or wronging me."

Repeat it a number of times, and try to feel forgiving, try to feel yourself giving up remnants of anger or righteousness towards them. If you are not sure with whom you're ready to do this exercise, do it with someone whose hurt to you was very minor — a driver who slipped ahead of you on the freeway, or a clerk who overcharged you by a few cents. Eventually, with practice, you'll be able to do this exercise with people who have caused you more serious pain.

Saint Augustine exhorted us to hate the sin, but love the sinner. It is crucial to remember that forgiving a person does not mean that you condone or accept their behavior. You are forgiving the person, not their behavior. And it's well worth doing, even for purely self-interested reasons, because letting go of anger, or of feelings of having been wronged, is a very freeing experience.

DAVID: For me, doing this exercise on the publisher who had "appropriated" my harmonica book and title concept (see "Why I Needed To Meditate") allowed me to stop wasting energy on anger and self-hatred, and to get on with my life.

Thoughts For The Day: On Forgiving Ourselves

Often the person it's hardest to forgive is one's self. We judge ourselves mercilessly, with recriminations for the things we should, or could, have done, but didn't. For the things we did, but now regret.

Unfortunately, blame is a dead end street with no place else to go, except towards more self-abuse. Forgiving one's self opens the heart, creating new awareness and new options. Instead of clinging to pain or defeat, forgiveness offers a clean slate for starting over.

NINA: I used to feel morally superior when I would give myself a hard time over perceived flaws and errors and then feel proud of holding myself to perfectionist standards. I've since realized that life contains quite enough pain without my extra efforts and have turned to forgiveness and compassion instead.

So please try the Forgiveness meditation on yourself, after you've done it a few times on other people. If this feels fruitful to you, Stephen Levine's "Who Dies" has much longer and more detailed meditations of this type.

On Illness, Blame, And Responsibility

People who become seriously ill sometimes blame themselves unjustly, as they seek out explanations for their misfortune in an effort to maintain an illusion of control.

DAVID: Sometimes, in my volunteer work with dying and grieving clients, the issue of "taking responsibility for one's illness" will arise. It's easy for a person (who is already in physical and/or mental pain) to interpret this as meaning that he or she has "caused" his or her own illness, and I've encountered a number of people who have used this concept as a great opportunity for unleashing self-hatred.

To me, taking responsibility means being responsible for our *response* to the illness, rather than believing ourselves to have caused the illness itself. One of Stephen Levine's clients puts it beautifully in "Healing Into Life and Death" (see bibliography, required reading for anyone dealing with these issues). He explains that events, such as illness, are like the wind that fill the sails of a boat. We can take responsibility for adjusting the sails and steering as well as we can, without needing to take responsibility for the wind.

On Envy and Compassion, And Secret Pain

As you recall, we discussed the problem of our insides vs. other people's outsides in Day 11. It's so easy to believe that others are as perfect as they look, while knowing exactly, in great detail, how imperfect we feel inside. So it's sometimes useful to consider the kinds of pain that people cover up so as to appear "perfect". For example, rich, sexy, famous Elizabeth Taylor fights a constant battle with weight and back pain. Handsome, famous Rock Hudson lived a secret life for decades. Gary Hart's sexual addiction destroyed his political career. Countless writers, musicians, politicians and TV stars who want nothing in the way of money, companionship, and popularity are waging lethal wars with alcohol and other drugs, with sex or money addictions.

The next time you begin to compare yourself to someone who seems impossibly, enviably to have it all together, do this meditation to put things in perspective.

Picture the person you're secretly envying — the corporate vice-president who flawlessly juggles career and family, the athletic star who is rich, talented, attractive and famous, your high school classmate who has lived up to the title "most likely to succeed". Consider the full reality of his or her life — that this person also has lived through a life full of ups and downs, unfulfilled longings and hidden fears, no doubt similar to your own. As you picture the darker side of this golden boy or girl's life, you'll begin to understand that, no matter how good someone else's life may look, that person has experienced pain — simply because he or she is human.

Feel compassion for all the hidden pain in that person's life. Do a moment of Compassion Breath, and see if you can visualize yourself being drained of envy and filling up with compassion. Acknowledging another's pain will let you see the common bond of humanity, of life's pain, that we all share. And in sharing this awareness, we can begin to let the pain of envy recede into compassion — both compassion for the secret pain of the other, and compassion for the painfulness of our own need to envy.

NINA: Several of my colleagues appear to be superwomen: they have successful careers, good marriages, delightful children, and appear to maintain flawless households with a minimum of effort. It's tempting to look at them and say "What's wrong with me? Some mornings it's a struggle just to tie my shoelaces and go to work!"

But, over time, I've begun to understand that these women are no different from me, facing their own compromises and choices. The outsides we present to the world belie the secret pain of our existence. As the old saying goes, " Walk a mile in the other person's moccasins" — both before judging them, and before using them as a standard by which to judge ourselves.

Day 17 Practice Plan: REVIEW

Formal Practice
- The Compassion meditation (page 121), for a *minimum* of three minutes.
- The Compassion Breath (page 130) for one minutes.
- The TV/Radio exercise (page 170, and below) for three minutes.
- The Forgiveness meditation (page 132) on yourself for at least three minutes.

Real Life Use: Use the Compassion Breath that you've devised (feel free to refine it or experiment with different ones as needed) as often as possible during the day. Try especially to use it with painful thoughts or emotions. Create a thought chain in which you apply a Compassion Breath to a fear or a desire as soon as you've noticed and labelled the thought.

The TV/Radio Compassion Breath

Once again, go back to your least favorite show. This time, instead of using breath counting to work with your negative reaction to the Six O'Clock News or reruns of Saturday Night Live, use your Compassion Breath while you subject yourself to the one-eyed monster. Try to experience compassion both towards yourself, for having to do this unpleasant exercise, and towards the people on TV that you don't care for.

Return for a moment to breath counting as you watch. Which (breath counting or the Compassion Breath) feels more effective in dealing with your feelings about the show?

If You're Ready To Work With A Real Person

By now you may feel ready to try either the Compassion Breath or breath labelling or counting while interacting with someone with whom you have a difficult relationship. It may be easier to try this on a person that you've already practiced the Forgiveness Meditation with.

If you are doing this with a real person, and it feels stressful, remember to use all of the techniques that you've learned so far.

Visualize yourself successfully doing the above exercise with that person, before you try it in real life. You may also want to visualize doing an "I-Thou" meditation on them, prior to your work with the person.

Do some mind clearing and relaxation just before the actual interaction. Label negative thoughts if they arise during the interaction, and try to return your attention to the breath as soon as you can. If you notice yourself tensing up physically, do a mini-relaxation; let those shoulders drop. And finally, if you were unable to maintain a meditative attitude during your face-to-face, do some compassion work with yourself afterwards. Using this material as just another club with which to beat yourself is *not* what meditation is all about...

Thoughts For The Day: Letting Go Of "Shoulds"

With the insight and awareness brought about by meditation, we can begin to recognize a whole array of subtle forms of "self abuse." For many of us , our "should lists" are a great way to create mental pain.

NINA: I used to be a list-maker. I would often find myself facing Saturday with a list of 18 errands to get through in half a day. My hidden message to myself was "You're not working hard enough if you don't get all of this done..." Or somewhat more benignly, "You'll deserve to relax when this is all finished."

Once I truly acknowledged the emotional sabotage of these lists, I was able to let go of the "tyranny of the shoulds", as psychoanalyst Karen Horney describes it. My strategy for planning activities now *incorporates* thought-watching and compassion exercises. For every thought that begins, "I should...", I now ask *"Why?"* I've realized that my own values have to be the basis for action — that reasons like, "Everyone else does it this way..." or "I've always done it like that" are nothing but indirect ways of denying my own needs. Of course, going against these ingrained shoulds is sometimes painful. So whenever I begin to feel sad or self-hating, I pour on an extra dose of compassion...

Think about your own plans for your next "free" day or lunch hour. What are your plans? How many of these plans are based on "shoulds"? How much is based on "wants?" What's the balance between them?

Think about the shoulds on your list. Why are they there? Are they essential? Are they manageable? What on this list makes you feel good about yourself? Is there anything that seems like a waste of time? What are your values? How do you want to spend your time? Your life?

Shoulds, of course, show their coercive faces in many more areas than list making. But shoulds of all types and sizes share a characteristic: when we spend too much time doing things we feel we "should" be doing, but that really don't matter to us, existence becomes a bit grayer, and we begin to wonder, "What does it all mean?"

Of course, we have to do things that we don't want to do. The art of compromise is vital to relationships, and obnoxious errands are a part of daily existence. But, it's the things that we don't want to do, don't have to do and do because we think we *should* that kill our souls. Understanding the need to recognize our priorities and order our lives around them makes it easier to avoid these insidious time-wasters that so often masquerade as essentials.

A Two Person Shared Compassion Breath

This is a surprisingly powerful experience that can be used in two ways. With a close friend, relative, or lover, it's a wonderfully intimate and co-operative thing to do together. Done unilaterally (that is, without the knowledge of the "partner"), it is a non-verbal way to connect, even with someone that you may not feel very close to at first. You can even do this with a pet (although you'll probably need to take the active role, as described below).

It's easiest to practice initially with a co-operative partner. Decide which of you will be the active partner, and which inactive. The inactive partner simply sits or lies comfortably, eyes closed, and breathes normally. The active partner sits nearby, close enough to see the rising and falling of the inactive partner's chest as they breathe, close enough to hear each in and out breath.

The active partner tries to match as exactly as possible the breathing rhythm of the other, to begin the in breath exactly as they do, to inhale exactly as long, to hold the breath exactly as long, to exhale for the same amount of time. It's not easy to do, and requires *intense* concentration! On each exhale, the active partner will release the breath with a sigh... "ahhh."

The inactive partner should try not to "help" the active partner by making breaths unusually regular or loud, neither should they try to hinder the other by holding their breath or breathing especially softly.

This exercise promotes a strong feeling of connection, compassion, and love between the partners. Couples will find this a lovely trust-builder, and especially powerful if eye contact is maintained. It's almost as though one breath is being shared between two people — sometimes it actually feels as though the two bodies are somehow merged.

Many nurses, therapists, and some physicians use this meditation with their patients, since it can be done with the inactive partner sleeping or comatose, and may be very calming and soothing for someone who is ill, as well as for the healer.

Doing this exercise with a non-co-operating partner who is not aware of what you're doing simply involves matching your breathing rhythm to theirs. In the interests of discretion, you'll probably want to dispense with the "aaah" exhale. Don't be surprised to find a feeling of increased closeness between you and your breathee, even though on a conscious level they are not tuned into what you are doing. The matching of breath rate is an important component of modern behavior change programs such as Ericksonian Hypnosis and Neuro-Linguistic Programming.

Day 18 Practice Plan

Formal Practice
- Two minutes of the Centering Balance exercise.
- At least two minutes of the Body Scan exercise.

Real Life Use: At least ten minutes (in segments of any length) of "Living In The Now" exercises during the day, while going about your usual routine.

Identify Opportunities: Choose a particular action that you repeat throughout the day (such as washing your hands, or drinking a glass of water), and make it into a "Now" meditation every time you perform it.

Note: As in earlier days, but to a greater extent, in today's instructions we blur the distinctions between formal practice and real life use, and between the actual exercises and inspirational sections. Although this may seem confusing, it is necessary if eventually meditation is to become a way of living, fully integrated, separate from nothing.

On Living In The Now

Most of us live most of the time in either the past or the future. Only rarely is our attention focussed on what is happening in the "Right Now." Is yours? You think so? Then quick — without thinking about it — are you inhaling or exhaling? You probably had to re-focus your attention onto the breath to answer that question. Where had it been?

Thoughts about what we just did, or didn't do, and thoughts about what we should do, or shouldn't do, or might do, continually clutter our minds. How often we use past thoughts in a self-hating way, "I should have done it differently," or "I sure messed that one up." How often we use future thoughts to upset ourselves, such as "What if that happens?" or "It probably won't work out."

Virtually all of our thoughts are either based in past or future, and absolutely all of our fears and desires. Desires are usually remembrances of past pleasures that we plan and hope to recreate in the future. Fears are usually memories of past pain that we plan and hope to avoid in the future.

Some memory-thoughts and some planning-thoughts are useful, or at least necessary, for functioning in this or any culture. But it's important to remember that when we focus our attention on a thought of the past or a thought of the future, we are bringing past or future into our present, thus pushing the actual present, the "Now," out of mind.

When we're thinking of how much work we have to do while our boss is talking to us, or thinking of what we'll say next during a conversation with a friend, we can't be present to listen and to respond meaningfully right now. Similarly, when we're busy filling our fork for the next bite while chewing the present mouthful, or pondering dessert during the entree, we're simply not present to enjoy our eating right now.

> Most people who meditate find that they don't have to do nearly as much "future planning" or "past remembering" as they once thought they did. A healthy, well-cared-for body can react quickly and naturally to the immediate physical requirements of any situation, whether they involve fighting or fleeing, sleeping deeply or remaining awake and alert. Likewise, a mind cleared by meditation tends to respond naturally and appropriately to the mental circumstances of the present moment, whatever those circumstances may be. Of course, this takes diligent practice, and time. But some serious meditators and many of the most experienced meditation teachers say that they rarely have to think much, that they just somehow know how to say and do whatever is most appropriate.

In a way, all of the meditations and exercises in this book are "Living In The Now" exercises. When we are Thought Counting or Slow Walking, there just isn't much time to think of the past or the future. We learn to let go of such extraneous thoughts, as soon as they arise and we notice them.

What's So Great About The Now?

There is something very satisfying about keeping your mind in the "Now," but it's hard to describe it precisely. All we can say is that the bite of food that you are savoring right now, is somehow quite different from the mouthful that you just ate (which you can only remember) or the mouthful that you plan to eat next (which you can only anticipate). Of course, thinking about either the past or future mouthful does bring it into the "Now" as a thought in your mind. But the actual food that's in your mouth can clearly be more satisfying than the *thought* of past or future food which may be in your mind right now. Better to be present with a potato than lost in thoughts of past or future banquets!

DAVID: I began to understand this as I learned to improvise on the blues harmonica. Worrying about the note I had just played, or planning ahead for the sequence that I wanted to play next, impaired my ability to create improvisations freely. I had to learn to *let go* of a note as soon as had I played it, without thinking about the note to come. Only then did my music begin to improve.

NINA: Employed in a think tank, exploring the future of aging in America, I often have to look 30 years into the future. Although my "Now" on the job may involve the year 2020, doing the Living In The Now exercises help me to stay centered in *my* "Now", moment by moment throughout the day.

DAVID: As a publisher, I often need to plan books, advertising, or marketing strategies far into the future. So my "Now" may involve initiating events that will not be completed for many months. It's confusing for me to separate the reality of the "publisher's Now" (which includes the next six to twelve months) from my "personal Now." In my personal Now I wish to savor the events of the present — smells, tastes, feelings — without over-influence by future and past-related fears and desires. It's a delicate balance, and one that I don't yet clearly understand. But I do know that the following "Living In The Now" exercises help! And, speaking of a delicate balance...

The Centering Balance Meditation
Stand up straight, arms at your sides, with your feet no more than six inches apart. Focus your attention on your sense of balance, your sensation of standing upright with your body weight centered over your feet.

Lean forward an inch or two, and feel the tension as your toes dig deeper into the ground to compensate for the forward incline, as you become a human Tower of Pisa. Lean backwards an inch, until most of your weight is on your heels. Lean slightly left and then right, noting the weight shift from foot to foot.

Do the forwards, backwards, left, and right leaning motions again, but more subtly, with less movement. See just how little you need to lean in order to feel not quite perfectly upright, not quite perfectly balanced. See how easy it is to over-compensate, in one direction or another. Is there any one position in which you do feel in complete equilibrium, when you really focus your attention on it? There may not be one.

You can do this exercise anywhere, without attracting much attention to yourself, if you use the more subtle motions of the second part. Since "feeling balanced" is often used as a metaphor for mental stability, this exercise is a useful one to do anytime you feel off-balance. The few moments' respite that you'll get from the tensions of past and future thoughts will help you to restore both your mental and physical equilibrium!

The Body Scan

Sometimes the body and mind seem to be in different parts of the planet, if not the universe. Have you ever gotten so involved in what you were doing that you didn't even realize your foot had fallen asleep —until you tried to shift positions and felt the pang of pins and needles? Or, perhaps you've scrunched up your neck talking on the phone, only to discover this painfully, after hanging up.

Taking even a few seconds to fully experience the body will remind you to stay in touch with each present moment.

This exercise can be done any-where, anytime. You can be sitting, standing or even lying down. It's actually a good idea to do it in a number of different situations, which will make it a natural part of your on-going awareness, wherever you are.

Bring your awareness to your entire body, as described below. Try to catch yourself "unaware", as you quickly begin this exercise. Don't relax or otherwise change your position in the second between your decision to do this exercise and when you actually do it. This exercise is designed to give you feedback on *tension* in your body at a given moment, *not* to help you relax.

As you focus your awareness, simply scan down your body. Forehead, eyes, neck, shoulders, back, waist, legs, ankles, feet. Is there any tension? Any tightness? Are you comfortable or uncomfortable in your present position? Are you hot or cold? Hungry or tired? Are you balanced or leaning slightly to one side or the other?

Right now, *after* you've finished your body scan, is a wonderful time to relax. Either use the general relaxation exercise on page 88, or concentrate on your particular areas of tension, and relax them!

After you've done this meditation several times, you'll have identified your most common tension spots. At this point, you'll be ready for a short-cut. Simply relax the trouble spots as soon as you identify them on your ten second mental scanning trip from head to toe.

NINA: I sometimes take a minute at the office to focus on my body sense. Often, sitting at my desk, I'll get hunched over a pile of papers, leaning forward uncomfortably, without even realizing it. Remembering to focus on my body sense allows me to release this tension and find a more comfortable position, a mini-meditation and a "spot tension check" at the same time.

Other Living In The Now Meditations

We can take almost any commonplace daily activity and easily convert it into an effective and interesting Living In The Now meditation. In effect, you've already done this with walking and breathing. As we've said before, anything done with a high degree of focussed awareness is, by definition, a meditation.

The Zen Buddhist tradition of Japan often utilized this approach. Flower arranging, the Tea Ceremony, Zen Archery, and most of the Japanese martial arts are used as forms of meditation. Their practitioners focus exclusively on the flowers, or tea, or bow and arrow, excluding all other thoughts. Sound familiar?

The Zen Lavatory Meditation

Perhaps the Tea Ceremony or the practice of blindfolded Zen Archery seem somewhat outside of our everyday routine. So why not choose some mundane repeated action and make it the focus of a meditation? Here are a few suggestions. Can you think of some more?

DAVID: Some days I decide that every time I need to wash my hands, I'll "just wash my hands". Instead of using those thirty seconds to plan my next move, or fantasize, or anticipate the meal that I'm cleaning up for, I focus exclusively on the sound and feel of the water on my hands, and the smell of the soap. Without really thinking about it, I often have a sense of compassion as hand glides smoothly and caressingly over hand, and a sense of cleansing on many levels, as in a ritual ablution.

NINA: I like to make a meditation out of taking a drink of water. No listening to the radio during it, or looking out the window, or letting my mind be on anything but drinking water. I focus on the subtle taste and smell of the water (it's there, if you make yourself sensitive to it), its weight, its coolness and smoothness in the throat. I appreciate, without words if possible, that every living creature must do this same thing, how the water is outside one minute, and incorporated into my body the next, going to each cell as needed, without conscious direction.

Roberta, an insurance underwriter in a large office, used to be a chronic clockwatcher. She still is. But now she tries to use every glance at the clock as a cue to remind her to meditate for just a few seconds, doing a single experienced breath or a ten second body scan/relaxation after each time check.

DAVID: Nina didn't really want me to mention this one (she thought it might gross some of you out). But I sometimes use going to the bathroom as the focus of a meditation (I learned to do this during a ten day Tibetan Buddhist retreat, where it's considered the proper thing to do). If it seems right to you, give it a try. It's a private space we all have many times a day, even for the busiest amongst us. And cultural considerations aside, it's both intrinsic to all living creatures (from bacteria to presidents), and absolutely essential to maintaining life. Plus, it can really put some rest in the rest room!

From Automatic Pilot To Meditation

So much of the time we get habituated to what we see and do on a daily basis. We go through life virtually on automatic pilot, passing the same house on the hill every day — but is it red, blue, or chartreuse? Who notices? You may think you know all there is to know about your route to work, your colleagues' attitudes, a common skill, your own body. But when you stop and look anew, with "the eyes of a child" (or a meditator), whatever you see can become the basis for a new meditation.

Opportunities for exploration exist everywhere, *if* we are open to them. The trick is "finding the time" to explore. Recognizing that each moment of our life has tremendous potential to be fully alive allows us to see each on-going moment as a resource for growth, instead of "something to be gotten through".

Take a minute to explore the Now and inject some extra aliveness into your life by taking a new perspective on some old activities. Begin by focussing your awareness on the action, without analysis or judging. Here are some suggestions:

Lift your gaze as you walk down a familiar street. We tend to be goal-oriented, creatures of habit, so focussed on getting to our destination that we forget to notice anything along the way. What does the skyline or horizon look like, from a few points on your route? Can you see any reflections in the windows of buildings? Are the trees or shrubs healthy or not? Any interesting smells? Are some parts of the street noisier than others?

Look at your own hand, foot, face, or body. Take a minute to truly see it. Notice the texture of your skin, the scars, beauty marks, the way those little hairs create their own patterns on your arms. Mess up those hairs and look again! Are they silky, long and smooth? Are they wiry and curly? Worn away at knee or elbow? When was the last time you noticed them at all?

Look at something manufactured: a woolen sweater, a car, a stone building. Without analysis, realize the billions of years or evolution, and hundreds of thousands of years of human development and culture needed for it to exist.

Watch your spouse, significant other, child. Create a "snapshot in time" — a loving portrait that you can review in your mind's eye. You've lived with this person on a daily basis, yet how clear an image can you call up at a moment's notice? How current are you with the loved ones in your life? Try living in the now for just a minute at a time with these persons as your focus. Doing so will help you to stay aware, and to cherish the fleeting moments that you have together, in this fragile and transient lifetime. Your focussed awareness will mark some of these "insignificant" daily moments as special memories. It's so important to realize that these are truly the "golden years" — because the Now is all we really have.

Thoughts For The Day

All of the above, plus any from other days that you'd like to re-read.

Day 19 Practice Plan

Formal Practice
- Five minutes of The Thought Judging meditation.
- Three minutes of The Acceptance meditation.

Real Life Use: Do a Particular Thought Counting exercise (page 105) with judging thoughts throughout the first half of the day, as often as you can remember to. Do the Thought Judging meditation throughout the second half of the day, as often as you can remember to and begin to consider using the Acceptance meditation whenever you notice judging thoughts arise during the day.

On Judging: The Double Ended Sword
Minds just love to judge. Events, other people, ourselves. Unfortunately, judging is a double-ended sword. And a double-ended sword has no safe place to grip. As we grab it, to swing at a real or imagined enemy, its razor-like handle cuts deeply into the flesh of our own hands.

"Judge not, lest ye be judged" is a statement that applies well to the mind. If we allow our minds to judge other people and events, our minds surely as boomerangs will turn around and judge us too. Quite literally, the sword that cuts both ways...

Learning not to judge so quickly has two great benefits. Firstly, as we begin to relax the mind's judgment mode, we will judge ourselves less often, and less harshly. So the judging and the compassion exercises complement each other nicely.

Secondly, as we try to suspend our judgments of both thoughts and events, we find, as Carlos Castaneda's Don Juan put it, that everything becomes not *either* a blessing if we like it, or a curse if we don't, but a *challenge*. And our challenge is to try to use every thought, and every event of our life to take us in the direction of increasing awareness and even Enlightenment.

It's quite a task. Maybe, indeed, a full 100,000 mahacalpas worth, as the Buddha claimed (see "How Long Should It Take," page 44). But the following exercises will help us get started, on a level that we can relate to, today.

The Thought Judging Meditation

This simple little exercise is rather like the Thought Labelling Exercise, only easier. Instead of watching each thought, and labelling each as to its category, just watch your passing thoughts and label each thought either as positive (you like the content of this thought), negative (you don't like the content of this thought), or neutral (no particular feelings toward this thought). If you find yourself getting *involved* with the specific content of the thought, as in "I really like Pontiacs — sure wish I had a Firebird — let's see, if I traded in the Hyundai...," gently note how you feel about getting caught up in content once again, and return to just noting: positive, negative, and neutral.

Noticing the constantly changing likes and dislikes of the mind without getting caught up in the emotions of liking or disliking will also help you to deal with actual events in the outside world as well. Instead of asking yourself "Do I like or dislike this event?", you'll begin to ask "How can I best meet this challenge in a way that will help me to go in whatever life direction that I choose?"

Since we hope that you are beginning see the satisfaction of a more meditative, calmer, less judgmental way of life, you'll find, more and more often, that you prefer calm acceptance (which does *not* mean resignation, as will be discussed later) to frenzied struggle, and compassion to anger. And whenever you "backslide," and yell, scream, or feel depressed, you'll be able to notice what you're doing, and gently, compassionately, return your mind to the way of the meditator.

On Acceptance

There are certain situations in which our knee jerk reaction is to judge. We may judge co-workers for not being fast enough, or other drivers for being too fast. We may be judgmental towards a friend for not seeing things our way, at our spouse or children for not doing what we want, at ourselves for not being perfect.

Fortunately, acceptance is a powerful antidote to judging. And a Breath Counting or Compassion Breath intervention is as available as the next inhalation.

The Acceptance Meditation

Choose and then visualize a situation in which you usually become judgmental. Bring it to mind as clearly as you can, and allow yourself to judge the person or event as harshly as you would in real life. Experience the sensation of judging. Does it contain helplessness? Fear? Anger? Maybe a thought chain of helplessness to fear to anger? An element of "I don't do this, how can they?", or "The world shouldn't be allowed to be this way"? Turn it over in your mind — are there any other thoughts or feelings you can find in judging?

Then do some breath counting, labelling, or experiencing, or the Compassion Breath for as long as it takes (three breaths? one minute? three minutes?) to soothe the angry, judgmental thoughts. Perhaps a quick relaxation scan will help here, a visualization of your special place. Use this interlude of acceptance to calm your mind. Recognize the urge to throw a mental temper tantrum, and let it go. Feel acceptance overcoming anger, even just for a few seconds.

Watch yourself throughout the day for judging thoughts. Do you find yourself getting upset and judgmental over someone else's mistakes ("What a jerk. I can't believe he did that!"), your own inadequacy ("I should have done more with this opportunity."), or events ("This is really a major bummer.")? Simply label the thought: "Ah yes, Judging", and turn your attention to your breath, or whatever meditative intervention seemed to work best in the formal practice.

> Feel free to use whichever of the meditations (or, of course, whichever combination of meditations) that seem to work best for you. Once again (and we can't stress this too strongly), learning and then using meditation to become more metaphysically fit is like learning and then using a martial art. You learn the various moves and techniques, and then when you need to use them in a fight situation, you use whichever ones (and combinations) that will work best in that situation.

NINA: Sometimes I get into a whirlwind of activity, wanting to have everything done yesterday and feeling annoyed at the things that get in my way. On days like that, I can get very judgmental. For instance, if I'm getting a busy signal on an important phone call, or if the person I reach is unable to help me I'm likely to take it personally, and blame myself for not being a more effective worker. But if I can just get myself to apply some meditative techniques, a few moments of experiencing breath, a healthy dose of compassion, and a brief Acceptance meditation helps me to relax around the difficulties and get back on track with the task at hand.

DAVID: I often find myself getting self-righteous about events, feeling that things "shouldn't be the way they are". Being a small business person in the highly competitive business of publishing, and often having to deal with far larger companies (who, naturally, hold all the cards and are not shy about using them) is difficult and often painful. When these judgmental feelings about events arise, I try to do some thought watching, and find that my judgments are usually preceded by feelings of helplessness, then fear, then anger. Soothing the helpless feelings with compassion helps, while reminding myself that my labels of good events as opposed to bad are likely, in the long run, to be erroneous.

The Good, The Bad, And The Judgmental

When we believe that we know what's best for us, then it makes sense to judge every event that occurs as good or bad. Yet the fact is that we can't really judge adequately from our limited perspective, so we waste tremendous amounts of time and energy in making meaningless judgments. The positive may flip-flop over to prove negative, and vice-versa.

DAVID: This was brought home to me when I realized that the two "worst" things that had ever happened to me eventually proved to be two of my life's most important catalysts for positive change, while one of the "best" and most wished for events had quite a negative long range effect in many ways.

The sudden accidental death (if you consider drinking and wrecking a motorcycle to be an accident) of my best friend Tim in late 1978 was terribly traumatic. I attempted to tough it out, but without much success. So, too proud to seek help for myself, I decided to try to help other people deal with their grief. I applied and was accepted for the Shanti Project's three month training in counseling grieving and dying clients, which proved to be the beginning of a process that opened my heart and allowed me to eventually drop my old "macho hippie" persona for a more mature and compassionate way of being in the world. Over ten years later, I still miss Timmy. But without his death I might still be stuck in a personality that I had adopted as a defense in high school.

Likewise, the intense pain I experienced when in 1984 another publisher (whom I had expected to publish my harmonica method) beat me to press with his own similarly-titled version, actually motivated me to seek a different and more meditative lifestyle. If it were not for the cumulative effect of these two "catastrophes", I might not have done the emotional work necessary to settle down in a relationship and have a child, and I certainly wouldn't be writing a book like this today.

On the other hand, despite mediocre grades, I desperately wanted to go to a prestigious college, and was overjoyed when Connecticut's Wesleyan University not only accepted me but offered a generous academic scholarship based on my "potential". Yet had I gone to the co-ed state university instead of all-male Wesleyan, I most likely would have developed a healthier and more natural way of relating to women, the lack of which plagued me for many years.

Since it's clear that my judgments at the time of these three major life events were laughably (cryably?) off-base, how can I have the nerve to seriously judge the goodness or badness of what befalls me?

On Denial And Projection

When we are judgmental of others, we will often find (if we're willing to look deeply and honestly within ourselves, which of course most judgmental folk are not) that we are projecting onto them characteristics which we prefer to deny in ourselves. If we cannot acknowledge our own cheapness, we'll accuse and despise others for penury. If we have lust in our hearts, we'll judge others harshly for the same feelings that lurk only in the shadow.

When we begin to accept ourselves, spiritual warts and all, it becomes harder and harder to keep anyone else out of our hearts. Because how can we judge them for that which we see in us?

So whenever judgment arises, look within. Remember that we can despise a sin, without hating the sinner. And it's so much easier to forgive the sinner, if we're aware that we have the same potential for sin within us, no matter how well hidden or well controlled...

Day 20 Practice Plan

Formal Practice
- Spend a few minutes ruminating on the koans, below.
- Do the Don't Know meditation for three minutes.
- Do the Don't Know Decision Making exercise for three minutes.

Real Life Use: Try to allow some "don't know" space around whatever questions that arise in your life today. If you have decisions to make, see if you can apply the Don't Know Decision Making exercise to them.

On The Zen Of "Don't Know"

At the heart of traditional Japanese Zen Style meditation is the "Koan." A koan is a question with no rational answer. Some favorite traditional koans are:

"What is the sound of one hand clapping?"

"What did your face look like before your mother's birth?"

"Can a dog achieve enlightenment?"

Observe your mind as you focus your attention on one of these questions. Does it strive for an answer? Does it want to reject the exercise by calling it ridiculous?

As you consider the koan, try to cultivate a sense of "don't know." It may not feel comfortable, at first. But just let it be okay not to know. Look for the empty, spacious feeling of the "don't know" mind. The "don't know" mind has room for absolutely everything!

The standard story used to illustrate this concept tells of the scientist who visited the Buddhist teacher, in order to learn about Buddhism from a "scientific" point of view. Before beginning, the Buddhist suggested having tea. He filled the scientist's teacup to the brim, paused, then poured more tea into the cup. The scientist leaped up as the hot tea cascaded into his lap. "A teacup that is too full," the Buddhist said, "can receive nothing additional. Neither can a mind."

Jesus' statement "Before Abraham was, I Am" (John 8:58) makes a wonderful Christian koan! And since the word that Jesus used for "I am" was also the sacred name for God, it fits in well with some concepts that I'll later present in the "I Am" section of the book.

Since childhood, we've enjoyed pondering the koan "Ice cream has no bones." And that, of course, is a classic ice cream koan (apologies to Ben Cohen [Koan?] & Jerry Greenfield)!

The Don't Know Meditation

Try working with the "don't know" by choosing a situation from your own life, whose outcome just cannot be predicted. It can be something as innocuous as "Will we win tonight's softball game?" or as serious as "Will I marry?" or "How long will I live?"

Focus your attention on the question, while trying to maintain a sense of "don't know" in your mind. Notice attempts to make rational predictions, "Our second base man has the flu, but their best pitcher's arm is sore...," but then gently return to the "don't know." Watch your mind as it vacillates between answer-seeking and "don't know." What does it feel like? Try to memorize that sensation of "don't know".

Try to cultivate a sense of "don't know", to incorporate more "don't know" into your daily life. Will you catch that bus? Don't know. And that's okay. Will you get that raise? Don't know. And that's okay.

You can continue to strive wholeheartedly to catch the bus or get the raise, even while allowing it to be okay that you don't know whether it will happen or not. And — one last question, or perhaps I should say koan — will you make meditation an ongoing part of your life? Don't know. And that's okay, too...

Laurel, a performing artist in her mid-thirties, described her fear before each performance. "Each time it's like I've never been on stage before. My mouth gets dry and my knees start to shake."

After a few weeks of thought watching Laurel became aware that much of her stage fright derived from her anxiety over the uncertainty of performing. "I want to go out there and know ahead of time that the show is going to be great. Will they love me or hate me? The uncertainty drives me crazy. Sometimes I just don't want to take the risk."

Laurel started doing some breath counting meditations to calm herself each time she began to get upset about performing. And she quickly realized that the Don't Know meditation could also be applied to her situation.

Wonder how the audience will react? Don't know. Will the performance be less than perfect? Don't know. And that's okay. Incorporating a sense of 'don't know' and nurturing compassion for both herself and her fears allowed Laurel to begin to face performances with greater equanimity.

"I used to think I'd have to stop taking gigs if I couldn't learn to handle my nerves any better. But, now the nervousness is more just a fact of life. I still get real nervous at times. But I have tools to work with it, and it doesn't seem so life-threatening any more."

Stan, an attorney in a small environmental law firm, described his feelings during a trial. *"I'm okay during the trial itself. I can think on my feet and score points on cross examination. No problem until it's time for closing arguments. Then it's hard because I care too much. Let's face it, someone's going to win and someone's going to lose. I just don't want the loser to be me.*

I get very judgmental about it. It feels like I'll be a bad person if I lose, not like just losing a case. And that's really hard to take."

Stan recognized the difficulty he was creating for himself. *"When I base my self-worth on the decision, I get tense, and I can feel myself losing control of my audience. Then I get even tenser. Kind of a vicious cycle, but it's so hard waiting for the outcome.*

I tried doing some breathing meditations before entering the courtroom, but I just couldn't sit still. I kept on pacing the hall. I finally realized that I don't have to sit still to meditate. I'm doing some step counting meditations while I pace up and down now, and trying to accept that jury decisions are just a 'don't know'. It's still really hard, though."

On The Don't Know Decision Making Meditation

Often-times, the act of trying to make a decision can be enormously difficult. Even small ones are hard enough, but the big ones may seem to threaten sanity, if not life or limb. When it comes to important life decisions, wanting to make the absolute "right" choice can make it impossible to decide. Many of us drive ourselves crazy with lists of pros and cons, with pressure for that "perfect" decision, which will be all gain and no loss. We mull over our options compulsively and obsessively, until, at least to an outsider, it becomes clear that we are just plain stuck, terrified to make a decision, yet unable to allow *not* making a decision to be okay.

The next time you find yourself faced with a decision that's driving you crazy, don't cogitate, meditate!

The Don't Know Decision Making Meditation

Choose a question or choice that requires resolution. Start with something that isn't crucial, but which requires a decision, like "Is this a good weekend to take a mini-vacation?" or "Should I buy a gym membership or put the money in the bank?"

Take a moment to relax your body, then do some meditative breathing. When you feel relaxed and your mind has cleared a bit, recall the sense of "don't know" from the last exercise. Let the choice float in the spaciousness of "don't know" for a minute or two. Surprisingly, the Don't Know meditation removes much of the discomfort surrounding decisions and makes it easier to choose a course of action. Perhaps you'll find that it really doesn't make a great deal of difference what you do, as long as you choose an alternative and commit yourself to it. As discussed yesterday, we can't really tell which events are good or bad, in the long run. So how can we ever expect to make the perfect decision?

Practicing this exercise on small decisions will help you have this skill available for big decisions when they come up. The choice between A and B may not be a simple one, but we often make it more complex and painful than it needs to be.

As we begin to recognize that no single right or wrong answer for anything exists, we can also begin not to judge ourselves so much on whether we've made a "right" decision.

NINA: My recent job change caused me a great deal of emotional stress. I agonized endlessly, made extensive (and repetitive) lists of pros and cons, and drove myself, my husband, and David to the brink of distraction trying to determine the "right" course of action. Had I begun a meditation practice earlier, and had we devised this exercise sooner, it might have saved me a great deal of pain.

DAVID: Back in the late 1970's, my pals Ben and Jerry were living in Northern Vermont and trying to decide between opening a bagel store and an ice cream parlor. Bagel equipment was more expensive, but would ice cream sell well in the frozen north? They decided to go with ice cream, and now sell $40,000,000 a year. Did they make the right decision? Don't know. Would they have had a $50,000,000 a year bagel business today? Don't know. Would they be poorer but happier bagelmeisters? Don't know. They committed to a choice, and pursued it with zest. And that's all that *any* of us can do...

Thoughts For The Day: On Decisions And Control

Much of the fear and anxiety attached to decision-making stems from our efforts to be "in control" of our lives, to make the "right" decisions, to move in an ever increasing spiral of money, happiness, satisfaction. But, the unhappy truth is that *all* of our plans may go awry at a moment's notice, despite the best decision making. As Robert Burns said, "The best laid schemes of mice and men gang oft a'gley."

The question, then, is how shall we deal with the pain of acknowledging the fragility of our very existence, the hidden gut knowledge that our lives and plans are built as a house of cards and may come tumbling down at any moment. How, indeed...

One way is to begin to accept the "don't know", to recognize with sadness and compassion that we are unable to control our lives to the extent that we would like to do so, that "don't know" is an unavoidable part of human life. The compassion must also extend to the fact that it is our own fear of loss of control that drives us to our compulsive efforts at maintaining control. Because as we practice the cultivation of "don't know", we begin to see how often our (futile) attempts to control cause as much pain as our actual lack of control. Self-caused pain is the saddest, and the most needful of compassion...

On Psychic Space

When the Buddhist teacher overfilled the scientist's teacup, he was presenting a very important point about the mind. Because the less full the mind is, the easier it is to deal with thoughts and feelings. For us, psychic space is the metaphor for allowing our thoughts to float loosely in the mind, just floating, not strongly attached. And as we discussed way back in Day 1, attachment to thoughts is what causes pain. If we are not strongly attached to a desire, it becomes merely a preference, to be satisfied if reasonably possible. If we are not strongly attached to a fear, it becomes a reverse preference, to be avoided if possible, and accepted if not avoidable.

A spacious mind has lots of room in it. Room for thoughts to float unattached, so that they can be seen simply as objects for thought watching, not as imperious commands that must be instantly acted upon. Room for lots of "don't know". Room for compassion. Room even to accept those elements of ourselves that we'd prefer not to see, would prefer to project outwards onto others. Room to seek the truth, rather than merely to protect old habits or self-images, as we'll consider tomorrow.

Day 21 Practice Plan: REVIEW

Formal Practice
- Three minutes of The Acceptance meditation (page 150).
- Two minutes of the Body Scan exercise (page 143).

Real Life Use: Spend some time during the day observing your thoughts and labelling them as positive, negative, or neutral (page 149). Do some of the "Living In The Now" exercises, (page 140). Choose one particular action that you repeat throughout the day (such as washing your hands, or drinking a glass of water), and make it into a "Now" meditation (page 144) every time you perform it.

Important: Keep doing breathing and walking meditation throughout the day, as often as you can remember to do so, for any lengths of time (no matter how short)!

Thoughts For The Day: Looking For The Truth Versus Protection Of The Self-Image

As we become less judgmental, less prone to denial, and more able to admit that we just don't know, we can begin trying to learn what is *"true"* about ourselves instead of trying to *protect* ourselves from pain with deceptive self-images. This would doubtless be considerably easier to do if the truth were always pleasant.

Unfortunately, many truths are painful to acknowledge. Some hurt because they contradict our ideas about what "a good person should be like", and thus we prefer to deny them rather than face them. Others, whether positive, negative, or neutral, cause pain because they contradict our ideas of what we ourselves are already like.

While we were growing up, we began to form a rather solid mental picture of who we were, our self-image. For many of us, this self-image has become something that must be maintained at all costs, whether appropriate or not.

NINA: I learned as a child that women and girls were not supposed to be angry. So for years I forced myself to repress a very real component of my personality. My angry feelings then had to be re-directed either towards myself in the form of self-hate, or transformed into more subtle methods of confrontation without being too *openly* hostile.

DAVID: I learned early on that boy children were tough, and never cried. As a young adult, I was then forced to deny my feelings of fear or sadness, since they just didn't fit in with my self-image. I would fight when challenged by the local "hoods," or else experience terrible self-hatred because I had been "unmanly." I also had to deny my love for and dependence on my first long-term girlfriend, since neither emotion fit my "tough guy" image.

As another example, although I'd loved music as a child, when my voice changed during puberty I was ignominiously kicked out of the choir, and told that I "just couldn't sing". Rather than face the pain and embarrassment that this caused me, I somehow decided that being "tonedeaf" (like my father thought he was) wasn't so bad. It seemed a tough, masculine, macho, trait.

I began to cut music class, and make fun of, even look down on, other kids who were members in the school band or orchestra. I absolutely ignored any evidence that I had been, or could be, a musical kind of guy.

After seven years of self-imposed "tonedeaf-ness," during the late 1960's (the most pliable period of my life, up to then), I was able to buy a harmonica to take on a hitch-hiking trip to Alaska. The fact that no one who picked me up knew me made it easier to go against my earlier unmusical self-image (however, a noticeable lack of virtuosity shortened many of my rides!).

The important part of this story is that for seven years I deprived myself of the joys of making music, because I was more interested in maintaining a particular facet of my self-image, than in looking for and learning about what was true.

On Habits

Often, we form habits at an early age, and rarely check in later life to see if we would still make the same choices around food, sex, intoxicants, clothing likes and dislikes, or anything else. As our minds begin to clear through meditation, it may be well worth the time to occasionally investigate whether old habitual choices still satisfy. We can do this by doing "just experiencing" and thought watching exercises while thinking about or indulging in the habit we want to investigate.

Even if the old ways don't gratify like they used to, we may still wish to maintain them for a while. But as we periodically check back on these old habits or choices, if they have lost much of their allure, we'll probably put less and less energy into fulfilling them.

DAVID: During my college years, I formed a habit of getting slightly drunk and watching old mysteries on television while eating junk food. For years afterward I continued to do this, not realizing that it was more habit than anything else. A few years ago, I began to observe how I felt when indulging myself thusly. I found that the idea or memory of doing so was more satisfying than the actuality. I kept doing it for a while, but tried to be aware of how unrewarding it actually was while doing it (which took most of whatever enjoyment was left out of it). Eventually I just quit. I may do it once in a rare while, just to make sure it's still not fun, but it certainly is no longer a habit.

NINA: Change is difficult in general and habits are especially hard to change. In fact, by letting us act without needing to think, habits "protect" us from change. They keep us in the region of the known, the safe, the path of least resistance.

I spent several years indulging an exercise habit in which I jogged religiously seven days a week, whether I wanted to or not. After beginning to meditate, I began to become aware of my thoughts and feelings while I maintained this supposedly healthful habit of exercise. I recognized, with some pain, fear ("Will I turn into a couch potato if I stop pushing myself?") and judgment ("I should exercise every day!"). Seeing these feelings and applying compassion helped me to moderate my need to exercise. With more time available for other things, I was able to explore some new dimensions of myself, like meditating and writing.

Taking It Farther

On a metaphysical level, learning to invest in the meditative view of the self (seeing ourselves as part of a much larger whole of consciousness, as opposed to seeing ourselves as individual body/minds only) is the highest application of self-image renovation. Rather than trying merely to polish up our individual, egotistical, narcissistic self-image, we gently remove our attention from and our attachment to it, and focus more energy on the connection with the Higher Power within. Paraphrasing Stephen Levine and Sri Nisargadatta, we can call this "learning to break out of jail instead of spending time decorating your cell".

Truth And Self-Protection In Relationships

This conflict between truth and self-protection is an unusually efficient producer of pain in our relationships with others. In our old relationships to family and lovers, we would invariably become angry rather than face even the slightest feelings of rejection. Of course, getting mad then increased the distance between ourselves and our loved ones (which usually resulted in even more feelings of rejection and thus more anger). Once we became able to notice our thoughts of rejection, and experience the pain of them, we then often became able to either console ourselves with compassion or share our feelings with the other person, and thus work together on the issue of closeness and rejection.

We strongly recommend the book "Do I Have To Give Up Me To Be Loved By You?" for anyone who'd like to work with issues of truth versus self-protection in the context of a relationship. The next two day's work, on softening around pain, will also help — both with developing a more realistic self-image, and with the pain that so often is a concomitant of trying to do so.

Day 22 Practice Plan

Formal Practice
- Do the Softening Around Physical Pain Visualization exercise for at least five minutes.
- If you like (with your doctor's permission, as discussed below) do any of the other exercises for as long as you like.

Real Life Use: Look for (but please don't create) opportunities to soften around any type of physical pain that may arise during the day.

Note: See "Two Warnings" below.

On The Vicious Cycle: Pain and Resistance

Imagine trying to push away a huge, thorny rosebush. The harder you push, the more its spines impale your hands. Pain often functions in this this same, "Catch-22" kind of manner, in which the more we resist it, the more it hurts. And the more it hurts, the more we attempt to resist it.

Learning to soften around pain, be it physical or mental, is difficult but rewarding. Often discomfort will diminish, or at least become more bearable, when we stop trying to push it away. We may be able to realize, eventually, how our attempts to avoid pain actually help bring it right to us. And when we can make even physical or emotional discomfort into "grist for our meditative mill", we can begin to live in the world with less fear of anything that might befall us.

Softening Around Pain

Yes, softening around pain either mental or physical is one of the best examples of using what seem to be "obstacles" to deepen our meditative practice. It's not easy.

For most of us, pain immediately brings up fear, anger, helplessness feelings, and other delightful thoughts. So when investigating this subject by reading about it, doing visualization work, or real life experience, we will need *every* skill that we have available to us. Virtually every exercise that we've practiced, from the breath count to the relaxations to the Compassion Breath, can be used to soften around pain. It's up to you to discover what tools or combinations of tools work best for you in the intensely personal science of softening around pain.

With lots of practice, you'll be able to create a type of thought chain in which the act of noticing physical pain will automatically give rise to the softening techniques that you find most effective.

Today we will focus on softening around physical pain. Tomorrow, we'll work with emotional pain.

On The Softening Around Pain Exercises

These exercises simply involve observing pain and our reaction to it as just another focus for meditation, like the breaths, steps, or thoughts we've been using as meditation objects. As we observe the pain sensations, we'll try to "soften" around them, and watch them, instead of tightening around them as we usually do.

So often, when pain strikes, the body and mind tighten up, often in a cramping of rage at the perceived cause. Who hasn't hit thumb with hammer, and at least wanted to fling the offending tool across the room?

There is also another dimension of tightening around pain. When it occurs, it often seems to expand to fill our entire consciousness. We seem to experience nothing but pain (and maybe anger). When pain engulfs all, there's no room to work with it. But observing, watching the pain can make it something outside of us, something that we can work with a little. And if we can loosen around the pain, we can let the pain exist in some psychic space, aware of the pain but able to focus on compassion and relaxation too, as well as any other thoughts that arise.

A Painful Admission And Two Warnings

Of course, working with pain is far from easy — we'd be lying if we said that anyone can begin to put these exercises into use after their next header down the stairs. It's almost impossible to loosen around severe pain without lots of practice. But it's absolutely impossible to loosen around any pain with no practice. So that's why we'll start now, with these exercises: utilizing either very moderate and self-controlled doses of discomfort, or visualization of pain instead of actual pain.

Two important warnings: These next exercises aren't to be performed competitively, with gritting of teeth, but with gentleness and compassion. If you find yourself trying to "tough these out," better do some more compassion work before returning to them.

Also, if you are under a doctor's care for any reason, or have any physical condition which might be affected by these exercises, you *must* ask your physician's advice before trying any of them.

The Hot Pepper Meditation

We both like spicy food. Even so, in Thai, Mexican, and Hunan restaurants, we often reach a point which is technically known as "hotted out." Mouth and lips burn, and we wish (once again) that we hadn't over-indulged *quite* so enthusiastically.

Although overuse of hot sauce or chili peppers can be momentarily unpleasant, it is not physically harmful, and the discomfort is of short duration. So it is a good way to practice softening against pain.

If you aren't a fan of hot food, be careful. Even one drop of Tabasco or other hot condiments may give you more of a reaction than you've bargained for! Remember, these are not endurance exercises!

Spend a moment doing your favorite mind clearing exercise, and then eat an amount of hot sauce that's a *bit* more than you'd usually use (don't overdo it, at first especially). Try to focus on the sensation of burning, just as you've focussed on so many other objects of meditation. No analysis, no "wish it would go away", no thought at all. Just "what is this sensation?"

As you experience the pain, also be aware of any thoughts. Do you want to take action: rush for a glass of ice water, yell at the waiter, be angry at us, or yourself ("What a dumb exercise!"), or cry? Does your body or jaw tense up? Your eyes tear? Your preferred thought, right now, is simply to *investigate* how you react to pain.

Try to relax, to soften around the sensations in your mouth. Even as your lips are burning, do the quick relaxation exercise, or a mind clearer, or a Compassion Breath. After the hotness recedes, try it again. See if you can push your limits while maintaining as clear and focussed a mind as possible.

The Cold Shower Meditation

You can perform a similar meditation while showering. Just make the water a *bit* colder than you normally prefer, while doing one of the mind clearing or relaxation meditations, and/or focussing on the sensations that arise, without thought. Once again, be compassionate. Compassion in this context means doing the exercise, and pushing your limits, *only* to the extent that you can do so without being self-punishing.

DAVID: I like to do this exercise using both *slightly* hotter and slightly colder-than-normal water. I just gradually change the shower

164

setting from a bit hotter than I usually prefer to a bit colder, while meditating and trying not to tighten up, either mentally or physically. I also sometimes use jumping into a cold swimming pool in a similar way.

I'm *not* recommending this exercise (if you feel that you must try it, ask your doctor about this if you are under a physician's care, and be very careful — *don't* burn yourself). But I like to use it as an analogy, as it gently approximates the experience of the Native American sweat-lodge, which I occasionally partake of, in which the participants alternate between hovering over steaming rocks in an enclosed shelter, and jumping into an ice cold river.

And the sweat-lodge is a metaphor for life, as well. Going back and forth between too hot and too cold can help remind us that we can stay centered within our minds, no matter what is happening on the outside. It's too hot now, in the sweat-lodge? Soon it will be too cold, in the river. Then too hot again. And life's like that, too much one moment, too little the next. Too busy today, too quiet tomorrow. Too this, too that. We can't control life. But we are learning to control our reactions to it.

Softening Around Physical Pain Visualization

Picture yourself stubbing a toe, or hitting your funny bone. Create a clear visualization of the situation, with as much detail in the form of sight, sound, smell, taste and of course sensation as you can manage. Watch yourself tensing up in pain, then visualize yourself doing either your favorite Compassion Breath variation, or a Very Quick Relaxation. Try to focus the compassion or relaxation especially on the hurting toe or elbow. Continue to use the compassion or relaxation techniques, or perhaps try a mind clearing meditation, like a breath label or count. Experiment! Use this visualization to try to identify the technique or techniques that will allow you to loosen instead of tighten around the pain. And then the next time you bang your shin on the car bumper, you'll have a tool to try. Instead of tightening and cursing, perhaps you'll be able to feel compassion and relaxation. It won't keep you from crying and hurting entirely, but it may shorten the period and intensity of the pain.

Thoughts For The Day: Softening Around Pain In Real Life

After you've experimented with either the self-controlled pain/ resistance meditations or the visualization above, try softening around minor pains or discomforts that you *cannot* control, those that come up in daily life. Remember, practicing on the lesser pains is what will enable you to deal with the greater ones. If a stubbed toe seems too much to work with today, don't be critical of yourself. Just choose an even lesser pain to begin working with.

DAVID: I use to curse and even throw things when I would give my toe a good stubbing. It never helped the toe much, although it did seem to take my mind off the pain in my toe somewhat by replacing feelings of pain and helplessness with anger. I now realize that a hurting part of me needs softness and compassion far more than anger or curses. In fact, when I'm hurting, mentally or physically, that's exactly when I *most* need my own compassion. What irony that it's usually then that my self-compassion is least available — and what a clear message that much practice is needed on this point...

So when I walk into the baby's carrier in the dark living room, and the thick wire divider at its base jams between my toes, I try to soften, drop my shoulders (which tighten up and raise at the first hint of pain or tension), feel compassion for the person who is undergoing this pain, and visualize an image of mentally "cradling" my aching foot in my hands, with gentleness and compassion. If tears come to my eyes, I encourage them.

Diane, a new mother at age 38, described a striking example of softening around physical pain. "I had a difficult pregnancy and was on bed rest for the last seven weeks. I couldn't do anything and I had plenty of time, so I started to work with 'The Three Minute Meditator.'

Of course I didn't know it at the time, but meditation turned out to be critical in getting through childbirth. Labor went on forever and I finally had an emergency C-section. I was in tremendous pain, yet I had to lie still for certain procedures. I softened around the pain, counted my breaths and it worked. My doctor even commented, 'You're so still.' It was the meditation!"

Softening Around Chronic Or Ongoing Pain

Not all pain is acute, short term, or accidental. But the same techniques can be used to work with illness or longer term pain. If you suffer from ongoing pain, please see the books listed below. They deal with the subject in great detail, especially "Healing Into Life And Death". Even if you're not chronically ill, it's well worth using softening techniques with toothaches, flu, lower back pain, or headaches.

DAVID: I find that I can sometimes work with headaches and backaches as well, just by consciously softening around them. When in pain, instead of gritting my teeth and tightening my muscles, I may consciously try to relax my stomach, my jaw, my back, my neck. I'll try to "just experience" the sensation of pain, without judging, or trying to do anything to it, Just watching. Perhaps I'll do a relaxation exercise. Maybe I'll even try to do visualizations of sending some love and compassion directly into the place that's hurting. And occasionally I still yell, and complain, and reach for the aspirin bottle! But a healthy dose of compassion helps me to recognize and accept that I handled the pain as best I could at that exact moment in my life...

Softening Around Chronic Illness

Some researchers working with cancer patients are finding that visualizations of sending love to their tumors may be more healing than sending the more aggressive visualizations (like tiny alligators eating the damaged cells) that had previously been used. It will be fascinating to all of us, patients or not, to watch this type of research unfold.

Once again, the bigger the pain, mental or physical, the more practice and effort it takes to soften around it. That's why it's wise not to wait until you're desperate to start working on these important skills.

If you suffer from ongoing physical pain, or are interested in pursuing this type of meditation in greater depth, Stephen Levine devotes careful attention to working with pain in "Who Dies", "Meetings At The Edge", and "Healing Into Life And Death". We cannot recommend his books too highly!

DAVID: My first ten day long meditation workshop with Stephen was a turning point in my life, and teaching him to play some blues harmonica a great privilege! Our meetings and workshops with he and his partner and wife, Ondrea, have truly been peak experiences.

Day 23 Practice Plan

Formal Practice
- Spend a total of ten minutes working with the softening exercises below. Do a few minutes of each, or do the one that seems most important to you for the entire time. Use a variety of techniques, as described, to soften during the meditation.

Real Life Use: Begin trying to soften around the variety of mental pains that arise in the course of daily life. Yes, it's a tall order, but we need to start sometime — why not today?

Softening Around Mental Pain

Softening around mental pain is really not much different than softening around physical pain. It's a matter of learning to watch the mind as it hurts, to make the pain in the mind the object of investigation as we did yesterday with the pain in the body.

Once again, it's not a skill that comes quickly or without effort. But, with practice, even fear, desire, and anger can be seen as just thoughts, floating through the mind...

As we said yesterday, feel free to use any technique or combination of techniques that you feel may work for you. There are many types of mental pain, the pain of fear, the pain of anger, the pain of self-abuse. We'll present a few possible meditations below, but please apply the techniques to whatever type of pain is most predominant in your own life. And, once again, with a great deal of practice, you'll be able to create a thought chain so that the very act of noticing mental pain will automatically bring up the softening techniques that work best for you.

Softening The Fist Of The Mind

In these following meditations, we sometimes like to use a visualization to help soften around mental pain. We picture the mind as a fist, clenched tightly around its pain or anger or self-criticism, just as the fist was clenched around a thorny stem in the introduction to Day 22. The tighter we clutch, the more it hurts. Then we just visualize that fist slowly relaxing, softening, opening into a flat palm on which gently rests the painful emotion — loose, unattached, simply sitting on the palm where it can be observed with clarity and compassion. Perhaps we'll let our body relax, sigh and shrug our shoulders, while we picture the mental fist loosening.

Keeping Open The Heart

When the fist of the mind closes around the heart, it closes the heart as well. And when the heart is closed, as when we feel engulfed by fearful or angry thoughts, compassion and acceptance are not accessible to us. But if we can relate *to* the painful thoughts, instead of relating *from* them, if we can soften around them, and just watch them, then our salves of compassion and acceptance, "don't know" and "living in the now" can now be applied to the situation that caused the mind to tighten around the heart.

Softening Around Self-Criticism

In this first exercise we'll practice softening around self-criticism, a form of pain that virtually everyone subjects themselves to at times. Choose something about yourself that you don't particularly like. It may be easier to begin with a physical rather than mental quality. Allow yourself, just for the three minutes of this exercise, to accept without the normal self-criticism that which you don't like. Watch your mind. Is it resistant? Most likely it is, but just try to soften around it. Observe the sensation of self-criticism if it arises. What does it feel like? Are there other components inside it, like guilt, or fear that "no one will like me if I'm like this", or anger? Can you hear the voice of a critical parent in the self-criticism? Just watch it. The Compassion Breath may help.

DAVID: I used to like to do this exercise in front of a mirror, and focus on the extra few pounds of flesh that stubbornly cling to my midsection, no matter how much I bike or kayak. But the more I meditate, the less concerned I can make myself about how I look, so long as the amount of extra weight I carry isn't a health hazard. I stick my belly out, and jiggle it, and it just seems funny rather than disturbing. So lately I tend to do this exercise with my self-righteousness. Maybe one day I'll let go of that one, too!

Softening Around Anger

One of the main qualities of anger is that it tends to harden the mind, and to fill it up. When we're angry, it's hard to think of anything else, to allow any space in the mind. So learning to loosen around anger — to just watch it in the mind as an object, nothing that needs to be acted on — is very useful.

Choose something in your life that usually makes you mildly angry, and use the variety of softening techniques that we've been discussing to soften around it, just for a few moments (you can always get mad about it later, if you like).

DAVID: I use a neighbor's barking dog for a meditation focus sometimes. Although listening to the dog's incessant barking can be annoying, when I just focus on the sound, the physical sensation, of each bark without thinking, "He shouldn't bark" or, "Why isn't it more quiet" or, "Why do I let him upset me" — the noise doesn't bother me anymore. And if angry thoughts arise, I just watch them too, although after doing this exercise for a while I just don't seem to get angry about it anymore. The barking becomes just another experience, nothing to judge or react to. By shifting my focus, the dog has, once again, become my teacher instead of my tormentor.

Softening Around Fear

Softening around fear is very simple, though often not easy. It can almost always be done by applying large doses of compassion. Since much of our fear tends to be based on thoughts dating a long ways back, the Compassion Exercise (page 121), in which we visualize soothing our child-self, is especially effective. If, as soon as we notice a fear thought arising (before we can unconsciously convert it into anger, or hopelessness), we do a quick relaxation and begin a child-self compassion exercise, we can soften around the fear. This doesn't mean that we cannot evaluate the validity of the fear, and if valid, work to evade the feared event. But we don't have to be in constant mental pain while doing so. And if we aren't flustered by fear, our actions are far more likely to be appropriate and effective.

Softening Around "Could've Would've Should've"

Here's another type of self-criticism to practice softening around. Do you sometimes find yourself reviewing an event and thinking, "I should have said... I should have done... I should have..." While it's important to understand our interactions with others, there's a big difference between useful introspection and mental self abuse. And since hindsight is always 20/20, while our foresight tends to be rather less eagle-eyed, these instant mental replays can go on endlessly. Fortunately, meditation can help us to let them go.

The next time you start spinning those cognitive wheels and putting yourself down, take a moment to meditate.

Much as you did on Day 22 with physical pain, begin to soften around your emotional pain. Watch your regret over actions not taken or words that would have been better left unsaid. Explore your reactions to being less than perfect. Acknowledge the pain and create some space by just watching how it feels to be self-critical. Bring some compassion into this space — compassion both for yourself as an imperfect being and compassion for yourself as someone who clings to emotional pain.

Everyone makes mistakes. Moments past can't be re-lived. Your most compassionate action is to recognize that next time, you can do it, whatever it is, differently.

Watch your thoughts throughout the day. Notice how many times you tell yourself, "I should have said... I could have done... I would have been..." How often does a twinge of regret intrude upon your thinking? What types of regrets do you tend to experience? In what situations? Are there times when you're more vulnerable than others?

Much as we judge our insides against others' outsides (see Day 11), we also have an invisible, but tyrannical, Ideal Self against whom we measure *all* our actions.

Using thought watching and compassion, we can become aware of these painful self-judgments and begin to soften around them.

NINA: In my Ideal Self, I'm *always* concerned with other people's feelings, needs and problems, always kind, loving, understanding, sweet-tempered, gracious and thoughtful. A saintly ideal, but not a very realistic expectation for daily living. Yet, I used to get annoyed with myself when I was anything less than perfect in meeting these impossible standards. What a set-up!

Meditation has helped me soften around the realization that I am not now, and never will be, perfect. Although it sounds silly when I say it (because of course I know I'm not perfect), my internal critic never used to let me forget it. With large amounts of compassion, I've become able to love and accept myself just as I am. And it sure feels better than constantly wrestling with self hate. Big surprise!

171

Softening Around Societal Pain

We live in a world full of pain, and our own nation is far from exempt. How can anyone *not* agonize over the fact that the world's richest and potentially greatest nation allows 25% of its children to grow up in poverty? A nation in which the streets of every large city are lined with the homeless and the unaided mentally ill. A nation in which large numbers of the urban poor see "crack" as their best hope, and whose senior citizens, far from being utilized as the incredible resource of wisdom and living history that they are, are often devalued and shunted into institutions.

Yes, it's painful. But take a moment of mind clearing or relaxation now, and try to momentarily bring a feeling of acceptance to some external condition that you dislike. You might choose one mentioned above, or any social or political issue that torments you. Or, if you prefer, choose something about your job or your life. Softly let it be okay for it to be exactly the way it is, just for three minutes. Watch the pain. If resistance arises, watch the resistance. If anger comes up, try to relax around it. Let it float free in your mind, unattached, just for these three minutes. Of course it's hard to do.

Acceptance Without Resignation

Acceptance doesn't mean that we won't try to change that which we dislike in the near or distant future. It merely means that we are allowing them to exist right now, without self-hatred, anger, or judgment. Since they *do* exist, we are better off recognizing that and accepting them for right now.

Every act can be accomplished *more* effectively when our minds are unobscured by the clouds of self-hatred, anger, or judgment. Living with increased acceptance, we find that we no longer need to use anger or self-hatred to motivate internal or external changes. We can simply *do* whatever's appropriate, with the well cleared mind of the meditator. With less internal struggle, we have more energy for change. And we're less likely to fall into the trap of fighting hatred with hatred, or anger with anger. Because fighting fire with fire, in the long run, only adds to the conflagration.

The Softening Around Mental Pain Visualization

As with the Softening Around Physical Pain visualization yesterday, create a clear mental image of a painful thought. If you like, you can use an actual painful thought. Or, if you prefer, you can create an imaginary situation that would be painful if it happened, as you did in the Experiencing Emotions exercise (page 127). Visualize yourself using compassion, relaxation, and whatever other techniques that you choose to soften around the painful thought, to create enough mental space for the thought to float freely for a moment. Not attached to the thought, just watching it, as an object in the mind. Treating yourself and the entire situation with calmness, acceptance, and especially compassion. This visualization will help you to identify the technique or techniques that will allow you to loosen around mental pain when it arises. And this is the Master Skill, the ability to keep your mind open and clear when painful thoughts or emotions of any kind pass through.

Thoughts For The Day: Pushing Our Limits

Of course it's hard not to resist pain. Although the top-of-the-line gurus seem virtually impervious to even terminal suffering, it's going to be a long haul before most of us can refrain from cursing even a severely stubbed toe, a missed opportunity, or a tailgating truck driver. And an equally long time before we can do the forgiveness exercise with a malevolent ex-spouse, or the thought watching meditation as the boss hands us the pink slip.

So let's be realistic. Would a good boxing manager match his promising new kid, fresh from a local Golden Gloves triumph, against the reigning Olympic champ? He'd be nuts to do it, and he'd risk ruining his protege. Instead, the manager would carefully match the young boxer against a series of challenging but not insurmountable opponents.

And when we begin to apply our new meditative skills to real life challenges, we'll begin with small ones. We'll try to soften around the pain of a disappointing dinner, rather than the distress of a divorce. We'll practice forgiving the annoying bus driver, rather than an unscrupulous business competitor, or an abusive relative. We'll cultivate a "don't know" attitude on whether our friend will show up in time to make the eight o'clock movie, rather than on whether we get that new job we want so much.

Perhaps we'll try watching our thoughts as a moment of jealousy arises when a friend gets a compliment that we'd like for ourselves. Instead of the usual harsh judgment ("How can I possibly be jealous? He's my friend! What an awful person I am..."), maybe we can even observe that jealous thought with a touch of compassion. And then let go of that jealous thought, just for this moment.

In any times of mental pain or disappointment, instead of tightening the mind up, and feeling fearful, angry, or somehow blaming ourselves, we just might try using one or more of the tools that we've learned these past few weeks. Perhaps a Compassion Breath or two would help. Or maybe a moment of step counting coupled with some thought watching.

Then maybe we'll be feeling anxious one day, but rather than immersing ourselves in the content of those fearful thoughts, as usual, we'll merely practice a mind clearing exercise for a few moments of relaxation and clarity.

> Using the exercises to work with even seemingly small challenges is actually of tremendous value. *Every* time we react in a meditative way instead of falling back on our habitual responses of judging, impatience, anger, or resistance—we push our edges, our limits, further out. Every event in our life can become an exciting opportunity to react as skillfully as possible at that moment. Little by little, we develop the ability to live a compassionate and relaxed life, highly aware of our thoughts but no longer controlled by them.

Day 24 Practice Plan

Formal Practice
- Do the Alarm Has Already Rung meditation for five minutes.
- If possible, do the Horn Has Already Honked meditation.

Real Life Use: As you read Day 24, be aware of painful feelings that may arise, and practice softening around them with whichever techniques you prefer to use, including lots of compassion.

On Impermanence

It's a cliche, once again, but true: *nothing* is permanent except for the fact that everything changes. Everything that you think you know about yourself, your body, your job, your loved ones, your country will alter with the passage of time.

Much of the pain that we experience in our lives comes from the desire to hold on to what must inevitably change. We hurt when our parents grow old and die, and we hurt when our children grow up and move away. We hurt when we lose the strength or beauty of our youth, or the prestige that our work brings us.

If our desire for protection from pain supercedes our desire to face what is true, we are doomed to live lives that attempt to limit or ignore change. And that's sure to hurt. Lots. Of course, facing change will bring pain also. But each meditative step that we take will lessen the amount of pain that we must experience when we face and accept change and impermanence.

This following two exercises are meant to be used as lightweight metaphors for the heavier and more painful transience that we all must eventually encounter in life. Many teachers (including Casteneda's Don Juan, Ram Dass, Stephen Levine, Alan Watts, and Elizabeth Kubler-Ross) stress using the knowledge of mortality to add vitality to life. If you find this concept interesting, read any of their books, as listed in the bibliography. John White's "A Practical Guide To Death And Dying" also has many exercises and meditations on this subject.

The Horn Has Already Honked Meditation

The car in which you are a passenger approaches an intersection, traffic light yellow or red. Instruct your driver not to move the car until the car behind you honks its horn.

Relax the muscles of your body, and focus your mind on the inexorability of that honking horn. It's going to honk, a rude, abrupt, noise. There is absolutely nothing that you can do to control the situation, except to accept the inevitable, and possibly by doing so to reduce your own impulse to jump or be startled.

Soften your mind around that impending honk. Witness your own tension, witness your resistance to this exercise. It's a hard one to do, because it goes against everything you've ever been taught. Observe your desire to tighten mind and body against the honk, and watch your desire to make judgments, like "This is a stupid exercise," or "What an impatient jerk the driver behind me is!" And perhaps also look at your own desire to somehow avoid the unavoidable...

The Alarm Has Already Rung Meditation

This is easiest to do as an early morning exercise, although it can be done at any time of day. Set your alarm a few minutes earlier than usual. When it rings, hit the "snooze alarm" or re-set the timer for five minutes. Begin your favorite breathing meditation. Watch your mind try to attach to the knowledge that the alarm is about to explode into noise.

You may feel your tension escalating as the minutes go by. If so, recognize that you are *anticipating* discomfort. Your pain is caused by anticipation, not by the moment itself. Or perhaps you wish you had more time. But if you can practice living in the now, you still have a quiet, peaceful space, because the alarm has not yet rung. There's still time to take another breath, to meditate for one more moment.

Relax and enjoy the moment, even as you recognize its impermanence. Soften around the anticipation, accept the impending intrusion of sound. And when the alarm inevitably does ring, observe your reaction. How did it feel? Was the anticipation worse than the actual event? How often we lose precious moments of our lives as we create our own suffering with fears and desires! Or were you able to overcome the anticipation by meditating?

More On Death And Dying

So many changes in life are inevitable. Death, old age, loss. Yet rather than accepting these as a natural part of life, we complain about them, we tighten against them, and we deny their existence.

The death of self or loved ones is perhaps the biggest, yet most inevitable, change. Every person now alive will be dead within ten, fifty, or a hundred years. It's difficult, and excruciatingly painful, to face what we call "The Devil's Contract": that we will all be forced to experience the death of everyone that we love, or else they will be forced to experience ours. There is no other alternative. And no easy answer.

Stephen Levine tells a story of a wise man who was given a beautiful and delicate goblet. It was knocked over, and broke, but the wise man only smiled. "Even" he said, "as I held it to the light and admired it, it was already broken in my mind...".

Every sensation we feel, every relationship we have, is made more real and poignant by the advance knowledge of its transitory nature. And how can we fail to develop a sense of compassion and camaraderie towards any being that must exist in this fragile and transient environment that we call life?

Dealing with the knowledge of one's own unavoidable death is the ultimate level of choosing truth over protection of self-image. It is neither a simple nor an easy thing to do. But meditation, and especially compassion, can help.

"I began using meditation to gain control of my thoughts in situations where I felt uncomfortable." Anna, a senior analyst at a computer company, talked about the way in which her view of meditation had changed after a family catastrophe.

"Meditation was helping me focus and I felt I was making great progress. Then my 18 year old grandchild was killed in a car accident. There's just no way to describe how I felt. Shaken to the core. Turned inside-out. In pain beyond belief. And feeling so helpless.

At that moment, I both fully experienced my agony and understood the meaning of impermanence. And it made me realize that I had to use meditation in a deeper way — to live and love and learn right now. Because that's all I have. The love and closeness that I'd shared with my beloved grandchild is the only thing that helps me to live with the loss now.

Why did this tragedy happen? I'll never know. I've stopped searching for answers, mostly. It may sound crazy, but her death has changed me. It still hurts terribly, every single day. But it's also strengthened my desire to step away from things that don't matter, like prestige and money, and towards the ones that do, like spending more time with my family."

DAVID: In my counseling work with grieving and terminally ill adults and children, I've found all of the meditative techniques described in this book to be valuable, both for me, in my counseling work and my life, and for those clients willing to try them.

To end on a slightly lighter note, I'll tell a story that dovetails with today's exercises. The last time I saw Stephen Levine and his wonderful partner-in-light Ondrea, in February 1989, they were leading a meditation for a large group of people. All sitting peacefully, eyes closed, meditating. Suddenly Stephen's microphone exploded with an unbelievably loud noise, as though he had struck it with a hammer. I began to wince, but almost instantaneously relaxed as I realized how perfect it was that Stephen was breaking our expectations for silence, and teaching us how to incorporate such intrusions into our meditations. Afterwards, I asked my friend George, who was doing the sound engineering, how they had made such an awful tone. They hadn't, he explained. It was an accident, and completely inexplicable.

Thoughts For The Day: Loving And Losing Is Loving

DAVID: For many years, one of my biggest resistances to having a child was my fear of the tremendous vulnerability that doing so would engender. How, I reasoned, could anyone face loving another being as a parent loves a child, and still live with the possibility of losing the child? On the other hand, if the only way to avoid that vulnerability was to withhold one's love, how could one be a decent parent? I vacillated between that rock and that hard place for a long time.

Eventually, after years of meditation, therapy, and other work on myself, I agreed to have a baby. But I hadn't really resolved the fear of loving and losing. Within a few weeks after the birth, a few weeks spent falling deeply in love with my new daughter, I began to notice once again some fears of loss in my mind. But then Lord Byron's famous quote came to mind: "Tis better to have loved and lost, than never to have loved at all".

Of course I was familiar with that line. Everyone is. But I had always interpreted it (in my typically macho way) as referring to two men competing for the love of a woman, with one suitor winning and the other rejected. Now, I realize that Byron was speaking of something entirely different — not about the value of competition, and the hope of winning the fruits of infatuation, but about the value of opening our hearts to love in spite of the transient nature of the world.

I then understood that the love shared with Katie was of tremendous and timeless value: "A treasure laid up", as Jesus said, "Where rust doth not corrupt". I suddenly understood how people of great strength could adopt babies dying of AIDS, and how Mother Teresa and her helpers could do incredibly important and valid work in the last few hours of a beggar's existence.

Realizing this has helped me to try to touch more people with love, and less with the businesslike attitude of "I'll scratch your back if you'll scratch mine", whether said scratches be mental, financial, sexual, or in any bartering mode. *I understand that my lifelong task is now to keep my heart open, no matter what thoughts pass through my mind.* My job is not to make money, not to polish and buff my self-image, not even to write books that help other people. My real job is to be compassionate, to keep enough spaciousness in my mind so that I can remember to keep my heart open whenever a moment of fear, or desire, or anger momentarily arises. I do it far from perfectly. But I'm working on it.

Day 25 Practice Plan: REVIEW

Formal Practice
- Spend a total of ten minutes working with the softening exercises for mental and physical pain described for Days 22 and 23. Do a few minutes of each, or choose one and work with it for the entire time. Use a variety of techniques, as described, to soften during the meditation.

Real Life Use: Begin trying to soften around any physical or mental pains that arise in the course of the day. It's going to take some work to do that, so try to make this an especially meditative day. Turn your mind to your favorite mind clearing exercises whenever you can remember to, and watch your thoughts as much as possible, so that you can identify opportunities to do the softening around pain exercises.

Thoughts For The Day: Meditation As Metaphor For Life
Yes, we are somewhat addicted to the use of the metaphoric. But that's because we tend to see everything as being interconnected, and thus the large can teach us about the small, and vice versa. The chemical composition of an ocean can be deduced from studying a single drop of its water, and the nuclear structure of an atom is strikingly similar to the way the planets are held in orbit around the sun. Perhaps the strangest metaphor that we'll propose is the use of our individual sense of "I Am" as representative of the Universal Consciousness (or God, if you prefer) — but that's another day. For now, we'll content ourselves by presenting a relatively more straightforward simile: that good meditation habits are very much like good living habits.

When we do a simple meditation like breath counting, we have to learn to notice when thoughts other than the count of the breath intrude, and then return our attention to the breath. We don't get angry or self-critical about the lapse, yet neither do we indulge ourselves by staying with the intrusive thought, no matter how pleasant or compelling it is.

As we learn to lead a more meditative lifestyle, we have to learn to notice the thoughts or events that take us from our new path. Once again, we don't get angry or self-critical about our lapse, yet neither do we indulge ourselves by staying off the path, no matter how pleasant or important the distraction may seem to be.

On Means And Ends

When we're meditating, thoughts on any "goal" of meditation ("Someday I'll be so Enlightened that I'll have my own cult following") only take us away from the meditation, rather than helping us to meditate. But each breath that we stay focussed on is not a means to an end, but a satisfying and worthwhile end in itself.

Likewise, in our lives an excessive focus on goals and ends instead of means and lifestyle will actually decrease our ability to reach the only "end" that really matters: living a balanced and compassionate life, which can only be built moment by moment. If we strive to "walk in a sacred manner", as the Native American spiritual traditions advise, then the walking itself becomes as important as the destination. With each sacred step, a means becomes an end in itself, and a life is judged not by what one accumulates in terms of wealth or ego-gratification, but by how consciously and compassionately one lived.

We can learn to make each moment of life an end in itself. We do this by living fully and consciously, by living in the now, by not getting caught up in the furious thoughts, emotions, fears, and desires that fill the mind. It's not easy to do, but it's worth working on. Far more worthwhile, in fact, than most of what we put our time and energy into, like making money or watching old re-runs of Star Trek and The Honeymooners. So let's think more about ends and means, after reconsidering the idea of cause and effect from the meditative point of view.

On Cause and Effect

In the Western world, each individual performs specific actions that have particular effects on the world. In the Meditator's worldview, everything we do is connected to and dependent on everything else.

An example: Think about your neighbor's cat. Its movements in the neighborhood, in the Western view, seem random, and completely independent of anything else. Yet, in the Meditator's view, the cat is drawn to one yard because of a honeysuckle bush that attracts hummingbirds, and avoids another yard due to the presence of a large dog. The honeysuckle bush was planted by a family who left the Old Country after an earthquake in the 1880's. The other family bought a watchdog after a neighbor's house was broken into by thieves. So in a very real way, the cat's movements today are connected to an earthquake in the past and the fear of potential crime in the future. This same "interconnected" viewpoint applies to any event: political, social, economic, or interpersonal. From this perspective, there really is no such thing as cause and effect — everything is as it is, because everything else is as *it* is!

NINA: When I first met my husband Bert, I wasn't yet aware of the interconnectedness of seemingly random events. Fortunately, my ignorance did not impede the workings of the cosmic chain of causality.

Bert's housemate briefly dated my roommate after the two of them had met at a surprise Golden Wedding anniversary thrown for her parents, by his parents. If the two parental couples had not been close friends, or if the "Golden Couple" had split up after their first date, I wouldn't be celebrating my own 15th anniversary this year.

Actions Versus Outcomes

Considering the meditator's view of cause and effect may help us to realize that actions and outcomes are not as clearly or directly related as we are sometimes tempted to think. How can we possibly expect to control anything as complex and inter-related as this crazy, mysterious world that we exist in? We can work with zest and enthusiasm towards any goal that we decide on, or struggle powerfully to oppose that which we believe to be wrong. However, even though we direct all our energy into *actions* aimed at a particular goal, we can try to remain unattached to the eventual *outcome* or *result* of our actions.

Whenever we make our happiness dependent upon specific results, we inevitably invite pain. Because although we can take responsibility for our actions, the results of our actions, the fruits of our labor, can *never* be controlled.

For example, Mahatma Gandhi's work towards India's freedom from Britain was intensely motivated and powerfully executed. But didn't this same work eventually "result" in the Bengladesh war and famine which killed millions? Einstein's theoretical breakthroughs were instrumental in ending World War Two. But now the fruits of his labor threaten to begin and end World War Three, and everything else, as well.

At first glance it may seem confusing and frustrating to realize that even the sages mentioned above had no true control over the outcome of their efforts. Yet acknowledging the fact that even these wisest of humans are as impotent in the face of the fallacy of control as the rest of us can be comforting as well. If their ends were beyond their control, why should we make any pretense at it ourselves? And once we abandon the fallacy of being in control of our ends, we become more able to concentrate on our means, and focus our attention on the conscious moment by moment living of our lives. In this direction lies the only hope of true freedom.

On True Freedom

We generally think of freedom as the ability to do whatever we want. But this type of "freedom" will always be limited, because no one can ever control what happens. Even kings and rock stars must contend with accidents, disease, aging, pain, and other people's conflicting interests, not to mention their own self-destructive fears and desires.

True freedom lies rather in the ability to face whatever is happening, moment by changing moment, with awareness and acceptance, with open mind and open heart. Without judging or resistance, and with compassion for both self and others. Using every thought and event as a meditation lesson, a challenge (neither curse nor blessing), an end in itself and not just a means to some end. Building a road towards Enlightenment out of the very rocks and obstacles that appear to block our way..

NINA: It's not easy to give up the illusion of control. I have to keep reminding myself to "plan *plans*, not results, " and to "write my plans in pencil." (Or, as David says, "Write softly and carry a big eraser.")

At times it's difficult to integrate the awareness that I must take responsibility for making choices or changing my life while knowing that actions and outcomes may not be directly related. Oddly enough, remembering this is *hardest* if I try to *think* about it. When I simply focus my attention on the moment, and do "the next right thing," my life seems to fall into place without so much conflict.

Day 26 Practice Plan

Formal Practice
- Do three minutes of The "I Am Happy," "I Am Sad" meditation.

Real Life Use: Do the "I am _____" Thought Counting exercise during the day, for as long as you like. And meditate as much as you can, today — because in tomorrow's meditations you'll need as clear a head as you can manage!
Also, see if you can remember to observe the "Am-ness" sensation when you first wake up tomorrow morning. It may help to re-read the entire day just before going to sleep, so that it percolates in your mind during the night.

Note: Today's "Thoughts" section comes before the exercises. Read the following slowly and carefully, and really try to locate and investigate the "I Am" sensation as we discuss it.

On The High Road Without Rails

As we said earlier, many meditators call exercises based on the following concept "the high road without rails." It is probably the most metaphysically sophisticated and least intuitively obvious style of meditation around. So read about it, think about it, try it for a moment. If it seems really interesting to you, get the Sri Nisargadatta book listed in the bibliography.

DAVID: It's one of my two or three favorite books — I've read it a dozen times, and occasionally even think I understand a paragraph or two! Another favorite book which tackles this subject (and a much easier read) is Stephen Levine's oft-mentioned "Who Dies."

On I Am

Consider the statements "I am happy," or "I am sad," "I am tired" or "I am bored." They are all statements of *temporary* validity. No one is ever permanently happy, or sad, tired or bored. Yet *one* part of each statement is permanently true — the *"I Am."*

We can also validly make the negative statement "I am not happy" or "I am not tired." But no one can ever truthfully make just the statement "I am not," or "I do not exist." As long as a person exists enough to say or think "I am," they just cannot honestly say, or think, "I am not."

Although your physical body and your intellectual makeup have probably changed significantly since you were a baby, this basic sense of "I Am" remains remarkably stable. Think back to an early childhood memory. The six year old that you were had a clear sense of "I Am." He or she could confidently state, "*I am* a first-grader" or "*I am* a good reader." That child's sense of "I Am" was and is the same as your sense of "I Am" right now, as you think, "*I am* a meditator" or "*I am* hungry."

"Am-ness"

Yet it's hard to describe the "I Am" feeling, although we use it as part of an expression dozens of times each day. Perhaps it is easiest to identify this sensation when we awaken in the morning. Just exactly as our eyes first open, before we know where, or even who, we are — there is always a sense of (for want of a better word) "Am-ness." Someone, or something, some awareness or consciousness, appears to be in the body, looking out. And this "I Am" feeling is always present, unless we are in a state of dreamless sleep. In some traditions, this sense of "I Am" is called "the witness." It's also known as the "sense of conscious presence". It's where the "thinking about thinking" ability that we discussed in Day 9 comes from.

This sense of existing, this sense of "Am-ness" that all people possess, is the basis for a series of the most subtle and difficult but important meditations. They are important because the "I Am" is, in a very real way, the connection between the small mind of the individual and the big mind of God, or the universal consciousness.

According to the Meditator's worldview, the "I Am" sense in your individual mind is a very small piece of consciousness that is a part of *all* consciousness, just as a tiny bay is a small, connected, part of the entire ocean. Unfortunately, we usually don't focus our attention on the "I Am" feeling clearly enough to realize and perceive the connection. Our minds are too busy with the day-to-day problems and gratifications of the workaday world. We constantly focus on "I am ____" thoughts such as "I am hungry," or "I am a smart person," but never just on the "I Am."

An analogy: On a windless summer night, the full moon is perfectly mirrored in the still waters of the pond. But agitate the water, and the moon's tiny reflection is jumbled, broken, perhaps unrecognizable.

Eventually, as your mind begins to quiet through meditation, the agitations of thought — desires, fears, thoughts of past and future, the "I am hungry" and "I am a good golfer"— become still and quiet for short periods of time. Then, like the moon, a reflection of the universal consciousness of the Meditator's worldview begins to shine in the "I Am" of your clear mental waters. Amazingly, you don't even have to believe in this, for it to happen. You just have to do it...

The "I Am Happy," "I Am Sad" Meditation

Relax for a moment with a mind clearing meditation, and then choose two contradictory "I am _____" statements, like "I am happy" and "I am sad," or "I am tired" and "I am alert."

Take one, and visualize it as clearly as possible. If you chose "I am tired," picture yourself yawning, and feel the sluggishness of your body. Then quickly visualize the other one, "I am alert." Picture yourself brimming with vigor, feeling energetic, eyes bright and watchful. Go back and forth between the two, and try to feel how neither is very "true."

Now just say "I Am" to yourself, sink deep into the sense of "I Am," and experience how "true" that seems. Try to observe the sensation "I Am." What is it like? Is some part of you, some awareness inside you, looking out? Who? Who is that "I"?

I Am _____: Thought Counting Exercise

This meditation uses the Particular Thought Counting technique (from Day 11) to explore the labels that we usually attach to the "I Am". But today, instead of using a grabby thought, like fear or desire, and following it throughout the day, simply notice each time you indulge in an "I am _____" thought. Try this exercise for an hour, a half day or a full day. Be aware that some of these self-labels are subtle, a *sense* of "I am a good (or bad) businessperson" rather than an explicit verbal statement. In fact, some of our "I am _____" labels exist almost entirely beneath the threshold of consciousness, as in "I am a man" or "I am an American". Also, virtually all "like" or "dislike" thoughts have an implicit "I am ____", since "I like ice cream" is really "I am a person who likes ice cream".

Just notice them, whenever possible. We'll *work* with them tomorrow.

"I am ____" labels are often a way of seeking to understand and categorize ourselves in the world, a way of trying to impose order on a potentially overwhelming array of experiences. As we develop a clearer sense of the "I Am" by itself, using the exercises in Day 27, we'll begin to find that we have less and less need to attach ephemeral labels to the "I Am", and are more able simply to *be*. So if we find ourselves using lots of self-labels, we needn't be judgmental or critical. We'll simply begin to watch the labelling movie in our mind and ask, "Who is it that's doing all this labelling?"

In doing this exercise, Alison, a very competent young executive in a small computer software company, discovered a negative self labelling pattern that surprised her. "It's as if I'm looking to support a negative image of myself. When I do something wrong, I tell myself, I'm no good at that, but when I do something right, I tend to overlook it." Using the insights gained from meditation, along with a lot of compassion, Alison was able to stop creating painful, and unnecessary, self labels. Gradually, a growing awareness of "I Am" by itself helped her to realize that it is okay simply to be, without having to be anything in particular. This discovery of hers was not really our intention as to the purpose of the exercise, but it was useful to her, and an important part of her desire to free herself of labels.

The Freedom Of I Am

Our self-labels often form a kind of cage about us, a cage whose bars are forged by the habits and happenings of the past. "I am a guy who likes a few beers every evening", or "I am a woman who gets frightened at the thought of anger" are confining thoughts, where just "I Am" has space enough for anything or nothing.

The clearer our mind becomes, the less we need to maintain a self-image of any sort. We begin to trust ourselves to say and do whatever is appropriate, without having to live up to any role or historical self-image that we may have created for ourselves. Although at first it may be difficult to let go of our carefully crafted personality to some extent, it may eventually seem quite a relief!

DAVID: During my "Wild Dave" years, from the mid-sixties to the early eighties, I felt that I had to be a funny, witty, hyper, outspoken and outrageous guy. Whenever I was with other people, I had to be "on". I was very popular at parties (although some people surely disliked my tendency to monopolize conversations), but I certainly grated on the nerves of even (or, should I say, especially) my closest friends. Now I find it tremendously refreshing to be able to just listen, or hang out with people, and not have to be the center of attention.

NINA: Dave sure is easier to be with nowadays! As our old pals Ben and Jerry said in their introduction to *The Three Minute Meditator*: "Dave never used to be what you would call a 'mellow' type of guy. Smart, definitely. Articulate, without doubt. Mellow, maybe when he was asleep. So we were kind of surprised when he started getting into this meditation stuff for relaxation a couple of years ago. And we were even more surprised when it seemed to be working!"

Day 27 Practice Plan

Formal Practice
- Do at least five minutes of the "Who Am I?" meditation. Consider each question below, while reading about it.
- Try the "High Road Without Rails" meditation for as least three minutes, using the Expansion Awareness exercise for a minute or two beforehand if it sounds like it will help.

Real Life Use: Ask yourself the "Who _____ s?" question as often as you can remember to throughout the day, especially when "I am _____" thoughts arise.

The Stream Runs Into The River

One of our favorite blues musicians, the late and lamented Muddy Waters, used to sing "The steam runs into the river...and the river runs into the sea". Likewise, the sense of "I Am" can be used to trace a track back to the God Consciousness that we've so often mentioned, just like one can track a trickle of water to a stream, which runs into a river, which eventually runs into the sea. As Nisargadatta was wont to say, the sense of "I Am" is our best clue, the only one which can be followed to solve the great mystery of the universe — Who and What Am I?

The "Who Am I?" Meditation

After a moment of your favorite mind clearing meditation, ask yourself the question "Who am I?" "Who am I *really?*" Some answers may come up for you, and you'll have to consider them.

Are you your name? Clearly not, since lots of people change their names (as David did — you didn't believe that he was *born* a harmonica player named Harp, did you?) and remain the same person.

Are you your memory? People suffer from amnesia, yet certainly retain a sense of conscious presence — they may not know who they are, but they know that they are.

Are you your reputation? That can change quickly, but you still stay you. And if you went to a place where no one knew your reputation, it might make a difference to how you would act, but not to who you were. Besides, living on your reputation is very dangerous. An insult

189

from a friend or a stranger, an accident, or a case of mistaken identity ("Yes officer, that's definitely the man who stole and ate my corset!") can destroy your reputation — if it's you, how then will you live?

Are you your body? Bodies can continue to exist without minds in them. If that happened, would your mindless body still be you? And clearly you could lose large chunks of your body, even most of it, and still be you. So you *have* a body, but your body is not you.

Are you your thoughts? No, because you've learned this past month to observe your thoughts as things outside of yourself, as you practice the thought watching exercises.

Try asking yourself "Who asks the question, 'Who am I?'" Or even ask yourself the question "Who asks the question: "Who asks the question, 'Who am I?'"" Hello? Anybody home? Someone must be, to be asking all these questions.

This exercise can function as a koan, a "don't know" meditation. Or perhaps, like many who have asked it, you will return to the Meditator's worldview, and conclude that the "I" of "Who am I?" is a piece of "recycled" consciousness, that *animates* the body it inhabits — the "witness" of so many meditative traditions, a little bit of God.

If you find the "Who Am I" meditation difficult, Sri Nisargadatta suggests that instead of asking "Who am I?", practice saying "I do not know what I mean by 'I'". What do we mean when we say "I"? We do it often enough! It's a good question! Consider again, as above, whether the I refers to the body? The thoughts? Our history? Perhaps your answer to those questions today will be a bit different than it might have been a month ago.

"Who _____s?"

Whenever you notice an "I am ____" thought, instead of just counting it as you did yesterday, ask yourself: *"Who* is afraid?", *"Who* is angry?", *"Who* is hungry?", *"Who* desires?", *"Who* is in pain?". Who is it that's doing all that thinking? Remember, you don't need to answer the question, only to ask it in good faith. *Who* ponders this question?

The "High Road Without Rails" Meditation

For most people, this will probably be the hardest meditation in this book. It's simple enough, but not easy. All it involves is focussing mental attention on the sense of "Am-ness" itself, just as we've learned to focus our attention on our breath, our thoughts, and even on our pain.

When first shining our mental attention on the "I Am", it may be easier to treat it as a thought, by mentally *saying* "I Am", or "Am". This is roughly equivalent to a labelling exercise, just as we labelled the breath (except that it's hard to label something that you can barely perceive yet, so we verbalize it instead).

But simply saying "I Am" is not enough. So after a moment of this, we can try to shift to a "just experiencing" of the "I Am", rather as we shifted, in Day 6, from labelling the breath to experiencing the breath. The perception (just experiencing) of an inhaled breath is very different from the thought of the label "in". Likewise "just experiencing" the actual sensation of "I Am" is very different from saying or thinking the verbal label "I Am".

The sense of "Am-ness" is as directly perceivable as a sensation of pain or pleasure, heat or cold, just a bit more subtle, since it's an internal sensation rather than an external one. But it's hard to just experience the sense of "Am-ness". Most people who can, say it's a feeling of sensitive, highly alert openness. No thought, no judging, just openness.

The Expanded Awareness Exercise

If you can't seem to make the jump from saying "I Am" to experiencing it, try this. Sit quietly, eyes closed. See if you can let your awareness expand to encompass the farthest sound you can perceive. A distant truck? Birds outside? A plane overhead? Pretend that your body, instead of being bounded by your skin, is bounded by the limits of your hearing. If you can hear it, it's part of you. Try not to analyze, label, or judge, but just cultivate a sense of openness.

Once you feel somewhat open, return to a focus on the sense of "Am-ness". It may be easier to perceive now...

Thoughts For The Day: More On The "I Am"

We certainly don't want to give you the impression that this "I Am" work is easy and accessible to most people right off the bat. It's not — if you can stay focussed on nothing but experiencing "Am-ness" for even a few seconds at a time, we're impressed!

NINA: Although I still have my mental hands full working with my thoughts and emotions, I've recently begun to work with the "I Am" meditations. Asking myself "Who _____s?" has brought to light a whole "array" of Ninas. Seeing the limited nature of each small piece of myself is making it easier to move beyond thought and into "Am-ness," although this awareness rarely lasts for more than a few moments at a time.

DAVID: It's really hard for me, too. I can rarely stay focussed *directly* on it for more than a minute or two, without beginning to label it, think about it or attempt to analyze it in some way, or without being distracted by other thoughts. I focus on it best when I first wake up, or towards the end of one of my longer formal meditations. During a ten day retreat, or while camping by myself are the only times when I can spontaneously revert to the "Am-ness" focus without needing to work at it.

On the bright side, when I am able to focus on it, even for a few seconds, I experience an incredible sensation of somehow being "Dave *illuminated* by the Higher Power" instead of just "Dave by myself". It's a wonderful feeling!

I seem to be best able to isolate the "I Am" by tracing it mentally from childhood. Because although my body is different, and my mind is different, and my thoughts are different, that sense of "Am-ness" is exactly the same right now as it was when I was four years old, or twenty four. So experiencing the sense of "I Am" as the only true constant in my life helps me to keep my mind on it.

Not Just Another Passing Thought

At first glance, it might seem that the sense of "I Am" is just another thought, passing through the mind. Yet with a moment's consideration, we see that in one crucial way the sense of conscious presence differs radically from any thought. Virtually all thoughts are temporary. They may be recurrent, but even recurring thoughts come and go, while the "I Am" remains solid as a rock for a lifetime (if not longer).

Most of our thoughts are also *based* on the sense of "Am-ness" — "I am hungry", "I am sad", "I am a good driver" would all make no sense without "I am". In fact, without the sense of conscious presence, thinking itself would be impossible.

I Think, Therefore I Think I Am?

Descartes' famous statement, "I think, therefore I am", makes little sense when one analyzes it. For without a sense of "Am-ness", *who* would be thinking? For example, the only time in our life when we are not aware of our "I Am", in deep sleep, is also a time characterized by a complete lack of thinking.

Had Descartes said, "I think, therefore I think I am", we'd have had less quibble with him, because it is certainly is possible to have "I think I am" as a thought in the mind. It's also possible to have "I am" in the mind as a thought, as we did when beginning the "High Road" meditation. But what Descartes really *should* have said (according to us 21st Century Rationalists), is "I am, therefore I think", because thoughts and the rest of the mind actually come after the sense of conscious presence. In the meditative worldview, the sense of "I Am" is the *screen* on which all thoughts occur.

Thoughts Make The Mind

Think about an atom. Although it may seem like a solid little piece of something, it's actually composed mostly of empty space, a few tiny electrons defining a shape by rushing madly around a nucleus. In certain ways, a mind is like an atom. From our point of view, a mind is composed of a bunch of thoughts appearing and disappearing on the "screen" provided by the sense of "I Am". When the thoughts change, we say that we've "changed our mind".

As we learn, through meditations like the thought watching exercises, to relate to our thoughts as somehow "outside" of who we really are, our minds seem less solid. A flash of physical pain in the lower back brings a moment of fear, which changes to self-hate or anger. A sensation of hunger brings up a desire thought, then a guilty one. Thoughts float around in the mind, unattached ones swimming by like fish, powerful emotions or attached desires like great ships on the surface of an ocean. We just watch. But deep underneath, far below the surface hubbub and turbulence, lie the undisturbed depths of "I Am", connecting directly to the God Consciousness.

When we realize that the only solid part of what we usually think of as our mind or personality is that sense of "I Am", that sense of conscious presence — we can then answer the question "Who am I?". "Who am I?" "That's who: I Am!"

Day 28 Practice Plan REVIEW

Formal Practice
- Do three minutes of The "I Am Happy," "I Am Sad" meditation (page 188).
- Do five or ten minutes of the "Who Am I?" meditation (page 189).

Real Life Use: Ask yourself the "Who ____s?" question (page 190) as often as you can remember to throughout the day.
See if you can periodically take a few seconds during the day, and focus your attention on the sense of "Am-ness". If that seems difficult, do some short Expanded Awareness Exercises (page 191) whenever you can.

Thoughts For The Day: Speculation On Why It Is How It Is
Since, as we said earlier, fools rush in where angels fear to tread, we'd like to talk about how we conceptualize the development of the mind. While of course no one can really know for sure how it all works, this scenario makes sense to us (and a variety of other metaphysicians). Also, David has been observing his new daughter closely, so the fruits of many long and late nights have been added to our reflections.

By the time a baby is born, the developing body in the womb has somehow been imbued with the sense of "Am-ness" that we've talked so much about lately. From the meditative point of view, we'd say that this "Am-ness" is the reflection of the Cosmic Consciousness or God, expressed in physical reality. But whatever it is, the late third trimester fetus *is* conscious. It can hear nearly as well as an adult, and can feel, and probably see to some extent (not that there's much to see in there). Of course, these physical senses do not add up to "Am-ness", because as we know creatures of all levels of complexity have senses. Although there is no way to test for "Am-ness", consider the following account.

DAVID: Throughout my wife's pregnancy, I talked, sang, and played music to our fetus, whom we'd nicknamed "The Tadpole" (that's what it looked like on the ten week sonagram). In the last two months I made sure to say, in exactly the same falsetto tone of voice three or four times a day, "What's that little baby *doing* in there?" I didn't really believe that the fetus could relate to me (guess I'm just not *that* New Age), but figured it was worth a try, and funny besides.

At the birth, after a hard forty hour labor, our baby girl popped out. The midwife gave her to the pediatricians for a quick check, and within thirty or forty seconds (about four howls worth) I heard the words I'd been waiting for: "She's all yours!"

Katie lay on her back in a high pediatric emergency cart, surrounded by casually talking doctors, floodlights in her face, her tiny eyes squinched shut, yowling. I bent down, covered her eyes with my hand, and said my line: "What's that little baby *doing* out here?"

She stopped in mid-howl, and opened her eyes to stare directly into mine. The obvious quality of her awareness staggered me as I took her into my arms. Her consciousness was the same as yours or mine, not backed by much experience, but without any doubt a sense of conscious presence. I didn't expect it, but it was there — I'll swear to that, to the end of my days.

What Happens Next

Taking as an assumption that the sense of conscious presence is inborn in the newborn (and thus even in the older fetus), we believe that thoughts begin to arise, built on the framework of the "I Am". Simple thoughts perhaps, in the womb, awareness of amniotic slooshings, mother's heartbeat, motion, crampedness. These thoughts build up, gaining in number and complexity to gradually form what we will eventually call the mind.

After birth, this newly minted mind becomes filled with thoughts about the "blooming, buzzing confusion" (as William James put it) of life outside the womb, so much more varied and interesting than the watery (and meditative) quiet to which it had become accustomed. Thoughts about the exciting new body, and its sensations and needs. Sights and sounds, hot and cold, smells, clothing on skin, the hands of an "other", whether recognized as such or not — an intoxication of stimulation! And so instead of looking back to its "roots", and identifying with the Universal Consciousness that gave it birth, just as surely as the mother gave birth to the baby's body— the new mind mis-identifies itself with the physical form. Thus begins the myth of the "I am my body" idea...

As the child grows, and the mind develops, this mis-identification increases. The parents and other people add to the mis-identification, due to *their own* case of mistaken identity with the body instead of with the God Consciousness. The child now believes itself to be a body with a mind — separate, individual, alone.

DAVID: The other night, I saw John Belushi, playing his classic role of the disgusting fraternity man "Bluto" in the movie "Animal House". It struck me that the actor Belushi so strongly identified with his character Bluto that he perhaps lost himself in the role. Instead of identifying himself with the larger role of actor, who could have played an immense variety of roles for a lifetime, he identified with one self-destructive role, in essence *became* that role. And within a year or two was gone, a two hundred pound killer bee who stung himself to death.

In essence, we do the same thing when we identify with the body/mind instead of with the Universal Consciousness. Don't get us wrong — it's not that the body/mind is bad, and the Universal consciousness is good, not at all. That's as silly, and erroneous, as saying that cells are bad, and the body is good, or that the flowers are bad, and the garden is good. The body/mind that each of us possesses is a wonderful tool for creative expression and love on this planet of physical reality — it's only confusing it with *who we really are* which is as limiting as Belushi's becoming entranced with and stuck in his Bluto role.

The Deceptive Councilors

Yet it's terribly hard to transcend the idea that the body and mind are all we are. For one thing, we are used to receiving all information through the mind, in the form of thoughts. It's as if a king wished to see the reality of his country, but was forced to receive all of his information from his advisory council, who might have a tremendous vested interest in keeping him in the dark, and themselves in control. "The war is going fine, and it's a just war, Your Majesty." "The peasants are happy, and they love you." "Just look at these reports that prove everything we say!"

"We are reality", say our thoughts, "The world is as we say it is, forget that meditative worldview stuff." And we are so used to listening to them, to letting our thoughts interpret reality for us, that it's often easier to believe them than to look or think for ourselves.

That's why it's so essential to clear the mind, and to learn to work with our thoughts as objects of attention, so that we can begin to see the reality that lies beneath thought, beneath the mind.

The Bridge Of Meditation

As we've been saying throughout this program, meditation is the bridge by which we cross from the old Western worldview, locked in the mind and body, to the meditative worldview. It's not a bridge that most of us can stroll merrily across in an instant. Perhaps a better analogy is that of turning on the windshield defroster on a wintry morning, when a thin sheet of ice covers the glass.

The windshield doesn't instantly become free of frost. Instead, a few dime-size areas will grow first translucent and then transparent, just barely enough through which to catch a glimpse of the outside world. Ultimately, the glass is entirely clear, and we can see all.

Perhaps one day, in the midst of a meditation, you'll have a fleeting perception (not a thought, but an actual sensation) of how the world *really* is. For a few seconds you'll feel the interconnectedness of everything to yourself, and yourself to everything. With time and practice, that perception will return, for longer and longer periods.

Living In The "Real" World?

Of course, believing and participating in the Meditator's worldview doesn't mean that we won't spend a lot of our day to day life in the so-called "real" world. And, that being the case, it's convenient, even necessary sometimes to act as *if* cause and effect, birth and death, good and evil, were real, and meaningful, to act as *if* the body/mind were our focus rather than the Universal Consciousness.

A theoretical physicist knows that his kitchen table is composed largely of the empty space between electrons. However, he confidently uses it to support his lunch. An Australian Aborigine believes in "Dream Time," a mystical reality in which dreams and spirits rule the earth, determining the outcome of all events. Yet he also depends on his knowledge of animal behavior and local geography in order to live.

We can live, and act, in the world using the Westerner's view. At the same time, we can begin to open our minds to the possibility that the Meditator's worldview has a validity of its own — there's no paradox in doing so. In fact, we believe that those who can accomodate both worldviews can exist most satisfyingly and effectively in the world, enjoying and participating in the intense joys and sorrows of physical existence without losing a more cosmic perspective.

Most of us have already, since infancy, bought into the prevailing non-meditative worldview. The following concept has helped us and many others to accept the Meditator's worldview (on an intellectual level, at least). It may help you.

Why We Can't Lose By Investing In The Meditator's Worldview

As you continue to meditate, the Meditator's worldview will begin to feel more right to you on a gut, or emotional level. But today, you probably feel doubtful about it, and wonder: Can the Meditator's worldview possibly be real?

Our answer to that is practical, rather than scientific or spiritual. And this same answer also works for what is perhaps humankind's oldest question: "Is there life after death?"

There seems to be a certain amount of evidence that some part of a person may persist after the body dies, although it's impossible to know for sure, until you die yourself. But we are sure, dead sure, that we just *can't lose* by maintaining a belief in continuing existence after the death of the body. "How can this be?", you may well ask. We'll tell you.

If we're right, we'll be prepared for our continued existence. And throughout this present life, we'll have had the faith and support that comes from a belief in undying consciousness.

If we're wrong, and absolute nothingness follows death, we'll never realize our mistake. But we'll still have gained the same benefits from that belief during our life! It's a bet that we really can't lose!

On the other hand, let's say that we may choose to disbelieve in consciousness after death. If we're right, and nothingness follows death, we'll never have the satisfaction of knowing that we were right. And if we're wrong, not only will we be unprepared for whatever comes next, but we'll have cheated ourselves out of the benefits of belief in some type of life after death during *this* lifetime! What a lousy deal!

We feel exactly the same way about the Meditator's worldview. If we're wrong in our belief, we'll never know. And right or not, our trust in the Meditator's worldview can help us to live our lives *now* with increased acceptance and confidence!

Day 29 Practice Plan

Formal Practice
- Spend ten minutes listing the exercises that you found most valuable, and the times or opportunities in which you can continue to use them on an ongoing basis.
- Identify some situations in which you'd like to use meditation, but can't seem to.
- Do a Meditation Visualization exercise (page 91) to help you use meditation in a situation in which you usually don't.

Real Life Use: Observe your meditation practice throughout the day. Are there opportunities for meditation that you are missing? Why is this? Watch your thoughts to find out. How can you improve the integration of meditation into your daily routine?

Developing Your Own MPF Maintenance Plan
We've provided a sampler of our favorite meditation techniques, and a month's worth of planned practice to give you a framework in which to use them. But the rest is up to you. By now, you've probably begun to know which meditations you like better than others, to see a pattern in your use, a sense of what works best in which situations.

Think about your own "meditational profile". Which exercises did you like best? When did you use them? Did you create any new meditations of your own? (If you did, we'd like to hear about them! Please send us a note using the address at the back of the book.)

As we requested above, identify times or situations in which you find it easy to use the meditations. These might be physical situations ("as I walk from my car to the office") or mental ones ("when someone is rude to me on the phone"). Even more importantly, try to identify situations in which you *need* to meditate, but *don't*.

Do certain types of thoughts, like fears about money, or anger at your significant other, seem to close your mind and heart? Are particular situations, like traffic jams caused by incompetent drivers, or long lines at the bank, hard to remember to meditate during? Make a list!

The Master Skill — A Visualization Exercise

The Master Skill, as we've repeatedly said, is the ability to deal skillfully with *whatever* comes our way. We can't control what happens. But we can control our mental and physical reactions to what happens. And so, to us, skillful dealing means using the meditative techniques that we've presented in this book. Today, choose a few of the missed meditation opportunities that you've just identified, and use the Meditation Visualization Exercise of Day 8 to see if you can learn to use a meditation in a place (mental or physical) where you usually don't. If you've been using the exercises in low stress situations (moderate traffic on the way to work), try raising the stakes a bit, and meditate when the car won't start at all, or when the bank statement isn't what you'd like it to be.

To Each Their Own

There is no one right meditational maintenance plan. It's a matter of figuring out and doing what seems to work best for *you*. Following are a few of the possible variations. How do they compare to what you plan to do on an ongoing basis?

"All I ever do is the breathing meditation, mostly breath counting and breath experiencing" says Rene, a warehouse supervisor. "But I've read all about the 'I Am' meditations, and I think I get some of those 'I Am' feelings sometimes while I'm doing breath experiencing. It feels good. I sort of forget about everything while I'm doing it."

Clara, a research biologist, has been reading the Nisargadatta book "I Am That". "I read Nisargadatta every night before I go to sleep, and I think I'm beginning to get an understanding of his view of the world. I try to focus my attention on the "I Am", but it's certainly difficult. I probably should do more of the other meditations."

DAVID: How would I describe my meditation practice? It varies a lot. I try to do breath and step meditations throughout the day, and just experiencing meditations (sometimes for only a second or two). I attempt to remember to do thought watching whenever a thought that has much force behind it (like fear, anger, or desire) comes up. I use the softening around pain a great deal, and some I-Thou. I also read and ponder my favorite spiritual authors, among them Nisargadatta, Stephen

Levine, and Ram Dass, at least once a day for ten or twenty minutes, and try to focus on "I Am" every morning as I wake up.

NINA: I do a lot of thought and emotion watching too. I find myself working at cultivating a sense of "don't know" to deal with my control issues. I love to do just looking and just listening exercises when I'm outdoors. I read less than David, probably do fewer breath and step meditations, and more work with the Compassion exercises.

When The Going Gets Tough, The Tough Meditate!

Creating your own MPF Daily Maintenance Plan isn't necessarily something you need to do formally. You don't have to write down the exercises you plan to do for each day, although it's fine if you choose to do so. The important point is to maintain an attitude, a meditative state of mind, that is primed to *recognize* occasions when meditation would be useful, or necessary, and to *act* on it.

Your meditational needs are likely to change from day to day, if not from minute to minute. In fact, we have only one guideline for MPF maintenance: When the going gets tough, the tough meditate! Using and maintaining your skills is virtually assured, if you can keep that in mind. Missed your bus? Meditate! The boss was unfair? Meditate! Your spouse was grumpy? Meditate! Banged your shin? Meditate! Lost your wallet? Meditate! Worried about money? Meditate! Feeling fat? Meditate! Get the idea?

Thoughts For The Day: On Separation, On Oneness

In the beginning of this book , we stated that there are three main levels of meditation: clearing the mind, learning to work with thoughts and emotions, and investing in the meditative worldview. As perhaps you now see for yourself, it's not quite as clearly defined as all that. We alluded to this lack of separation in our baseball training analogy, in which our young players did basic calisthenics, learned to throw and bat, and studied teamwork and baseball strategy, all simultaneously.

Obviously, clearing the mind and learning to work with thoughts and emotions are two facets of one process, as supportive to each other as the two sides of an arch. As we clear the mind we can see (and thus work with) our thoughts and feelings. As we learn to control our thoughts and feelings our mind gets clearer.

Similarly, the progressive investment in the meditative worldview, which could just as easily be called the search for connection with the Universal Consciousness, is not a process separate from the other two. As the mind clears through working with thoughts, that connection eventually becomes clearer automatically, whether we work at it or not. A dirty, cobweb covered mirror naturally begins to reflect us when we clean it (even if we didn't realize that it was a mirror at all, and only wanted to wash the dirty panel on the wall). As our mind becomes somewhat cleared of the dirt and cobwebs of fears, desires, angers, plans, and other thoughts, we begin to see the reflection, in the deepening sense of "I Am", of who and what we *really* are.

Expanding The Circle

As the entire meditative process unfolds, and we grow in under-standing, clarity, and compassion (not to pretend that the process is smooth or easy — *of course* we'll backslide, fall off the wagon, and otherwise act unskillfully at times — at least *we* plan to!), a parallel process begins to take place.

We start to move away from the "I-It" relationship to other people, and to the world in general, in which we are the only subject, the only point of view that counts. We develop (in dribs and drabs at first, later on with more consistency) an "I-Thou" relationship to others, in-cluding people, animals, and even things.

As a illustration, contrast the "I-It" relationship of the average American to the cow which provides the package of ground beef in the supermarket, to the "I-Thou" relationship of the Native American hunter who studied and stalked, and even prayed for and apologized to, the deer that was to be killed and eaten. (We may not become vegetarians, but we can be aware, and appreciative that a living creature not completely unlike ourselves died to feed us. And no living creature likes to be killed...)

With time and practice, the "I-Thou" deepens into a general sense of non-duality, of being connected in some way to *everything*, animal, and vegetable, mineral or empty space. Distinctions fall away, as we develop an awareness of the "non-separateness" or "non-duality" of everything from everything else. All seems of a piece, forming one seamless and integrated whole — including us.

The Universe, All-That-Is

When we no longer need so much to analyze, to plan, to control, to judge, especially to judge — we no longer need to set anything apart from anything else. That which we used to think of as disconnected — mind from body, meditation from daily life, even ourselves from God — we can learn to see undivided, as part of the entire unfolding of the All-That-Is.

And nothing is really separate, in this amazingly interconnected universe in which we exist. Rather than thinking of the universe ("uni" meaning one) in an astronomical way, as some mostly empty and mostly dead physical immensity spinning through the infinity of space, we learn to think of the universe instead as the "unicity" (oneness), the All-That-Is — including events both physical *and* mental, objects *and* thoughts, present and past *and* future, emptiness as well as substance.

The Responsibility Of The Meditator

Meditation is a powerful tool. For that reason, we're concerned that our writings help to promote it in a healthy and socially responsible way. Because, to be quite honest, in the beginning stages, meditation can conceivably be used as a "Band-aid®", a symptomatic relief, to help a person function better in an amoral or unhealthy lifestyle.

But we're not in the business of teaching meditation techniques so that you can work longer hours at the local chemical weaponry plant, or better handle the cutthroat climate at B.S. Shark, Inc. Certainly, meditation could help you to do so. But by presenting a meditation program that emphasizes and integrates *both* the pragmatic and the spiritual, we're banking on the fact that sooner or later you won't *want* to. Because if you really work on the program, it will work on you, as a vehicle for deep spiritual change.

By changing ourselves, we begin to change the world. And there's nothing wrong with the world that a change in humankind's attitude wouldn't cure. The planet has sufficient resources to satisfy every person's needs, although not enough to satisfy every person's greed. As Jack Kornfield says, "It's not a problem of insufficiency, it's a problem of distribution".

If we all saw each other, neighbor or across the seas, as connected, as 'Thou's rather than 'It's, the stronger would help the weaker, and the richer would help the poorer. Imagine a world where infant health care didn't have to be cut so that the richest .01% of the population could avoid a tax raise that would reduce their income by one-twentieth, an amount that would affect their opulent lifestyle not at all. Imagine a world whose nations saw the preservation of the planet as even more important than the expansion of their individual spheres of influence. Imagine a world where all the borders were carefully, meticulously, eventually, made as secure by mutual trust as the imaginary, unfortified line that divides Canada from the United States...

The Spirit Of Generosity

To our way of thinking, we're lucky to be meditators, lucky to have a way of escaping from the isolation and meaninglessness that plagues so much of modern life. And one way of expressing our gratitude for this is to cultivate a spirit of generosity, of giving back some of what we get to this wonderful, challenging, painful and awesome world.

In a famous photo, the silent Indian saint Hari Dass is seen holding up the chalkboard by which he communicated, on which was written "We must do all." He was right. We must do all. Whenever we allow a single issue, no matter how important, to close our minds and hearts to the rest, we have lost our way.

There are an extraordinary number of ways in which to be generous. While we cannot actively partake of them all, we can be aware of as many as possible, and support the ones that we can. We must save the rain forests of Brazil, and the *"flagellados"*, the poor people of Amazonian Brazil as well, who are often forced to work at destroying those same rain forests. We must protect the world from the arms race, while taking care of the people who depend on that race for their livelihoods. We must save the children, and the whales, and the whalers, and ourselves — all the time remembering to remember that if we put *anyone* outside of our heart, make anyone "the enemy" — we have lost our own connection to the heart as well.

Some Resources

In the resources section towards the end of this book, we have listed a few of our favorite "causes". Many more are equally worthwhile. We believe that investing energy into good works, without expectation of results, is an enormously valuable way to develop a spirit of generosity. For a much deeper investigation into this subject, we strongly recommend Ram Dass and Paul Gorman's book "How Can I Help", as well as the chapter entitled "The Path Of Service" in Jack Kornfield and Joseph Goldstein's "Seeking The Heart Of Wisdom", and the chapter entitled "Stopping The War" in Stephen Levine's "Healing Into Life And Death".

Day 30 Practice Plan

Formal Practice
- A full ten minutes of counting the breath (page 47), from one to four, seated in a quiet place with eyes closed.

Real Life Use: Try to "walk in a sacred manner" as much as possible throughout this day.

Walking In A Sacred Manner

We've spoken about the Native American concept of "walking in a sacred manner", in which we attempt to imbue *every* action that we undertake with as much awareness as we can muster. Because when we make everything special, sacred — then each action becomes an end in itself, rather than a means that we rush through on automatic pilot in the pursuit of some imagined end that we crave.

To illustrate the importance of each and every part of whatever we do, today we'll return to the first exercise in the book. We'll do it carefully, lovingly, attentively, for a full ten minutes, with conscientiousness and compassion each time our attention lapses, as it no doubt will. And we'll be aware that this most basic exercise is fully as important as the more advanced, complex, and theoretical meditations of the later days. Not as a means to the completion of the program's thirty days, but as an infinitely valuable end in itself, in the Now.

When we bring our clearest meditative consciousness to every action, doing our best from moment to moment, life becomes impeccable. Because if we do our best from moment to moment, life takes care of itself, just as not drinking "one day at a time" every day yields a lifetime of sobriety.

Doing our best doesn't mean trying to be perfect. It "only" means really trying to be diligent in our attention. It means trying to notice when we're being lazy, and admitting it to ourselves, and trying to be a little less lazy in the next moment, without self-criticism or discouragement.

You Can If You Want To

Making a serious attempt to integrate meditation into our lives is *simple*. You already, by having read this far (whether or not you've done the exercises), *know* everything that you really need to know. But it's not *easy*. It requires the three C's: Commitment, Conscientiousness, and Compassion. However, if we apply the same effort to meditation as many of us have at times applied to sex, or sports, or job, or school, success in meditation is virtually guaranteed.

Success doesn't involve "becoming a great meditator", whatever that might entail. (We don't know; we're not great meditators.) Success in meditation is simply doing it as much, and as well, as you can, in any given situation. How much, and how well that is, will depend on you, and on the situation.

When Events Get You Down

There will be times when events seem so discouraging that the mind will rebel, and want to take refuge in old habits of self-hate or denial rather than in meditation. When this happens, as it will, here are three reminders:

Firstly, it may help to remind ourselves that the Master Skill of being able to use meditative techniques in any real life situation is *far* more important than any specific event, no matter how important that particular event may seem at the moment. Instead of focussing attention on how what is happening is not what we wish, we can focus on the great value of responding meditatively to the traumatic situation. While this may seem like a rationalization (and our mind will certainly try to convince us that it is), it's absolutely true. Meditative skills will help us through times of great pain and stress far better than money and power, or fame and good looks will. You don't buy that? Ask Howard Hughes or Marilyn Monroe.

Secondly, it will help to recollect that one of the most important MPF techniques is the application of Compassion. Even if it feels like we just can't meditate, we can probably try to have Compassion for that being who is in such pain that he or she can't even meditate. And if we can muster even a tinge of Compassion, well, that's a great meditative skill. We are then using meditation, so refer back to reminder number one for some more reassurance.

Thirdly, recall that none among us can foretell what will ultimately prove to be "a good thing" or "a bad thing". These terms, tempting as they are to use, are virtually meaningless. As David pointed out, two of what at first appeared to be the worst events of a lifetime proved to be of great benefit in the longer run, as he wove their lessons into the fabric of his life. Some people win the lottery, and have their lives destroyed by it. Others lose a love or a business, and go on to far more deeply satisfying ways of living. It's how we *react* to events that count, not the events themselves. If we can react meditatively, all that happens can only help us to learn and grow.

That doesn't mean that events won't be painful. They will. But as Nisargadatta says, "Pain takes you deeper than pleasure". When we can remember these points, we can really begin to view whatever happens as a challenge — rather than attempting to label it as a blessing or a curse as we used to. Everything then becomes grist for the mill, as we use the slings and arrows of outrageous fortune to hone and refine our meditative skills.

An example: in writing this book, we were forced to confront some old behavior patterns between us that were painful to admit. We had to use meditation, sometimes on a minute by minute basis, to smooth out our working relationship. It hurt. But doing so strengthened our meditation abilities, our commitment to the meditative process, and our relationship.

The Universe As Guru

When the mind is clear, we can learn from literally everything: the face of a passerby, a story in the newspaper, a single scene in an old movie, an encounter between two pigeons by the park bench on which we sit. We learn from loss, we learn from gain. We learn from pleasure, we learn from pain. We learn from watching fear, from watching anger, from watching desire. Our lives become an investigation of the truth, instead of a futile attempt to hide from it. In a very real sense, the entire universe becomes our guru, sending us a multitude of lessons which we only need to see and interpret.

The Rest Is Up To You

Reading this book is a step in the right direction. Using it will change your life. We have introduced you to techniques that can make meditation an incredibly powerful tool in daily life. Every new moment that arises in your life is now a point of choice, in which you can choose to use these techniques to investigate fear, anger, or desire instead of just mindlessly acting on them. A new moment, in which you can choose to live in the Now, instead of living in the habits of the past or the wishes for the future. A new moment in which you can choose to treat yourself and others with compassion rather than judgment. A new moment, in which you can choose the path towards rather than away from the Higher Power. The rest is up to you...

The Special Sections

Following are some suggestions and exercises aimed at particular groups of people. We'll also refer back to portions of the main text when they are appropriate. If you have any specific suggestions on ways that a person in *your* particular circumstances, whatever they may be, can use meditation, please let us know by writing to the address on the last page of this book.

Commuters

Obviously, the act of commuting offers numerous opportunities for meditation, since it so often involves time that can't be used for too much else. Instead of reading the newspaper, or perhaps even instead of reading your least favorite section, why not devote a few minutes to your favorite exercises, whether in car pool or on the bus?

I used to chat with the other guys in my car pool during the forty minute commute to work," said Jay, a data processor for a downtown law firm. "I didn't have much in common with them, but reading made me nauseous and I wasn't sleepy in the morning. Now I close my eyes and do a variety of meditations for the entire time. I like breath labelling and focussing on "I Am" the best. I do lots of thought watching, too. The others probably think I'm sleeping. That's fine with me."

For those that drive in to work, the following is an exercise that will enhance driving skills and mental concentration at the same time.

Conscious Driving

Driving is one of the most hazardous things that we do on a daily basis. Yet often, as we drive, our mind is lost in the past or the future, far from a clear focus on the manipulation of tons of iron at high rates of speed. We talk, listen to the radio, eat, drink or smoke, keeping "half an eye" on the road and other traffic.

In conscious driving, we focus our attention exclusively on the elements important to automotive safety, as intently as though we were Monte Carlo racing drivers, participating in the race of our lives. But

210

far from concentrating on speed alone, we pay attention to many factors: the road in front of us, the positions of other cars near us, our speed, driving conditions, and road conditions. Our mind and eyes stay on the road, not wandering to our passengers, or to attractive pedestrians that pass by. We are aware of the intense, life and death responsibility of safely shepherding our metallic steed along its way.

Should any thoughts not germane *only* to safe and alert driving enter, we notice them and gently but immediately return our attention to our driving. If this exercise seems to you, *for any reason*, to be unsafe, *please* don't do it. But we are convinced that if more people did focus their attention exclusively on their driving, that the highways would be much safer places for all of us and our loved ones. How could they not be?

Jason, a copier repairperson, found that this exercise really slowed him down. "I used to drive at 65 or 70 minimum. When I tried this exercise, I noticed how much time I had to spend looking for the highway patrol. It made it really hard to concentrate on the exercise. I also realized that I wasn't watching the road enough, I was always in my rear view mirror. I realized for the first time how wild it is to go down the road in a sitting position at a mile a minute, made me feel kind of fragile. Now I usually stick to under 60, and try to spend at least some of the time focussed on driving by itself. It's surprising how much less stressful that is."

New Parents

This section, though billed on the rear cover as for Parents, was actually intended for *New* Parents (the typesetter had other plans). But most of the ideas are appropriate for experienced parents, as well.

Children can provide a delightful and challenging focus for your attention. The Shared Breath meditation of Day 17 is an easy way to use your child as an object of meditation, and older kids will love to return the favor (simply ask them to watch closely, and breathe with you). A great variety of just listening or just looking meditations can be fun, too.

Day 5's Meditative Listening can be a great way to hear what a child is really saying, and the sections on Acceptance, "don't know", and softening around pain have obvious applications (especially for parents of teens and pre-teens, we're told).

DAVID: Infants can really help us to focus on the present, as they always live in the Now. They can be perfectly happy and content one moment (or even one second), and then crying piteously the next, or vice versa, all for reasons entirely obscure to you. So if you want to relate to them, you just have to meet their moods instant by instant. When they are crying and miserable, you can't let the fact that they were completely ecstatic only a minute ago affect your response to their condition now. And you impair your own ability to enjoy them if you let the crankiness of a few seconds past interfere with your reaction to their blindingly joyful now.

And consider this: the times that they are most acutely miserable are exactly the times when they need compassion the most — and (especially at 3 AM) exactly the times that compassion may be least available to us. Perhaps we can learn from this to provide compassion to *ourselves* also when it's most needed, and least available.

Paula, single mother of a colicky three month old boy, found softening and compassion to be of great use. "Michael would cry unconsolably every day from about three in the afternoon to ten at night. It was horrible. I'd find myself getting really angry, and I didn't know what to do. The only thing that seemed to help was to try to soften around the physical pain of being so tired and the mental pain of his howling. I would just cry right along with him. That somehow helped me to feel more compassion for him, like we were both in it together. I also tried to soften around how painful it was not to be the perfect mother. When I let go of that, I was able to call the local children's help line, and talk to other women who had been through the same thing."

Teachers

The teaching profession has had an impact on virtually all of us. The lucky ones among us have been given a lifelong affinity for education by a favorite teacher whom we still remember fondly. The less fortunate may have been turned away from academics at an early age by an impatient or critical teacher, of whom we also carry vivid memories.

NINA: Hello, Mrs. Sorkin from second grade wherever you are!

DAVID: If I said what I really felt about my kindergarten teacher, I'd be sued for slander. The pain of that first year had a negative impact on my entire primary and secondary school career.

But as much as we students have been shaped by the teaching profession, the hundreds of thousands of men and women who have chosen to make teaching their livelihood have been affected even more deeply. This section describes some of the many special stresses faced by educators within academic environs, and some uses of meditation to deal with them.

Evelyn, an English teacher at a private girls school, described her annoyance with parts of the system. "All I want to do is teach, because that's what I love doing. But there are some things that make it difficult, if not impossible, to do my job. For example, the school just sent our band and chorus on a field trip to Atlanta. That took half the school out for a week. I'm delighted that the kids will have this experience, but what am I supposed to do with the rest of the class? Crossword puzzles?

I know it's partly my own need for control that tenses me up. But I want to make sure my kids learn what they need and it hurts me to think they might be shortchanged. Watching my thoughts has been helping me get in touch with what's really going on inside my head. It's not so much that I'm angry at the system, it's more sadness, mixed with large amounts of frustration!"

Steven, a high school math teacher and basketball coach, described his interactions with parents. "Most of them are reasonable.

214

If they care about education, they're very supportive. Otherwise, they leave you alone. But I've had a few who are real humdingers.

One mother called me because her son was getting a D for the year. She was pretty belligerent, asking why she hadn't been informed and how could we let something like this occur with no parental notice. I pointed out that she'd been signing report cards all year and that deficiency notices were mailed home on a regular basis.

Her son had been intercepting her mail and who knows about the report cards.. I felt attacked by her, but I didn't take it personally. Doing an I - Thou meditation was a way of understanding that she felt disappointed by her son and pained by her own lack of attention to her child. In a very human way, she was seeking to put the blame elsewhere."

Some teachers, like Steven, are fortunate in having an administration that will back them up in a difference of opinion with a parent. But others face difficulties on both fronts when a problem emerges.

Janice, teaching history at a junior high, found herself encouraged to re-grade a paper after a parent complained. "It was a difficult moral dilemma for me. I was angry with my principal for putting me in that position, very angry. But I knew that I had to keep working with her. I did a forgiveness meditation many times and put a lot of effort into understanding that I could forgive the person but not the action. It's still hard to work with her. But I haven't had to quit."

Other stresses in teachers' lives come from the daily pressures of being in the classroom, trying to communicate effectively, planning lessons, grading papers, and being responsive to the needs of the many children that pass through in a single 24 hour period. Several teachers have described to us their use of mini-meditations to clear some mental space. Some use step counting between classes or during lunchroom duty, and many use the quiet time of a quiz or test to do a variety of exercises. Nearly all of them experience pain as a result of expanding needs and diminishing resources.

"Seeing my students as individuals and not just one huge herd is my biggest challenge. It's probably the most satisfying aspect to my work and also the most painful," Elizabeth, a 25-year veteran of the

public school system noted. "There have been times when I've watched children go through a lot of trauma. Divorces, death in the family, I can see the suffering. It's hard to simply stand by.

In fact, there have been times when I haven't stood quietly. In a few cases, the changes were so vivid that I felt I had to intervene. When I saw an out-going child become withdrawn, his good grades falling to failure, and became aware of his increasing demand for my complete attention, I had to say something to the school psychologist.

It was an agonizing choice. Am I doing the right thing? Am I making too much out of this? Will he snap out of it if I keep my mouth shut? I played that tape over and over in my mind. Watching my emotions and thoughts helped me clarify my actions. I let everything flow through my mind, got it all out on the mental shelf and then looked at what really mattered. I realized if I didn't say anything and he, God forbid, committed suicide, I'd never be able to forgive myself."

Being a teacher is one of the most important positions in the world. Unfortunately, our society, with its emphasis on money and visibility, undervalues as "unglamorous" the millions of men and women who devote their lives to the education of the next generation. Therefore, it is especially important that those committed to the noble profession of teaching marshall their resources of compassion and acceptance, and work to cultivate the meditative mindset that allows us, once again, to make bridges out of obstacles that appear to block our path.

Sales Personnel

Whether you work at the checkout counter of the local health food store, or on the floor of the New York Stock Exchange, sales is a job with high pressure and much stress. With so much people contact, the pressure to please the customer, and the stress of closing sales, it's no wonder that interviews with salespersons revealed many instances where meditation could be useful.

Vanessa, manager of a children's clothing store that's part of a large East coast chain, described pressure to equal or exceed sales from the previous year. "I'm under constant pressure to 'make my day,' meaning I have to compare my day (or week, or month) with last year's and try to come out ahead.

We're in a slump right now and even if I make my day on Tuesday and Wednesday, I could fall short by the end of the week. I take this pretty seriously and, in a really bad stretch, I may wake up at night thinking about it.

I'm just experimenting with meditation and trying to use the 'don't know' techniques when I get really uptight at three in the morning. Will I make my week? I don't know. It's really hard to sit with the uncertainty. But I guess I don't really have any other choice. I'm also trying to feel some compassion for myself. I don't have to make myself into a failure over this."

Matthew, a salesperson in a camera store, talked about the stresses of working the floor. "There's only one cash register for four salespersons. Sometimes we'll have twenty customers on a busy Saturday. And, of course, that's when the computer goes down. You can't do checks and credit cards without it and no one's paying cash. Everyone gets annoyed. My customers start complaining. I feel frustrated. And there's absolutely nothing I can do, except apologize.

When the system goes down, I want to leave the room. Just bail out for a while. But I have to stay put, keep my cool and try to keep my customers from taking a walk. The most useful thing I can do is count my breaths. It calms me down and give me something else to focus on. And no one has to know I'm doing it."

Commission work is another aspect of sales that can lead to high stress situations. Using the "don't know" meditations ("Will I close the sale? Will I keep the commission? Don't Know.") may allow you to both relax and to focus on the client during times of uncertainty, instead of wasting energy on fearful or self-critical thoughts. And compassion — both for self ("My feet are hurting, it's been a long day!") and others (the indecisive customer, the unpleasant client, the colleague who is competing for your business) — can help ease difficult situations.

At perhaps a deeper level, certain meditations can improve one's sales skills. The meditative listening exercise of Day 5 can increase sensitivity to the customer's needs, concerns, and wants. Even more importantly, cultivating an "I-Thou" awareness as regards your prospects will help to promote a sense of "win-win" in the sales situation. By caring about the customer and their needs as well as about your own, you will create a relationship condusive to ongoing business and increased referrals.

Therapists And Their Clients

An increasing number of therapists are incorporating meditation into their work with clients. We know this ourselves, since many of them are using *The Three Minute Meditator*. There are two main ways in which they do this: by meditating themselves, and by encouraging their clients to meditate.

We believe that a meditation practice can increase a therapist's efficacy by helping them to keep their attention focussed on the client and by developing a non-judgmental attitude. Of course, it may be the cultivation of compassion that has the most impact on the relationship between client and therapist, since many genres of psychotherapy are based on unconditional regard and transference between the two. Interestingly enough, the father of modern psychology (like it or not), Sigmund Freud, recommended for the therapist a mental state that he referred to as "evenly suspended attention". As he put it, "(the therapist) should simply listen, and not bother about whether he is keeping anything in mind."

DAVID: In the past, I often found myself planning what I was going to say to a client while they were talking. Meditation has helped me to become more present while in a session, because I can just listen (with or without a breath focus). At first, I used to worry that if I didn't think while the client was speaking, that I wouldn't have "anything helpful to offer" when it was my turn to speak. Now I realize that not only are my insights and suggestions clearer when I spend less time planning my response, but that the entire idea of "fixing things" for my clients is erroneous. My job is to create a space in which an "I-Thou" relationship can blossom, and not to "help" them, but to help them to help themselves.

The benefits of meditation for the client are equally clearcut. Mind clearing meditations help to allow previously unconscious material to rise towards the surface while minimizing denial and pain. The ability to understand motivation and defense mechanisms is facilitated by working with the thought watching exercises. And the progressive investment in the meditative worldview can provide a context for ameliorating the estrangement and isolation that so many in our society feel.

Last summer The Inquiring Mind journal (see Resources) published a comprehensive and superlative edition devoted exclusively to the intersection of psychotherapy and meditation. Although out of print, it appears that it may be re-released in some form, if enough people want it. If this would be of interest to you, please drop us a line, and we'll let you know if it happens.

Food And Dieting

Our society gives us many mixed messages about food. We use it to give ourselves love by eating exotic chocolates, tantilizing treats and tempting tidbits. Yet we also punish ourselves and use food to withhold self-approval, with crash diets and lifelong obsessions about those few extra pounds of flab. We pay lots of attention to what we eat, but little to how we feel while we eat. Often we avoid feeling entirely while eating. We do this by eating and conversing in the company of others, and when alone will eat while reading, or in front of the television set. Or, we may stuff ourselves compulsively without even tasting the food.

The Eating Meditation

A conscious focus of attention on feelings and sensations while eating can be a most powerful experience. Someday, perhaps when eating by yourself, try this "Conscious Eating" meditation.

Once your food is in front of you, spend a moment with a mind clearing exercise, perhaps one of the breath-based meditations. Then, slowly, begin to eat. Focus your attention on each part of the eating process, lifting the fork or spoon, choosing which forkful of food to pick up, lifting the food to your mouth, placing the food into your mouth, lowering the fork, chewing the food and noticing the taste, swallowing the food, and then lifting the fork once again.

If you like, label each action, as you did in the Slow Walking Meditation: lifting, choosing, lifting, placing, lowering, chewing, tasting and swallowing. If other labels seem more appropriate to you, by all means use your own.

Perhaps you would prefer to concentrate on how each action feels, rather than labelling them, as you did in the Experiencing Walking meditation. Simply slow down and concentrate on your eating. Some people find that this is easier to do if they hold their fork in the hand that they don't usually use, as this will increase the concentration on the fork hand.

Notice the sensation of metal against mouth, the muscular actions involved in lifting, chewing, swallowing. Feel each motion of your tongue, your lips, your throat. Concentrate on the texture and taste of each type of food. Be as specific as possible in your investigation. Do the skins of peas taste different from the insides? How close to your mouth is the food before you smell it? What else can you notice? As usual, be aware of thoughts as they arise in the mind, and then return your attention to your food.

DAVID: I often notice a desire to choose and lift the next forkful before I'm done chewing and swallowing the one in my mouth. This desire is then usually followed by a guilty thought about greediness. If similar thoughts occur to you, note them, perhaps label them ("aha, there's greed..."), then let them pass, and return mindfully to your dinner. If sad or lonely thoughts (especially around eating alone) come to you, as they often do to me in the course of this meditation, a moment of Compassion Exercise or Compassion Breath may well be in order.

An interesting duo exercise for friends or couples is to take turns feeding each other, while silently focussing on physical or mental sensations. For some, this brings up compassionate feelings for the feeder, and vulnerable or infantile feelings for the one being fed.

Meditations on Hunger

For many of us, food is more than sustenance or simple nutrition. It can be a companion, friend, painkiller, or enemy. For women, especially, the act of eating may be an experience that goes beyond hunger, into the realm of desires, needs, and fears. And of course meditation is the most effective method of dealing with such feelings. The following exercises deal with hunger, food, and dieting. They are quite new, and we would love to have your feedback on them. If you write to us at the address in the back page, we'll be glad to keep you posted on our work with meditation and food issues.

The Hunger Scan

Have you ever found yourself eating when you weren't really hungry? Eating to avoid work? To stuff down feelings? Out of boredom, or tiredness perhaps? If so, this meditation may help you to better understand why you eat, when you eat.

We'll start by doing a "body scan" meditation (similar to the one on Day 18). Doing this while eating will help get you in touch with sensations of hunger and fullness, or satiation.

To do this exercise, choose a snack or meal during which you won't feel rushed. And, at least for the first time, we suggest you try this when eating alone or with a friend who'll also try it, or who will at least respect your need to focus within.

Before you begin, spend a moment or two with your favorite mind clearing meditation, and relax your body. Then focus on the sensation of hunger, asking yourself "How hungry do I feel right *now*?"

Explore your hunger. Are you feeling just a little hungry? Moderately hungry? Ravenously hungry? Think about these levels of hunger: how might each of them feel? After you've begun to eat, continue to check your sensation of hunger. Does it change during the course of the meal? How does that feel?

Doing this mini-meditation for even a few seconds at the beginning, middle and towards the end of a meal will help focus your consciousness on your degree of satiation, help you realize when you're hungry, when you're full. It's also interesting and important to realize how much of our food may be ingested out of "greed", avoidance, or for other reasons, and not out of "need."

Labelling Types Of Hunger

If we can become more aware of our sensations around hunger, and at the same time watch our thoughts, we'll notice that there are many types of hunger. Sometimes hunger seems to be at a "panic" level — we feel we *have* to eat or we'll starve! Hunger sometimes feels "picky" — we're not really hungry, but we'll manage to chow down if the food smells/looks/tastes appealing. Hunger may also be "compulsive" — when we start eating to avoid certain feelings, thoughts or activities but are not really hungry, or perhaps when we start but just can't seem to stop. "Induced" hunger occurs after we've just seen an advertisement or some other cue that "reminds" us to be hungry. Occasionally, we may even find ourselves eating out of "normal" hunger — simply ready to dig in and really enjoy the food.

Hunger And Compassion

If you do this exercise, and find yourself unwilling to stop eating even though it feels like "greed", you may feel self-hate beginning to creep in. If so, just return to the Compassion exercise (page 121) or the Compassion Breath (page 130)and remember to be gentle with yourself.

As we've said so many times, the Master Skill of being able to use meditative techniques skillfully in difficult times is far more valuable than is having things go the way you want them to go. Nowhere is this more true than as concerns dieting. Treat yourself with loving acceptance and compassion, *whether or not* your figure or your eating behavior meets the standards that you set for yourself (or the standards set by Madison Avenue). If it seems to be hard to allow yourself to be compassionate just remember: Compassion will get you through the absence of slimness better than slimness will get you through the absence of compassion.

NINA: Our culture's relentless focus on women's bodies and thinness makes it difficult to stay in touch with a realistic body image. Many women diet on and off throughout their lives, sometimes compulsively, with greater or lesser degrees of "success". We feel the pain of denying our body sense, ignoring our hunger. Unfortunately, the more hunger is denied, the more it attempts to creep in around the edges, in compulsive little nibbles...eating past satiety...lusting after the forbidden foods. This above meditation has helped me get back in touch with my body's ability to know what it needs in terms of food. But even more important than eating "correctly" is the ability to apply compassion to feelings about food and eating.

I now try to define dietary "success" more in terms of health and self-acceptance than in terms of conforming to unrealistic (and perhaps misogynistic) advertising images. If I do start to feel compulsive around food and end up making eating choices that I regret the next day, I'm now more able to notice and clear away that old self-hating mental chatter, replace it with compassion, and start anew in the Now. And that's worth a lifetime of dieting...

Working With Food Issues

Understanding why we eat will help us to control our eating patterns. But it is also important to understand *why* we want to control our eating. Thought watching, the acceptance and compassion exercises, and softening around the pain of realizing that we've allowed others to dictate how we must look may all help us to face the food issues that occupy so many of us.

If we do decide to diet, we can try to make sure that we are doing it for reasons of self-love rather than self-hate. And we can then use meditation to help us achieve the goals that we've set, as David describes below.

DAVID: During my wife's pregnancy, I practiced a ritual known to anthropologists as the *couvade*, in which the husband sympathetically shares in the wife's symptoms. I cleverly did this by gaining nearly as much weight as she had. Unfortunately for me, she lost most of hers in one grand and productive gesture, while my excess clung stubbornly to the middle of my body.

Interestingly, though, the 25 or 30 pounds I was overweight bothered me far less than the three or eight extra that I had carried throughout high school and college. Instead of obsessing about the weight, and being self-hating and judgmental as I used to be (even when the actual poundage was far less), I simply began to exercise more and ingest fewer calories. Whenever I felt deprived by my avoidance of sugar and fat, I would use a Compassion Breath exercise, coupled with the thought that lighter was healthier and that each exercise session or low calorie meal was a step on my path to increased health. I've lost most of it, and plan to lose the rest. Someday. But I generally feel okay about myself regardless of how fat or trim I am. I think that it's easier for men to learn to feel this way than it is for women, as men tend more to be judged on how "successful" they are than on their figures.

Compassion And Meditation Will Get You Through Times Of No _____ Better Than _____ Will Get You Through Times Of No Compassion And Meditation!

Sometimes it seems as though we are all judged by how we look or what we do rather than by who we are. Women judged by their looks, men by their success, children by their satisfaction of mom or dad's expectations, executives and executrixes by how much they've contributed to the company bottom line this past quarter.

When we find ourselves beginning to judge ourselves by these external and erroneous standards, it may help to remember the quote from the previous page, re-stated above as the heading of this section. If we fill in both of the blank spaces with *whatever* it is that we are judging ourselves harshly for lacking: money, sex, fame, a flat stomach — they all make the statement true. And realizing the truth of this statement will help us in the direction of the increasingly compassionate and aware lifestyle that we are choosing to lead.

The "Why I Don't Meditate" Test

DAVID: Ten years ago, Nina's expertise in psychology and experimental testing combined with my interest in teaching music to people who considered themselves "unmusical" or even "tone-deaf." We developed a test to help people discover the roots of their musical blockage.

The insights offered by this test were so useful that we decided to use this same approach to help resistant would-be meditators explore their own "meditational blockage." In doing so, Nina conducted many interviews with would-be meditators around the country and found a remarkable consistency in their reasons for an "approach/avoidance" (I want to meditate/I'm not making any attempt to do so) conflict.

The following quiz is designed to help you explore your own meditational blockage. This test is not intended to predict how motivated a meditator you will become or how useful the effects will be for you. Your answers to those questions will only come in time. It can, however, help you understand and overcome the excuses which may have prevented you from exploring your own meditation potential.

As you take this quiz, recognize that there are no right or wrong answers. Please be as honest as possible. Simply write whether you agree or disagree with each of the following statements.

The Test

1. Meditation is not worth doing unless you can devote a lot of time to it.   Agree/Disagree

2. I'm the kind of person who will tense up and not be able to get into meditation.   Agree/Disagree

3. Meditation pulls a lot of people in at first, but then most of them seem to drop out. If it really worked, people would stick with it.   Agree/ Disagree

4. Meditation takes years of work and practice. A book this simple can't possibly teach me anything.   Agree/Disagree

5. Meditation might work for some people, but it probably won't work for me.   Agree/Disagree

6. I won't have the will power to stick to a meditation program.   Agree/Disagree

7. People are fooling themselves if they think meditation really makes a difference.   Agree/Disagree

8. My life is too busy to fit meditation into it.   Agree/Disagree

9. This book looks like the "Mickey Mouse" version of meditation. I'm better off waiting until I have the time to do the real thing.   Agree/Disagree

The value of this test lies in the four separate themes that your answers will now help you investigate. Please refer back to your answers for the designated questions as you read the following paragraphs. Most people who are resistant to the idea of meditating will find that at least a few of these erroneous beliefs are blocking their progress.

The Myth Of Innate Ability: Refer To Questions 2, 5 and 6

Many people who foreclose on their own meditative potential share a belief in a widespread and damaging myth. Do you believe that "All successful meditators are *born* with an innate ability to clear their minds, to focus their thoughts and to concentrate on their inner lives?" If your answer is "yes," you are *wrong*!

The truth is that meditators are made, not born. The ability to meditate is a characteristic that every human being has — an ability that must be nurtured and encouraged in order for it to bear fruit. No matter how tense or unspiritual you now think yourself to be, rewards await you, but only if you *try*.

Once you begin to believe this, you can turn your wistful would-be meditator self-image into a beginning meditator self-image, and thus start to enhance your own life with these tremendously useful techniques. Vividly visualizing yourself meditating will help you begin taking the steps to unblock your meditative potential. Not all of us will have the time or the inclination to spend hours a day meditating. But anyone with a sincere desire to meditate can begin to learn and use these techniques immediately.

Big Is Beautiful: Refer To Questions 4 And 9

If you think that this book is too simple to teach you anything, then you may be suffering from the "Big Is Beautiful," or rather "Complicated Is Better," syndrome. Why is it that we often need to make things appear complicated, difficult and/or expensive before we value them?

Much of the beauty of meditation lies in its exquisite simplicity. And simple as they may seem, these Three Minute Meditations are *the* basic tools which anyone who wants to meditate will eventually have to master. If this book makes these tools appear obvious, so much the better!

The fact is that as much or as little as you do, simply getting started is what counts. And that's what this book is designed to help you do. Once you've begun, you can then expand your practice of meditation in any direction you choose.

Lack Of Time: Refer To Questions 1 And 8

When you view meditation as an exercise which requires clearing a large time slot each day before you can begin, chances are that you will never get started. Today will not seem right and tomorrow will seem even worse. Life is so hectic for many of us that clearing half an hour or so daily may seem like an impossible task. And to think of doing so repeatedly, perhaps even twice a day, may be enough to leave most of us thinking, "Maybe next year, when things ease up!"

For those of us who feel pressured by lack of time, meditation is likely always to remain in our vague and distant future. Ironically, the time spent meditating, even three minutes worth, is often enough to clear the mind so that the rest of the day seems to flow more smoothly, as if time has somehow expanded to meet the needs that arise. This erroneous belief in the time demands of meditation has blocked many a would-be meditator (including for many years, both David and Nina)!

Meditation Doesn't Work, Anyway: Refer To Questions 3 And 7

Some people believe in the aggressive tenet that "the best defense is a good offense." Attacking the usefulness of meditation is a means through which many who have considered meditating are able to assure themselves that they are not really missing anything by their meditational blockage.

Much of this attack may be based on a pre-programmed sense of failure. Would-be meditators who suffer from this blockage often are asking themselves, "Why even try meditating, since it obviously doesn't work?" Another element of this attack consists of denigrating meditation because everyone who tries it does not continue. Yet this fact may be more a reflection on ineffective teaching techniques and the unrealistic demands that many disciplines try to impose on busy Westerners, than a reflection on the value of meditation itself.

Meditation techniques are identifiable in every major religion since the beginning of recorded history. Meditation has clearly stood the test of time, so if you are using this excuse, it's long out of date! Time to give up your excessive skepticism, and become a Three Minute Meditator.

Bringing Meditation Into Our Lives

Once you understand the four most common barriers that would-be meditators face, we hope you'll agree with our final analysis, which is: The only thing that now stands between you and meditation is the willingness to begin right now!

So let's briefly reconsider the four obstacles. The idea of "innate ability" is just a myth, because everybody has the God-given ability to meditate. The "Big Is Beautiful" concept is mostly a form of spiritual snobbery, counter-productive although understandable in our highly status-conscious culture. The "Meditation Doesn't Work" justification is strictly sour grapes. Meditation doesn't work only if you don't do it. Finally, "Lack of Time" is no longer an excuse — because the Meta-Physical Fitness method demonstrates how meditation can be effectively done in small chunks of time. And, even in small doses, meditation is effective in improving the quality of one's life.

If your goal is realistic ("I will begin learning to clear my mind") rather than perfectionistic ("I must achieve Enlightenment right away"), then your progress towards this goal is virtually guaranteed from the outset. All that you need to do is take a few deep breaths, relax — and go back to the beginning of the book!

Bibliography

Benson, H.: The Relaxation Response. Avon, 1975

Borysenko, J.: Minding The Body, Mending The Mind. Addison-Wesley, 1987

Casteneda, C.: Journey To Ixtlan. Simon & Schuster, 1972

Garfield, Charles: Peak Performers. Avon, 1986

Goldstein, J., and Kornfield, J.: Seeking The Heart Of Wisdom. Shambala, 1987.

Harmon, W. and Rhinegold, H.: Higher Creativity. Tarcher, 1984

Hay, L.: You Can Heal Your Life. Hay House, 1984.

Kornfield, J.: A Still Forest Pool. Quest, 1985

Kubler-Ross, E.: On Death And Dying. MacMillan, 1969

LeShan, L.: The Medium, The Mystic, And The Physicist. Ballantine, 1975

Levine, S.: A Gradual Awakening. Anchor, 1980

Levine, S.: Who Dies. Anchor Books, 1982

Levine, S.: Healing Into Life And Death. Anchor, 1987

Maltz, M.: Psycho-Cybernetics. Prentice-Hall, 1960

Nisargadatta, S.: I Am That. The Acorn Press (Box 4007, Duke Station, Durham, NC 27706), 1982

Ostrander, S., and Schroeder, L.: Super-Learning. Delta, 1979

Paul, J. and M.: Do I Have To Give Up Me To Be Loved By You? CompCare, 1983

Prudden, S.: Meta Fitness: Your Thoughts Taking Shape, Hay House, 1989.

Ram Dass, and Levine, S: Grist For The Mill. Unity Press, 1977

Ram Dass, and Gorman, P.: How Can I Help. Knopf, 1986

Rubin, T.: Compassion And Self-Hate. Ballantine, 1976

Rubin, T.: Reconciliations. Viking, 1980

Siegal, B.: Love, Medicine, And Miracles. Harper and Row, 1986

Silva, J.: The Silva Mind Control Method. Pocket, 1977

Thich Nhat Hanh: A Guide To Walking Meditation. Fellowship Publications (Nyack, NY 10960), 1985

Trungpa Rinpoche: Cutting Through Spiritual Materialism. Shambala, 1973

Watts, A.: The Book On The Taboo Against Knowing Who You Are. Collier, 1966

White, J.: A Practical Guide To Death And Dying. Quest, 1980

Resources

"**How Then Shall We Live**" is an eight hour video series featuring **Ram Dass, Stephen Levine**, and others. It is often shown on PBS, and information is available from: Original Face Video, Oakland, California, (415) 339-3126.

"**The Inquiring Mind**" is a semi-annual magazine for meditators. It features articles and a calendar of retreats and seminars led by **Stephen Levine, Jack Kornfield, Joseph Goldstein, Jamie Baraz** and many other fine teachers. It's a good mag — I always look forward to my copy! It's free, but funded almost entirely by donation (average $10-15/year). Write to: P.O. Box 9999, North Berkeley Station, Berkeley, California 94709.

"**The 1% For Peace Proposal**" is the brainchild of my friend Ben Cohen. As he puts it: "We really love our country. So we want it to be as safe and secure as possible. But we're really not sure that the best way to create a peaceful world is to spend 300 billion dollars a year preparing for war. Instead, we believe that it would be more cost-effective to use just 1% of that amount, every year, to prepare for peace. Directly."

Ben & Jerry's "Peace Pops" are now available, with the profits going to 1% For Peace. Ben's new endeavor is a variation on the peanut brittle theme called "**Rain Forest Crunch**", with cashews and brazil nuts bought from small farmers in the Amazon rain forest. As Ben says, "Brazil nuts can't be cultivated. They only grow wild. By increasing demand and paying top prices for them, we are using the power of business to encourage preservation of the Amazon and the original culture of its inhabitants." For more info, contact: Cultural Survival, 11 Divinity Ave., Cambridge, MA 02138 (617) 495-2562.

The Seva Foundation is a non-profit organization devoted to world service, from eradicating blindness in Nepal to providing goats for widows in Guatemala. With **Ram Dass** and **Wavy Gravy** as very active board members, Seva (108 Spring Lake Dr., Chelsea, MI 48118 (313) 475-9737) is a no-nonsense, low-overhead organization that does what it purports to, unlike certain "glitzier" service groups. Well worth your time and energy! Wavy also runs **Camp Winnarainbow**, a summer circus arts camp in Northern California that provides a crucial respite for inner-city children, among others. Its week-long camp for adults helps to subsidize the kids, and might be just the unusual vacation you're looking for next summer! To send donations or get more information, contact 1301 Henry St., Berkeley, CA 94709.

Beyond War is a non-sectarian grass roots group promoting world peace. They have a very meditative orientation and a great volunteer program. Contact them at: 222 High St., Palo Alto, CA 94301.

Sales Pitch

If you've enjoyed *MetaPhysical Fitness*, you may want to check out some of our other material. The following is a listing and very brief description of David's other books and tapes:

Instant Blues Harmonica, or Zen and the Art of Blues Harp Blowing: includes book, 98 minute cassette and high-quality harmonica, $19.95.

Instant Flute: 64 page book (folk, blues, country, classical, Irish, and more) and flageolet-style flute, $14.95.

Make Me Musical: Instant Harmonica Kit for Kids (ages 4-10): 64 page book, 90 minute cassette and high-quality harmonica, $19.95.

Instant Blues and Jazz Improvisation for the Chromatic Harmonica: book and 90 minute cassette, $12.95.

Instant Guitar: book, 98 minute cassette, and the amazing "ChordSnaffle™" (our invention that allows complete beginners to play chords instantly using just one finger!) $12.95.

Me and My Harmonica: (ages 3-6), 30 minute cassette $4.95. With high-quality harmonica $12.95.

Instant Blues and Rock Harmonica: 60 minute video and high-quality harmonica $49.95.

Bending The Blues: Booklet and 90 minute cassette (intermediate harmonica instruction) $9.95.

Harmonica Positions: Booklet and 90 minute cassette (intermediate harmonica instruction) $9.95.

How To Whistle Like A Pro: Book and 36 minute record $7.95 (Oct. 1989).

And, of course, with Nina: *The Three Minute Meditator*, on which this book is based. Good for people who'd like a shorter and more concise version without the 30 Day format. 128 pages, $6.95. Attention therapists, doctors, chiropracters, ministers, and people with lots of friends: Volume discounts (50% off retail) on ten or more copies! The same great volume discount applies to *MetaPhysical Fitness* ($7.95 single copy price).

Not to mention: *The Three Minute Meditator Audio Cassette!* Great for inspiration! Listen to it anywhere! Featuring both David and Nina reading from the 3MM, with the foreword by Ben & Jerry actually read by Ben & Jerry! 90 minutes, $9.95. And available November 1989, *MetaPhysical Fitness Audio Cassette*, $9.95.

And: We enjoy accepting *speaking engagements* when our schedules permit, either together or solo. We can custom tailor our program to fit the needs of any group!

If you'd like more details, send a stamped, self-addressed envelope to the address below for our brochure. We'll also put you on the mailing list for our occasional newsletter. Or, if you already know what you want, you can order right now. We accept checks or money orders by mail, or Visa/MC and UPS COD (in USA only, additional $3.00 COD charge) by telephone.

All orders shipped UPS unless otherwise specified. Please add $2.00 shipping and handling for the first item, and $1.00 each additional item. Canada please add $4.00 for the first and $2.00 for each additional item, Overseas please add $6.00 and $3.00. Free shipping (USA only) on all orders of $50.00 or more.

mind's i press P.O. Box 460908
San Francisco, California 94146 (415) 821 - 0809